DEVELOPMENT OF MANAGERIAL ENTERPRISE

DEVELOPMENT

The International Conference on Business History 12

OF

Proceedings of the Fuji Conference

MANAGERIAL

edited by KESAJI KOBAYASHI   HIDEMASA MORIKAWA

ENTERPRISE

UNIVERSITY OF TOKYO PRESS

89507

The Fuji International Conference on Business History has been held annually since 1974, with the third series beginning in 1984. We would like to express our deepest gratitude to the Taniguchi Foundation for their continuing sponsorship of the Conference.

Published by University of Tokyo Press
Printed in Japan

ISBN 4–13–047032–9 (UTP 47325)
ISBN 0–86008–397–7

Contents

Notes on Style and Usage

1. Japanese personal names appearing in this volume are given in the order customary in Japan: family name followed by given name. The exceptions are the names of the editors and contributors, which are given in Western order to avoid confusion for librarians and bibliographers.

2. Macrons have been used to indicate elongated vowel sounds in transliterated Japanese terms, personal names, and names of organizations. They have not been used, however, in names of places, e.g. Osaka or Kyushu.

3. Transliterated titles of Japanese language books with no English translation are given with only the initial word capitalized; English-language book titles have all important words capitalized.

Introduction

Kesaji Kobayashi
Ryukoku University

I

The theme of the first Fuji International Conference on Business History, held in 1974, was "Strategy and Structure of Big Business," and the proceedings of the conference were later published under the same title.[1] As the theme indicates, most of the papers presented related to the relationship between the strategy of enterprises and their managerial structure. The framework used in analysis was formulated mainly by Alfred D. Chandler, Jr. Since then, the problem of strategy and structure has become one of the most popular subjects among business historians, and intensive studies have been conducted. Meanwhile, through the works of Chandler and other business historians, such terms as "managerial enterprise," "managerial capitalism," and "managerial hierarchies" have become widely accepted among students of business history.[2] Those interested in this subject have also studied Japanese industrial enterprises. As a result, "Development of Managerial Enterprises" was selected as the theme of the second meeting of the third series of the Fuji Conference, held January 5–8, 1985, at the Fuji Education Center in Shizuoka Prefecture.

Nine papers were presented at the conference, most of them closely related to this theme. Brief comments on the papers by nominees were followed by lively discussion at each session. This volume contains the papers, comments, responses, and summary of the concluding discussion. Needless to say, the contents are based on years of study. As co-editor of this volume, I feel that it is pertinent here to trace the process that led to the emergence of managerial enterprises in Japan, introducing some representative works

ix

by Japanese business historians, so that non-Japanese readers who may not be familiar with Japanese studies will be able to gain a better understanding of the historical background of the conference theme as it relates to Japan.

The following remarks are divided into three parts: the relationship between owners and managers in the Edo period (1603–1867), the formation of managerial hierarchies in the Meiji era (1868–1912), and the emergence of salaried managers, who eventually came to control such hierarchies. Although there are a large number of studies relating to these issues, I will confine myself to works that relate directly to the theme of the conference.

II

If managerial enterprises are defined as firms in which top-level management decisions are made by salaried managers who own few shares of the company's stock, and if the process leading to the formation of such enterprises began with the employment of managers at the top level of managerial hierarchies, the prototype of such enterprises in Japan is to be found at a rather primitive stage of business development. In the Edo period it was the rule for big merchant houses to recruit competent men from among the employees and delegate managerial functions to them.[3] This type of manager, called a *bantō*, was promoted from among the *kumigashira*, or section heads. Starting as an apprentice at the age of 12 or 14, employees of the merchant houses had to climb more than a dozen steps on the hierarchical ladder to attain the position of *kumigashira*. Moreover, competition for the position of bantō was so intense that only a small number of employees attained this managerial post. In his study of the house of Mitsui from 1696 to 1730, Nakai Nobuhiko estimates that only 5% of apprentices became managers.[4]

Once promoted, however, managers were in a very powerful position, and they were often recognized as the key men who controlled the future of the enterprises they served. Referring to the importance of managers, one document states that a manager is "the leader of the commercial house and bears the heaviest responsibility. The rise or fall of the merchant house depends completely on his strategy. In extreme cases, the house delegates to him not only the responsibility for both the business and the household but also the authority to check the behavior of the owner if he indulges in bad habits."[5] In the Edo period many merchant houses identified their business with their household, so the failure of the business brought shame on the family.

In a sense, it was more convenient for a family to have daughters than sons. On the one hand, a son, if incompetent, often brought about the ruin of both the family and the business. On the other hand, a good-looking daughter meant there was a good chance of finding a capable young manager who would be willing to marry into the family. In fact, Yasuoka Shigeaki's study of Mitsui reveals that in only 13 of 51 cases, or 26%, did a son inherit; in the remaining 38 cases (74%), a son-in-law inherited. Yasuoka assumes that this does not necessarily mean that in 38 cases there was no son; instead, "it must be presumed that in many cases the son was incapable of running the business. The case of Daimaru, whose family preferred daughters because of the prospect of selecting better successors, indicates such a situation."[6]

Although, as we will see, the origins of salaried managers in the Meiji era were quite different from those of bantō managers in the Edo period, through these studies of the business and *ie* (house, in the sense of the extended family or household) system in traditional society we can see that the owners of businesses in the Edo period showed an active inclination to hire managers, delegate responsibility and authority to them, and take them into the family through marriage. This inclination or propensity was transmitted from generation to generation and also characterized the attitude of business owners in the Meiji era, an attitude described by Morikawa Hidemasa, the project leader of this conference, as the "progressiveness" of owners and one of the preconditions for the development of Japanese managerial capitalism.

III

The Meiji Restoration of 1868 was an epoch-making event in Japanese history. With the Restoration, Japan abandoned its closed-door policy and turned to introducing new technology, institutions, and ideas relating to business from the advanced countries. The corporation was among these. At first there was confusion and misunderstanding over the function and mechanism of a corporation. As is customary with late-developing countries, it was the government and the intellectuals who took the initiative in transplanting the new institution. To promote the establishment of corporate enterprises, the government issued the National Bank Ordinance in 1872. This resulted in making the national banks the pioneers of modern business enterprise although they lacked important qualifications to be called corporations, since the liability of investors was unlimited and shares were not transferrable. However, following the banks' lead, financial intermediaries, such as stock exchanges and insurance companies, incorporated themselves. After the establishment of the central bank in 1882, the corporate system spread to textile, railway, and many other industrial enterprises.

Two intellectual figures made major contributions to the adoption of the corporate system. One was Shibusawa Eiichi, and the other was Fukuzawa Yukichi. At the time of the Restoration, Shibusawa was overseas and had a chance to observe the practicality of businesses based on huge amounts of capital collected from social funds. Upon his return to Japan he obtained a post in the government and, through his recommendations and writings, promoted the establishment of Western-type enterprises. In later years, through his efforts as a promoter of new ventures in various new industries, Shibusawa came to be known as one of the greatest figures in the Japanese business world of his time. Fukuzawa also had an opportunity to travel abroad before the Restoration. While working for the Tokugawa government, he published a book explaining "Western affairs" in which he demonstrated his knowledge of corporations, especially in relation to the issuing of stocks and bonds. In 1867 Fukuzawa established Keiō Gijuku (later Keio University) and is said to have lectured on joint-stock companies in his economics course. Two years later, when a bookstore opened in Yokohama, Fukuzawa advised the owner to set up a company that was separate from his private property.[7]

After much painful trial and error, the company system was widely adopted in the business community by the end of the 1880s.

According to a study by Imuta Yoshimitsu, 54% of 4,039 business companies had a form that could be called a corporation.[8] With the enforcement of the Commercial Code in 1893, the corporate system became the legal foundation for business management. At the turn of the century, leading firms that were organized as corporations began to build managerial hierarchies with directors and managers at various echelons.

The work of Yui Tsunehiko deserves mention in connection with academic studies on managerial hierarchies. The paper he presented at the 1978 annual meeting of the Business History Society of Japan, whose theme was "Management Organization in the Meiji Era," analyzed the process of the formation of managerial hierarchies, with emphasis on the structure of top-level management.[9] Starting with a simple form, the top management of leading firms adopted a hierarchical structure consisting of chairman, president, senior executive director, executive director, and junior executive director. This trend in the formation of the hierarchical structure is seen not only in ordinary business firms but also in the huge zaibatsu enterprises with their dual structure consisting of a central headquarters with many subsidiaries. At the same meeting Nagasawa Yasuaki presented a paper analyzing the case of Mitsubishi and provided evidence supporting Yui's generalizations.[10] In discussion at that meeting, Nakagawa Keiichirō pointed out that it was clear that one of the most peculiar characteristics of Japanese top management was the formation of a hierarchical structure without the system whereby the board of directors, representing the stockholders, rigidly controlled the executives. Possibly this is related to Japan's economic processes in general.[11]

Returning to the theme of the Fuji Conference, we see that the important thing was not the formation of managerial hierarchies per se but the formation of such hierarchies controlled by salaried managers. In the cases discussed in Yui's paper, most members of top management in the early stage of managerial development were large stockholders, and except for the president, most of them were not interested in management. Who, then, actually took on the responsibility of running the business? Commenting on a paper written by a journalist who criticized do-nothing directors, Yui pointed out the importance of managers and chief engineers: "Except for the president, the directors did not fully recognize their responsibilities as members of the board of directors, nor did they perform their functions to the fullest. Under such circumstances, except in cases where the president held all managerial functions and carried them out himself, it was often managers and chief engineers who took over the directors' functions. While supporting the president, they were often effectively in charge of the functions of top management to some extent."[12] Thus was the way to the managerial enterprise paved.

IV

In the last 20 years of the Meiji era, or from 1893 to 1912, as the managerial hierarchies of enterprises grew in size and complexity, the top echelon was increasingly filled by salaried managers. This process began with the appointment of a senior executive director, who was promoted from the rank of manager or chief engineer, and then spread to other directorial posts in top management. The senior executive director, *senmu torishimariyaku* in Japanese, held the strongest position after that of the president. Theoretically he could be separated from the ownership of the company, but to meet the requirements of the Commercial Code, which stated that the directors be elected from among the stockholders, he had to acquire a certain number of shares in various ways, including buying or borrowing them.[13]

Morikawa has produced an outstanding study of the process by which salaried managers emerged in top management.[14] He notes that there were two patterns of promoting capable men to top management: in one pattern the company promoted capable employees, and in the other the company recruited men with higher education. Many business historians identify the former pattern with the bantō management of merchant houses in the Edo period and consider it a continuous process from that period. But Morikawa repudiates this view, insisting that the latter pattern was the mainstream of the process leading to the emergence of the managerial enterprise.

To support his proposition that the Meiji entrepreneurs preferred educated young men to employees who had started out as apprentices, Morikawa cites the following remarks addressed to Fukuzawa Yukichi by Iwasaki Yatarō, founder of Mitsubishi: "When I went into the steamship business, I first tried hiring young men from ordinary families. It is true that they are naive, obedient, and useful for temporary routine work, but unfortunately they have no education and cannot see things in their true proportions. So they are not only likely to make foolish mistakes but also are often inclined to make serious mistakes, which must be avoided at all costs. I therefore changed my policy and began employing scholarly young men, but again they were the cause of many embarrassing moments. Their manners are so rough that once they are behind the counter, their words and appearance seem to drive customers away, which is intolerable. However, looking on the brighter side, they are well intentioned and sincere, and they are more knowledgeable [than the other type of employee] and are never afraid of trouble. So I always rely on them whenever I have to deal with others in difficult negotiations or situations. Although there are advantages and disadvantages to both types, it is hard to train ordinary young men to acquire a scholarly inclination; it is easier to teach scholars to change their manner."[15] In fact, in the rapidly changing environment of the Meiji era, business was looking for a new type of personnel with enough knowledge and insight to see things from a wider perspective. How and where, then, did business recruit these personnel? Who in fact became the first salaried managers?

In a study analyzing the emergence of salaried managers in the Meiji era, Morikawa has selected 170 cases of salaried managers in the top management of companies established in the Meiji era and examined them from various angles.[16] His findings may be summarized as follows: First, the ratio of salaried managers was higher in the zaibatsu type of enterprise than in the non-zaibatsu type. This meant that because of their huge diversified enterprises, from an early time the zaibatsu families had to rely on professionals to manage their businesses, whereas in the non-zaibatsu type of enterprise large stockholders controlled top management for the time being.

Second, enterprises used three methods to recruit salaried managers. The first was the promotion of managers or engineers from the lower echelons of the hierarchy, the second was the recruitment of managers or engineers from other organizations, and the third was the transfer of directors from other firms. The proportion of directors brought in from outside was very high. The second and third methods combined accounted for more than 70% of managers in the zaibatsu enterprises and for 77% of managers in the non-zaibatsu enterprises. This phenomenon indicates that it was difficult for firms to supply directors from within the organization.

Third, salaried managers were relatively young. Nearly half of them were in their forties; only 15% were over 50 years of age. Many members of the younger generation were engineers, and this meant that businesses had to recruit directors with technical knowledge, regardless of their age.

Fourth, the managers' educational level was very high. Sixty-eight percent had received higher education at an imperial university, private university, commercial or technical college, naval academy, or educational institution in a foreign country. There were three uneducated men, but they were geniuses of a kind in either management or technology.

Finally, one of the main sources of salaried managers was the government. About 46% of directors brought in from the outside were former government officials, while the rest were managers and chief engineers from other companies. Taking advantage of the scarcity of managerial resources, these men with managerial as well as technical abilities occupied positions in top management and shared decision making with the owners.

V

In this introduction I have deliberately placed the emphasis on top management, ignoring the problem of middle and lower management. Although it is a self-evident truth that the lower echelons of the hierarchy were also filled by hired managers, insofar as the formation of managerial enterprises is closely related to that of managerial hierarchies, studies on this aspect are worth deliberating. Chokki Toshiaki's study on management organization addresses the problem of managerial innovation in the electric machine industry in relation to business performance.[17] According to his study, the electric machine industry was very backward in management, especially in comparison with the textile industry. Just as was the case in many advanced countries, the textile industry was a leading sector of industrialization in Japan. In the pioneering companies, such as Kanegafuchi and Mie, business was managed by a well-organized hierarchical structure, with professional managers in top management. Therefore the latecomers often modeled their management system after that of these companies. After 1888, when Kurashiki Bōseki, a cotton-spinning company, was established, the volume of business was not very large at first, and management was correspondingly simple. However, in 1908, when the company purchased one of its rival companies and added the acquired company's factory to the original one, coordinating the flow of raw materials and products in the two factories became a serious problem. Although the company was busy in running the enlarged business, organizational reformation was immediately initiated, and a hierarchical structure with three levels of management was established. The company also adopted a line and staff system. As a result, "young college graduates were promoted to head each department, and the company was filled with an invigorating atmosphere." This is an example of organizational innovation at the middle and lower levels of management.

Unlike the textile industry, the electric machine industry experienced serious problems in managing its enterprises. The latter industry was not only newer but also more complex than the former. The main cause of the trouble, however, was not technological but managerial deficiencies. In fact, when Shibaura Seisakusho, a manufacturing company that was a forerunner of today's Toshiba, was set up in 1893, it was technologically outstanding in terms of quality as well as of its wide variety of products. But the company's management was so poor that even after 1900 the operation remained in confusion. "The inefficient floor plan for the placement of machines threw the flow of work off balance; in some parts of the operation workers were idle, while in other sections they were working day and night without a break. The situation was just like that of a river whose bed was so narrow that at some points the water overflowed, resulting in no water downstream." At that time the company had five factories under the Production Department. But at the middle level of management there were no functional departments except Production. How closely this department coordinated the operation of the factories is not clear in Chokki's study, nor is any information available to indicate the way in which the flow of raw materials and products at the factories was coordinated and monitored. This chaotic situation appears to have been the cause of the company's poor business performance. Then, under the leadership of Ōtaguro Jūgorō, the company undertook a series of management modifications at the middle and lower levels, including the abolition of the *sewayaku* system (similar to the inside-contractor system in other countries) and the introduction of welfare programs for workers. As a result, in 1901 the company recorded its first profit.

Although these echelons of the hierarchy were now headed by managers, it again became necessary for the company to remold its management structure. By 1920 the company had built up a functional, departmentalized management structure similar to that of American big businesses. In fact, the company had been introducing technological know-how from General Electric. It was quite plausible that the company could learn from the experience of GE not only in technology but also in management. Chokki also points out that other electric machine manufacturers in Japan, such as Hitachi and Matsushita, faced the same problem, which derived from the gap between strategy and structure in their early stages of development, and solved it by rationalizing their lower and middle-level management and, more important, by recruiting capable young men and posting them appropriately as middle or lower-level managers. Indeed, these levels of management became a far more important source of salaried managers for top-level management than did outside sources.

In the foregoing I have traced the general process of the formation of managerial enterprises in Japan by introducing some of the representative studies pertaining to this area. But as far as the present level of research is concerned, analysis seems to be rather static, although it presents much evidence and many findings covering a short period. I therefore feel that it is necessary to conduct studies, especially those based on dynamic analysis, covering a longer period. In addition, if this is done on a worldwide basis, we will have an international comparison to enable us to reach a deeper understanding of the managerial enterprise, or managerial capitalism, of each nation in historical perspective. This was also a major consideration in the selection of the development of managerial enterprises as the theme of the 1985 conference. The following papers are the result of an effort to approach this theme from various angles as well as from numerous assumptions developed by business historians in many countries. I hope this volume will encourage readers to delve more deeply into the important issues raised by the participants in the conference.

NOTES

1. Nakagawa Keiichirō, ed., *Strategy and Structure of Big Business: Proceedings of the First Fuji Conference*, Tokyo, 1976.
2. Alfred D. Chandler, Jr., *The Visible Hand: The Managerial Revolution in American Business*, Cambridge, Mass., 1977. Alfred D. Chandler, Jr., and Herman Daems, eds., *Managerial Hierarchies: Comparative Perspectives on the Rise of the Modern Industrial Enterprise*, Cambridge, Mass., 1980.
3. Yasuoka Shigeaki, *Zaibatsu keisei shi no kenkyū* (A historical study of the formation of the zaibatsu), Kyoto, 1970. Sukudō Yōtaro et al., *Nihon keiei shi* (Japanese business history), Kyoto, 1979. Horie Yasuzō, *Nihon keiei shi ni okeru "ie" no kenkyū* (A study of the ie in Japanese business history), Kyoto, 1984.
4. Nakai Nobuhiko, "Mitsui ke no keiei: Shiyōnin seido to sono un'ei" (Business management of the house of Mitsui), *Shakai keizai shigaku* (Socioeconomic history), Vol. 31, No. 6, 1966.
5. Horie, *Nihon keiei shi*, p. 46.
6. Yasuoka, *Zaibatsu keisei shi*, p. 231.
7. Yui Tsunehiko, "Meiji shonen no kaisha kigyō no ichi kōsatsu: kaisha chishiki no dōnyū to sono rikai ni tsuite" (A study of business companies in the early Meiji era: On the introduction and interpretation of the corporate system), in Ōtsuka Hisao et al., eds.,

    Shihonshugi no keisei to hatten (The formation and development of capitalism), Tokyo, 1968, pp. 143–47.

8. Imuta Yoshimitsu, *Meiji ki kabushikigaisha bunseki josetsu: Kōgi yō text* (Introduction to the analysis of Meiji-era corporations: A textbook), Tokyo, 1976, p. 141.

9. Yui Tsunehiko, "Meiji jidai ni okeru jūyaku soshiki no keisei," *Keiei shigaku* (Japan business history review), Vol. 14, No. 1, 1979; translated by Stephen W. McCallion as "The Development of the Organizational Structure of Top Management in Meiji Japan," in Nakagawa Keiichirō and Morikawa Hidemasa, eds., *Japanese Year Book on Business History: 1984*, Tokyo, 1984.

10. Nagasawa Yasuaki, "Meiji ki Mitsubishi no top management soshiki" (The formative process of Mitsubishi's top-management organization during the Meiji era), *Keiei shigaku* (Japan business history review), Vol. 14, No. 1, 1979.

11. See Nakagawa Keiichirō's comment in *Keiei shigaku*, Vol. 14, No. 1, p. 84.

12. Yui Tsunehiko, "Nihon ni okeru jūyaku soshiki no hensen: Meiji-Taishō-ki no kenkyū" (The development of the top-management organization in Japan: 1868–1920), *Keiei ronshū* (Meiji business review), Vol. 24, No. 2–3, 1977, p. 32.

13. Yui, "Meiji jidai ni okeru jūyaku soshiki," p. 20.

14. Morikawa Hidemasa, *Zaibatsu no keiei shi teki kenkyū* (Business history of the zaibatsu), Tokyo, 1980.

15. Morikawa, *Zaibatsu no keiei*, p. 14.

16. Morikawa, "Meiji ki ni okeru senmon keieisha no shinshutsu katei" (The growth of salaried executives in the Meiji era), *Business Review*, Vol. 21, No. 2, 1974.

17. Chokki Toshiaki, "Keiei soshiki" (Management organization), in Nakagawa Keiichirō, ed., *Nihon teki keiei* (Japanese-style management), *Nihon keiei shi kōza* (Studies on Japanese business history), Vol. 5, Tokyo, 1977, pp. 90–129.

Prerequisites for the Development of Managerial Capitalism: Cases in Prewar Japan

Hidemasa Morikawa
Yokohama National University

I

Managerial capitalism refers to a capitalist economy in which managerial enterprises dominate. Managerial enterprises are defined as "firms in which representatives of the founding families or of financial interests no longer make top-level management decisions—where such decisions are made by salaried managers who own little of companies' stock."[1] Accordingly, a study on the development of managerial capitalism and managerial enterprise must focus upon the processes by which salaried managers acquire the power to make top-level management decisions.

Up to the present, many scholars have examined the reasons salaried managers came to take charge of top management in large enterprises and have pointed out the following three factors: (1) dispersion of the stockholding, (2) the financial situation, and (3) formation of a managerial hierarchy. None of these, however, provides a fully adequate explanation.

First, dispersion of the stockholding can lead to an increasing number of stockholders with a few percent of shares who struggle for status within top management and consequently exclude salaried managers from that status. As I will mention later, there were a number of cases in prewar Japan in which big stockholders controlled the top management of large-scale public utility companies with widely dispersed stockholdings, while salaried managers virtually controlled the top management of big zaibatsu companies under completely closed family ownership.

Second, the financial situation cannot be the decisive factor for producing managerial enterprises, either. Companies that rely on

1

self-financing are apt to maintain the power of the founding family in exchange for freedom from outside financial interests. By comparison, the top management of companies that introduce vast sums of money from the outside are easily permeated by financial interests, while the power of the family declines. Neither of these financial situations can independently ensure the domination of top management by salaried managers.[2]

Third, most business enterprises came to require a large number of salaried managers and organized them into a hierarchy for administrative coordination in proportion to the growth of the scale of the enterprise, increases in its units, increases in the complexity of its structure, and advances in its technology. The formation of such a managerial hierarchy shows that salaried managers play an indispensable role within big enterprises.[3]

Although the formation of a managerial hierarchy alone can explain the fact that salaried managers increase in number within middle management, it cannot fully explain why salaried managers are advanced to top management and dominate it.

It can be asserted that owners—founders, founding families, big stockholders—are unable to supply large numbers of people to fill top management posts in big enterprises and that therefore big enterprises have to depend on salaried managers. But this is too general a statement.

In this paper, therefore, I aim to find the direct cause of the process by which salaried managers of big enterprises came to dominate top management in Japan and to show the inevitability of this process. Generally speaking, managerial resources consist of money, goods, and manpower. When goods are divided into hardware and software, the former is obtained by money, while the latter pertains to manpower. Therefore we can regard money and manpower as managerial resources. Until now, however, the interest of business historians in Japan has been too narrowly focused upon money. By contrast, I have always aimed my business history research at manpower and will continue this approach in this paper. At this point, I should touch on the problem of definition.

The main topic of this conference is the managerial enterprise, or the salaried manager. But there is an inconsistency in the definition of managerial enterprise, or salaried manager, among us. Some participants take managerial enterprise to be an enterprise vested with a managerial hierarchy. But a managerial enterprise is not always the same as an enterprise vested with a managerial hierarchy. To discuss the topic fruitfully, we should use the term "managerial enterprise" with the meaning given in Professor Chandler's definition, which I cited at the outset of this paper. Some scholars are accustomed to using the term "professional manager" as meaning the same as "salaried manager." I believe, however, that they are not the same. A professional manager is the opposite of an amateur manager, whereas a salaried manager is the opposite of an owner-manager. The term "professional" means full time and specially trained. Accordingly, professional managers are found not only among employees but among owners. If we use the term "professional manager," we cannot clearly separate owner-managers and top managers promoted from among employees of the company.

II

Using the two dichotomies between owner-manager and salaried manager and between personal (family) enterprise and joint-stock enterprise (plural owners), four types of top management can be said to exist: X, Y, Z_1, and Z_2 (Fig. 1). I would like to observe the changes in relationships among these four types in prewar big Japanese companies. Specifically, I will compare the composition of top management in 65 big enterprises between 1913 and 1930.[4] Here I define big enterprises as joint-stock corporations, limited partnerships, and unlimited partnerships with paid-up capital above the following levels:

1913	Banking, electricity, mining	¥3,000,000
	Other	¥1,500,000
1930	Banking, electricity	¥20,000,000
	Other	¥10,000,000

Although the number of big enterprises in terms of these criteria totaled more than 65 in both 1913 and 1930, those on which we can compare data between the two years were limited to 65. Stated

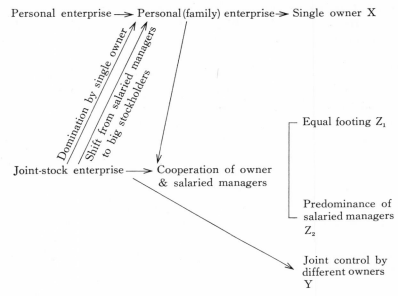

FIG. 1   Shifts between Types of Enterprises.

more accurately, there were 65 big enterprises in 1930 but 69 in 1913. The reason is that four companies in the 1930 list were amalgamations of two companies in the 1913 list, as follows:

Tōyō Bōseki (cotton spinning)	Result of merger of Osaka Bōseki and Mie Bōseki in 1914
Dai Nihon Bōseki (cotton spinning)	Result of merger of Amagasaki Bōseki and Settsu Bōseki in 1918
Nihon Sekiyu (petroleum)	Result of merger of Nihon Sekiyu and Hōden Sekiyu in 1921
Tōhō Denryoku (electric power)	Result of merger of Nagoya Dentō and Kyushu Dentō Tetsudō in 1921 and 1922

The composition of top management is shown by the ratio of

owners to salaried managers in the board of directors (or institution corresponding to it). In this paper salaried managers are defined as directors who *in principle* had no stockholding.

I should comment on two points here. First, for a long time boards of directors in Japanese joint-stock companies were the sole top management institution holding both policy-making and executive functions.[5] Before the 1910s, in many big enterprises *shihainin* (senior salaried managers) executed the policies decided upon by the board of directors. But shihainin never qualified for top management because of their concentration on day-to-day operations, and thereafter their functions were absorbed into those of the board of directors.

Within the board of directors, up to six different levels of directors existed: *kaichō* (chairman), *shachō* (president), *fukushachō* (vice-president), *senmu torishimariyaku* (senior executive director), *jōmu torishimariyaku* (executive director), and *(hira) torishimariyaku* (director), each with a voice in policy making according to the level.[6] Here, however, I have no space to deal with this structure in detail. In prewar Japanese joint-stock companies, the post of *kansayaku* (inspector) also existed and was held by someone elected from among big stockholders in order to monitor the operation of the board of directors. The kansayaku, however, did not qualify for top management because he had no policy-making or executive functions.

A second point that I need to make is the reason I define salaried managers as "directors who *in principle* had no stockholding." The reason lies in the fact that it is difficult to differentiate clearly a salaried manager from an owner in the prewar period, especially in the earlier part of the period. At that time a salaried manager generally earned a large salary because of the scarcity of managerial talent. A number of salaried managers employed in joint-stock companies that had offered their shares to the public bought their companies' shares using their high income, and became big stockholders. A few of them became big stockholders before advancing to the post of director by receiving the right to buy their companies' newly issued shares at face value as a reward for their services.

For example, Kagami Kenkichi and Hirao Hachisaburō, both among the ablest managers of Tokyo Kaijō Hoken (Tokyo Marine

Insurance Co.), joined the board of directors in 1917. However, at that time both were already big stockholders of the company. The stockholdings (number and ratio) of both had increased over time as follows[7]:

	1904	1907	1919
Kagami	500 (1.6%)	2,300 (3.8%)	10,000 (3.3%)
Hirao	241 (0.8%)	1,500 (2.5%)	4,700 (1.6%)

In 1906 Tokyo Kaijō doubled its capital and gave the priority to apply for the newly issued shares to Kagami (1,500) and Hirao (1,000) as a reward for their contributions to the company.[8]

Referring to the above types of cases in the earlier part of the prewar period, I classify stockholding directors as salaried managers when this stockholding was based upon their activities as salaried managers. Such cases, however, were limited to salaried managers who really held their companies' shares. In prewar Japan's joint-stock companies, every director was required to be a stockholder according to the Commercial Code, and as a result almost all salaried managers who had no shares could acquire the position of director by borrowing shares from someone else and transferring the title. These cases, however, differ from the above.

I distinguish the four types of top management, X, Y, Z_1, and Z_2, on the basis of the ratio of owners and salaried managers on the board of directors, as follows:

X	Family members+joint stockholders>salaried managers
	Family members > joint stockholders
Y	Joint stockholders > salaried managers
Z_1	Owners (family members or joint stockholders) account for less than half but more than one-third of all directors
Z_2	Owners account for less than one-third of all directors

In case of X and Y, if the ratio of salaried managers is close to half of all directors (and thus close to Z_1), I deal with them as X' and Y'.

Using the above categorization, I compared the composition of the boards of directors of 65 companies in 1913 and 1930. But before discussing my results, I would like to refer to some other procedural problems I encountered, some of which go beyond the scope of Japan and are related to the fundamental part of the development of managerial enterprises.

1. When a salaried manager of a parent company or a subsidiary company of Company A became a director of A in the capacity of a delegate, there arises the problem as to whether he was an owner or a salaried manager. I classify him as an owner-manager of Company A. There were many such cases in zaibatsu enterprises.

2. When a big stockholder of Company B lent shares of B to somebody who was not an officer of B and let him become a director of B as his agent or representative, the agent must be regarded as having been an owner-manager. But when somebody with managerial talent was made a director of Company B, he is better classified as a salaried manager of B. Theoretically it is easy to differentiate between these two types of directors. But in actual historical research it is sometimes difficult. Therefore, I regard all directors brought in directly from the outside as salaried managers except those who were clearly the agents of big stockholders and held positions in different companies simultaneously (in these cases they were often agents).

3. A director who did not hold any of his company's stock and functioned as the agent of a financial interest cannot, in theory, be defined as a salaried manager. Yet it is impossible to distinguish him from a salaried manager on the basis of ordinary company records. Directors who had a close relationship with a bank cannot always be inferred to have been the agents of a financial interest. Therefore I only classify as agents of financial interests, and thus as owners rather than salaried managers, those who became directors of Company C under the strong request of Bank D, from which C had borrowed much money, and who resigned as directors of C when the financial tie between C and D disappeared.

For example, Kasahara Kanmi, a director of Nihon Kōkan (NKK) from 1926 to 1933 (the last year as executive director), assumed this post in 1926 on the strong recommendation of Yuki Toyotarō, vice-president of Yasuda Ginkō (Yasuda Bank) until 1929 and president of Nihon Kōgyō Ginkō (Industrial Bank of

Japan) from 1930. Thereafter Kasahara functioned as the agent of
Yasuda Ginkō and Nihon Kōgyō Ginkō, the biggest lender to NKK,
and guided NKK's top management through its financial difficulties,
especially after 1930. However, in 1933, when NKK was able to
escape from its dependency on Nihon Kōgyō Ginkō, Kasahara
resigned.[9] A director like Kasahara cannot be classified as a
salaried manager.

4.   I classify high-level former bureaucrats who assumed directorships of companies (so-called *amakudari*) as salaried managers unless
there was some proof that they were the agents of big stockholders
or banks.

Using the above definitions, I compared the types of boards of
directors of 65 big enterprises in 1913 and 1930. My results are
given in Table 1.

TABLE 1   Classification of 65 Big Companies.

1.	Daiichi Ginkō	(First Bank, a forerunner of Daiichi Kangyō Ginkō)	$Y' \rightarrow Z_2$
2.	Yasuda Ginkō	(Yasuda Bank, today Fuji Bank)	$X \rightarrow X$
3.	Mitsui Ginkō	(Mitsui Bank)	$X' \rightarrow Z_1$
4.	Jūgo Ginkō	(Fifteenth Bank, absorbed into Mitsui Ginkō in 1944)	$Y \rightarrow Z_2$
5.	Sumitomo Ginkō	(Sumitomo Bank)	$Z_1 \rightarrow Z_2$
6.	Sanjūshi Ginkō	(Thirty-fourth Bank, a forerunner of Sanwa Ginkō)	$Y \rightarrow Y'$
7.	Mitsui Bussan	(Mitsui Trading)	$Z_1 \rightarrow Z_1$
8.	Nihon Menka	(today Nichimen; Trading)	$Y' \rightarrow Z_2$
9.	Nihon Yūsen	(NYK; shipping)	$Z_2 \rightarrow Y$
10.	Osaka Shōsen	(OSK; shipping)	$Y' \rightarrow Z_1$
11.	Tōshin Sōko	(Tōshin Warehouse)	$X \rightarrow Z_1$
12.	Mitsubishi Sōko	(Mitsubishi Warehouse)	$X \rightarrow X'$
13.	Kanegafuchi Bōseki	(Kanegafuchi Cotton Spinning, today Kanebo)	$Z_1 \rightarrow Z_2$
14.	Tōyō Bōseki	(Tōyō Cotton Spinning)	$\left.\begin{array}{l} Y \\ Z_1 \end{array}\right\} \rightarrow Z_2$
15.	Dai Nihon Bōseki	(Dai Nihon Cotton Spinning, today Unitika)	$\left.\begin{array}{l} Z_2 \\ Y \end{array}\right\} \rightarrow Z_1$
16.	Osaka Gōdō Bōseki	(Osaka Gōdō Cotton Spinning, absorbed into Tōyō Bōseki in 1931)	$Y \rightarrow Z_2$

TABLE 1   (*continued*—2)

17.	Fuji Gas Bōseki	(Fuji Gas Cotton Spinning, today Fuji Bōseki)	$Y \to Z_1$
18.	Nissin Bōseki	(Nissin Cotton Spinning)	$Y \to Z_2$
19.	Naigai Wata	(Naigai Cotton Spinning, today Shin Naigai Men, a subsidiary of Shikishima Bōseki)	$Y' \to Z_2$
20.	Nihon Keori	(worsted and woolen cloth)	$Y \to Y'$
21.	Tōkyō Muslin	(today Daitō Bōshoku)	$Y \to Y$
22.	Teikoku Seima	(linen spinning)	$Y \to Y'$
23.	Ōji Seishi	(Ōji Paper Mill)	$Y' \to Z_2$
24.	Fuji Seishi	(Fuji Paper Mill, merged with Ōji in 1933)	$Y \to Y'$
25.	Dai Nihon Seitō	(sugar plantations and refining)	$Y \to Z_2$
26.	Meiji Seitō	(sugar plantations and refining)	$Y' \to Z_2$
27.	Ensuiko Seitō	(sugar plantations and refining)	$Y \to Z_1$
28.	Taiwan Seitō	(sugar plantations and refining, today Taito)	$Y' \to Y'$
29.	Teikoku Seitō	(sugar plantations and refining, absorbed into Dai Nihon Seitō in 1941)	$Y \to Y'$
30.	Dai Nihon Beer	(divided into Nihon Beer and Asahi Beer in 1949)	$Y' \to Z_2$
31.	Nihon Beer Kōsen	(beer brewing and mineral water producing, absorbed into Dai Nihon Beer in 1933)	$Y \to Y$
32.	Dai Nihon Jinzō Hiryō	(today Nissan Kagaku; chemical fertilizer)	$Y \to Y$
33.	Nihon Chisso Hiryō	(today divided into Chisso, Asahi Kasei, Sekisui Kagaku; chemical fertilizer)	$Y \to Y$
34.	Onoda Cement		$Y \to Y'$
35.	Asano Cement	(today Nihon Cement)	$X \to X$
36.	Kawasaki Zōsensho	(Kawasaki Shipyard, today Kawasaki Jūkōgyō)	$Y \to Z_2$
37.	Nihon Denki	(NEC; electric machinery)	$Y \to Y'$
38.	Shibaura Seisakusho	(a forerunner of Toshiba; electric machinery)	$Y' \to Y$
39.	Nihon Seikōsho	(steel and arms)	$Y \to Y'$
40.	Mistui Kōzan	(Mitsui Mining)	$X' \to Z_2$
41.	Ōkura Kōgyō	(Ōkura Mining, dissolved in 1949)	$X \to Z_2$
42.	Fujita Kōgyō	(Fujita Mining, today Dōwa Kōgyō)	$X \to X$
43.	Hokkaido Tankō Kisen	(coal mining)	$Y' \to Z_1$

TABLE 1   (*continued*—3)

44. Nihon Kōgyō	(Nihon Mining)	$X \rightarrow Z_1$
45. Meiji Kōgyō	(Meiji Mining, dissolved in 1969)	$X \rightarrow Z_1$
46. Nihon Sekiyu	(petroleum)	$\left.\begin{array}{c}Y\\Y\end{array}\right\} \rightarrow Y$
47. Tōbu Tetsudō	(Tōbu Railway)	$Y \rightarrow Y'$
48. Nankai Tetsudō	(Nankai Railway)	$Y \rightarrow Y$
49. Keihan Dentetsu	(Keihan Railway)	$Y \rightarrow Z_1$
50. Hanshin Kyūkō Dentetsu	(Hankyū Railway)	$Y \rightarrow Y$
51. Hanshin Denki Tetsudō	(Hanshin Railway)	$Y \rightarrow Y'$
52. Nagoya Tetsudō	(Nagoya Railway)	$Y \rightarrow Y'$
53. Tokyo Dentō	(Tokyo Electric Power)	$Y \rightarrow Y'$
54. Daidō Denryoku	(Daidō Electric Power)	$Y' \rightarrow Y'$
55. Tōhō Denryoku	(Tōhō Electric Power)	$\left.\begin{array}{c}Y\\Y\end{array}\right\} \rightarrow Y$
56. Ujigawa Denki	(Ujigawa Electric Power)	$Y \rightarrow Z_1$
57. Kyoto Dentō	(Kyoto Electric Power)	$Y \rightarrow Z_1$
58. Kinugawa Suiryoku	(Kinugawa Electric Power)	$Y \rightarrow Y$
59. Tokyo Gas		$Y \rightarrow Y$
60. Osaka Gas		$Y' \rightarrow Z_1$
61. Tōhō Gas		$Y \rightarrow Z_2$
62. Mitsui Gōmei	(Headquarters of Mistui zaibatsu)	$X \rightarrow Z_1$
63. Mitsubishi Gōshi	(Headquarters of Mitsubishi zaibatsu)	$X \rightarrow Z_2$
64. Yasuda Hozensha	(Headquarters of Yasuda zaibatsu)	$X \rightarrow X'$
65. Furukawa Gōmei	(Headquarters of Furukawa zaibatsu)	$X' \rightarrow Z_1$

Source: Shōgyō Kōshinjo, Nihon zenkoku sho kaisha yakuinroku (Japanese directory of company directors).

Note: The electric power industry in Japan was drastically reorganized by the wartime government, and companies 54–58 no longer exist.

As a whole, the trend was toward a movement from X or Y $\rightarrow$ X' and Y' $\rightarrow Z_1 \rightarrow Z_2$. This trend shows the rising status of salaried managers within the top management of big enterprises. Of 65 big companies, only 2 exhibited a regressive trend (Nihon Yūsen [9], $Z_2 \rightarrow$ Y, and Shibaura Seisakusho [38], Y' $\rightarrow$ Y), while 13 showed a trend toward stagnation, hovering around the X or Y level:

Yasuda Ginkō (2)	Nihon Chisso Hiryō (33)
Tokyo Muslin (21)	Asano Cement (35)
Nihon Beer Kōsen (31)	Fujita Kōgyō (42)
Dai Nihon Jinzōhiryō (32)	Nihon Sekiyu (46)

TABLE 2   Shift in Type of 65 Big Companies.

Type	1913	1930
X	11	3
Y	36	12
X′	3	2
Y′	13	14
Z_1	4	16
Z_2	2	18
Total	69	65

Source: Same as Table 1.

Nankai Tetsudō (48)   Tōhō Denryoku (55)
Hanshin Kyūkō Dentetsu   Kinugawa Suiryoku (58)
   (50)   Tokyo Gas (59)

If 2 Y′ → Y′ companies (Taiwan Seitō [28] and Daidō Denryoku [54]) are added to the above, "stagnation"-type companies total 15. The other 50 companies consisted of 49 of the "advanced" type and one (Mitsui Bussan [7]) remaining as Z_1. The 65 big companies in 1930 can be classified as follows: X(3), Y (12), X′ (2), Y′ (14), Z_1 (16), and Z_2 (18); the 69 companies in 1913 can be classified as follows: X (11), Y (36), X′ (3), Y′ (13), Z_1 (4), and Z_2 (2) (Table 2).

From this we can clearly observe the remarkable development of managerial enterprises. However, in 1930, companies in which salaried managers exceeded owner-managers ($Z_1 + Z_2$) totaled 34, accounting for only a little more than half. Thus, at this point managerial enterprises were still not dominant among Japanese big companies. Accordingly, we have to say that in 1930 Japanese managerial capitalism was still developing or in a transitional stage.

III

According to data from the 1930 edition of the *Japanese directory of company directors*, there were 158 big enterprises in 1930. Of these, 27 can be classified as Z_2. The reason this number exceeds the number of Z_2 companies in 1930 in Table 2 is that it includes companies for which there were no data in 1913. The fact that the number of Z_2 companies in 1930 was only 27 and only 17% of all big enterprises indicates again the transitional stage of Japanese managerial capitalism. Yet however small this number may be, by studying these 27 most advanced managerial enterprises we can understand the basis for the steady trend toward managerial capitalism that arose within Japanese big companies between 1913 and 1930. The names of the 27 companies are given in Table 3. The meaning of columns I, II, and III will be explained later.[10]

The reason these 27 companies could become pioneers of managerial enterprises does not lie in the industries to which they belonged. They belonged to many different industries. Moreover, within one industry there coexisted companies with a high degree of advancement of salaried managers to top management (Z_2) and those with a low degree (X, Y), such as Daiichi Ginkō and Yasuda Ginkō in banking, Yamashita Kisen and Nihon Yūsen in shipping, Tōhō Gas and Tokyo Gas in gas production, and Mitsui Kōzan and Fujita Kōgyō in mining. The industry to which the company belonged thus did not automatically determine the ratio of salaried managers in its top management. Some of these 27 companies were large in scale and technologically advanced, held high market shares, and employed a number of salaried managers in a bureaucratic hierarchy. However, we cannot explain the advanced nature of these 27 companies only by such characteristics of big modern enterprises, since X and Y types of big enterprises in 1930, such as Nihon Yūsen, Tokyo Gas, Dai Nihon Jinzō Hiryō, and Nihon Sekiyu also possessed a hierarchy of salaried managers.

To explain the causes of the advanced nature of these 27 companies, therefore, I have classified them into types I, II, and III according to their character in 1930. Type I indicates zaibatsu joint-stock companies, and Type II, non-zaibatsu joint-stock companies. Type II companies, except for Yamashita Kisen, were owned and controlled by more than one rich man. Type III indicates big companies that went bankrupt during the 1927 economic crisis and were rebuilding in 1930. Of the 27 companies, types I and II are important, while III need not be considered. The reason is that type III companies only appeared to exhibit the progressive aspects of managerial enterprises, since their owner-managers had

TABLE 3   27 Z$_2$ Companies in 1930.

Industry / Type	I	II	III
Bank	Sumitomo Ginkō 5	Daiichi Ginkō 1	Jūgo Ginkō 4
Trading	Mitsubishi Shōji (Mitsubishi Trading) Tōyō Menka (Mitsui Bussan subsidiary)	Nihon Menka 8 Gōshō (a forerunner of Kanematsu Gōshō)	
Shipping		Yamashita Kisen	
Shipbuilding	Mitsubishi Zōsen (today Mitsubishi Jūkōgyō)		Kawasaki Zōsensho 36
Cotton spinning	Kanegafuchi Bōseki (Mitsui affiliate) 13	Tōyō Bōseki 14 Osaka Gōdō Bōseki 16 Nissin Bōseki 18 Naigai Wata 19	
Rayon			Teikoku Jinzō Kenshi (today Teijin)
Paper manu- facturing	Ōji Seishi (Mitsui affiliate) 23		
Beer brewing		Dai Nihon Beer 30	
Sugar plantations & refining		Dai Nihon Seitō 25 Meiji Seitō 26	
Department store	Mitsukoshi (Mitsui affiliate)		
Mining (including iron)	Mitsui Kōzan 40 Mitsubishi Kōgyō (Mitsubishi Mining) Ōkura Kōgyō 41 Kamaishi Kōzan (Mitsui Kōzan subsidiary)		
Gas production		Tōhō Gas 62	
Zaibatsu headquarters	Mitsubishi Gōshi 64		

Source: Same as Table 1.

resigned to take responsibility for bankruptcy and had been replaced by former bureaucrats and salaried managers.[11]

Type I companies were almost totally owned by zaibatsu families except for some Mitsui affiliates. While Tōyō Menka, as a subsidiary, was completely owned by Mitsui Bussan and Kamaishi Kōzan by Mitsui Kōzan, the ratio of stock held by the Mitsui family and Mitsui enterprises in the total stock of Kanegafuchi Bōseki, Ōji Seishi, and Mitsukoshi was not so high in 1930. These three, however, were influential companies within the Mitsui zaibatsu until the 1900s and kept their stockholding and financial relationship with the Mitsui zaibatsu until 1930. In regard to type I companies, it is significant that in prewar Japan these most advanced companies in terms of the promotion of salaried managers to top management belonged to big zaibatsu with extremely closed familial structures.[12]

Of the four zaibatsu represented in type I companies, the big three, Mitsui, Mitsubishi, and Sumitomo, were especially eager to employ highly educated personnel from an early period. Mitsubishi Kaisha (Mitsubishi Company), a shipping business before 1885, and Mitsui Bussan, for example, began to employ a number of highly educated men in the mid 1870s, while Mitsui Ginkō, Mitsui Kōzan, and Sumitomo Ginkō followed suit around 1890. As a result, at the turn of the century a hierarchy of salaried managers was built up within the three big zaibatsu, and senior members among these managers were promoted to top management.

The employment and promotion of many highly educated personnel was made possible by progressive top managers who recognized the need in the new era for new managerial talent. Examples of progressive top managers were Iwasaki Yatarō and his brother Yanosuke, both owners of Mitsubishi; Masuda Takashi, Nakamigawa Hikojirō, and Dan Takuma, all three salaried managers of Mitsui; and Iba Sadatake and Suzuki Masaya, both salaried managers of Sumitomo. These top salaried managers of Mitsui and Sumitomo were brought in from outside and had influence over the owners. In old family enterprises with long histories extending from the Edo period (1603–1867), such as Mitsui and Sumitomo, a tradition was maintained by which top management was delegated to a representative of the employees. Owing to this, the shift in top management toward highly educated employees and away from old-style employees (*bantō*), who lacked much education, was more easily accepted by the zaibatsu family and proceeded smoothly.[13]

I am not saying, however, that the favorable treatment of highly educated, salaried managers in Mitsui and Sumitomo derived from the tradition of the old merchant houses. Another old merchant house, Kōnoike, which was a rival of Mitsui in terms of wealth, was not at all ardent in the employment and advancement of highly educated, salaried managers, and as a result could not develop into a big modern zaibatsu.[14]

In the Ōkura zaibatsu, founder Ōkura Kihachirō, who lacked a formal education, nevertheless recognized the necessity of new-style managers in order to succeed in commerce, civil engineering, and construction business for the government, and hired such highly educated young men as Takashima Kokinji, Itō Kumema, and Kadono Chokurō. Furthermore, he had his daughters marry Takashima and Itō and sent his eldest son, Kishichirō, abroad to study at Cambridge. The top management of the Ōkura zaibatsu, composed of the Ōkura family and top salaried manager Kadono, tried to promote the development of salaried managers.[15]

The above description of type I generally holds true for type II, as well. Type II companies also had progressive owners and top salaried managers who committed themselves to employing and promoting highly educated salaried managers.

Among such owners were Yamashita Kamesaburō, the founder of Yamashita Kisen; Shibusawa Eiichi, the leading stockholder of Daiichi Ginkō; and Taniguchi Fusazō, the leading stockholder of Ōsaka Gōdō Bōseki. Fukumoto Motonosuke, the owner-manager of Amagasaki Bōseki (a forerunner of Dai Nihon Bōseki, which is not listed in Table 3 because it was a Z_1 company), was another such progressive owner. Fukumoto, as president and the representative of the big stockholders, overcame the latter's hostility to the participation of salaried managers in top management and promoted Kikuchi Kyōzō, the company's chief engineer, who had graduated from Tokyo Imperial University, to the post of director in 1893 and to that of president in 1901.[16]

Examples of progressive top salaried managers in type II companies were Kita Matazō of Nihon Menka, Nose Shichirōhei of Gōshō, Yamanobe Takeo and Saitō Tsunezō of Tōyō Bōseki, Miyajima Seijirō of Nissin Bōseki, Takei Ayazō of Naigai Wata, Makoshi Kyōhei of Dai Nihon Beer, Fujiyama Raita of Dai Nihon Seitō, Sōma Hanji of Meiji Seitō, and Okamoto Sakura of Tōhō Gas. Leading a corps of junior and subordinate salaried managers, they pioneered the way toward managerial enterprises. Such progressive top salaried managers were found among Z_1 companies, as well. Kikuchi Kyōzō of Dai Nihon Bōseki, Wada Toyoji of Fuji Gas Bōseki, and Hori Keijirō of Osaka Shōsen were examples.

Wada sought to promote salaried managers to the board of directors by using his power as president and to exclude big stockholders from the board, but he died in 1924 before accomplishing this. The diary of Asakura Tsuneto, a top salaried manager of Fuji Gas Bōseki who was promoted by Wada, tells of the difficulty such top salaried managers as Mochida Tatsumi and he had in their dealings with big stockholders and in enlarging the number of director's posts held by salaried managers.[17] This shows that it was very difficult for salaried managers to enter the board of directors and dominate top management in opposition to big stockholders.

IV

Next I would like to discuss big enterprises that had a low percentage of salaried managers in top management and examine the factors behind this.

Among the big enterprises in 1930 that lagged in the promotion of salaried managers there were three family enterprises (X): Yasuda Ginkō, Asano Cement, and Fujita Kōgyō, all of them zaibatsu enterprises. Among joint-stock companies established by plural owners, however, there were 12 Y enterprises, including Nihon Yūsen and Tokyo Gas.[18] Of all these, I would like to choose four companies as case studies: Yasuda Ginkō, Asano Cement, Nihon Yūsen, and Tokyo Gas. Nihon Yūsen is a particularly interesting example of a retreat from Z_2 in 1913 to Y in 1930.

Yasuda Ginkō: The attitude of Yasuda and Asano toward the employment and promotion of highly educated personnel differed greatly from that seen in the other big zaibatsu—not only Mitsui and Sumitomo, descendants of old and traditional merchant houses in existence since the Edo period, but also Mitsubishi and Ōkura, which like Yasuda and Asano were established after the Meiji Restoration of 1868.

Yasuda Zenjirō, founder of the Yasuda zaibatsu, lacked the keen awareness of the need to hire highly educated officers that other entrepreneurs who ran factories, mines, and trading firms had, because he had made an enormous amount of money as a financier, starting as a small money-changer. He did not recognize the value of an academic education because of his overconfidence in his own successful career, in which he had relied on his own experience alone. Furthermore, he was healthy until 83 and retained tight control over his zaibatsu. Consequently, it was impossible for any highly educated, salaried managers to rise up within the Yasuda zaibatsu.[19]

However, apparently sensitive to his reputation for holding higher education to be irrelevant, Zenjirō hired Iomi Teiichi, a graduate of Tokyo Imperial University, married Iomi to his daughter in 1897, and adopted him as his son, Iomi's name thereby changing to Yasuda Zenzaburō. Zenjirō also made Zenzaburō his heir rather than any of his own sons. As an owner-manager, Zenzaburō, unlike Zenjirō, sought to develop the manufacturing, mining, and trading businesses within the Yasuda zaibatsu and modernize it. In 1909 Zenjirō retired, and Zenzaburō assumed the posts of vice-president of Hozensha (the headquarters of the Yasuda zaibatsu) and *kantoku* (top-level monitor) of Yasuda Ginkō. However, his policy making was strongly checked by Zenjirō, who continued to hold de facto power and persisted in concentrating on financial business. In addition, the failure of nonfinancial businesses led by Zenzaburō weakened his influence. For example, although Zenzaburō had promised that Yasuda would invest in the newly established Nihon Kōkan, he had to withdraw this promise because of Zenjirō's opposition.[20] Finally in 1919 Zenzaburō, discontent with Zenjirō's interference, retired from top management and left the Yasuda family.[21]

Dictator Zenjirō was killed in 1921 by a fanatic who had been refused a donation. Zenjirō's sons, sons-in-law, and nephews were too incompetent to take charge of top management after his death, and as a result they asked Yuki Toyotarō, executive manager of the Bank of Japan, to assume the post of vice-president of Yasuda Ginkō and entrusted him with top authority over the Yasuda zaibatsu. Yuki followed Zenzaburō Yasuda's path toward modernizing the zaibatsu and adopted a number of highly educated, salaried managers. However, Yuki was unable to carry out his policies because of opposition from the Yasuda family, which was afraid of his radical reforms. As a result, he eventually left the Yasuda zaibatsu.[22] In 1930 the salaried managers of the Yasuda zaibatsu hired and promoted under Yuki's policy still had not reached the boards of directors of Yasuda Hozensha and Yasuda Ginkō.

Asano Cement: The Asano zaibatsu, including Asano Cement, did not allow salaried managers to advance to top management. The founder, Asano Sōichirō, was as uneducated and dictatorial and stayed in power as long as Yasuda Zenjirō—Asano died in 1930 at the age of 82. However, unlike Yasuda, the Asano zaibatsu did acquire a number of highly educated, salaried managers owing to the fact that Asano ran such wide-ranging businesses as cement, petroleum, shipping, shipbuilding, steelmaking, mining, banking, and trading.[23] But Sōichirō did not promote salaried managers to top management.

Although Sōichirō attached importance to the participation of highly educated personnel in top management, he required them to become members of the Asano family. Sōichirō formed a top management team consisting of himself, his sons Taijirō (Waseda University) and Ryōzō (Harvard University), and such salaried managers as Shiraishi Motojirō (Tokyo Imperial University), Suzuki Monjirō (Tokyo Kōtō Shōgyō, the forerunner of Hitotsubashi University), and Kaneko Kiyota (Tokyo Imperial University). Shiraishi, Suzuki, and Kaneko established kinship relations with the Asano family before being promoted to top management: Shiraishi and Suzuki married daughters of Sōichirō, and Kaneko married a granddaughter. This emphasis on kinship was similar to the case of Ōkura, but the Asano family did not bring forth such top salaried managers as Kadono in Ōkura. Isaka Takashi, a salaried manager graduated from Tokyo Imperial University, did assume the post of director of Tōyō Kisen (the shipping company of the Asano zaibatsu), but this was nothing but the temporary compromise of Sōichirō, the president, when he was called to account by big joint stockholders during a financial crisis in 1910. Isaka resigned his position in 1914 when Sōichirō recovered his power.[24] Kondō Kaijirō, a chemical engineer graduated from Tokyo Imperial University, could only attain the post of director of a small subsidiary of Asano Cement in his last years despite his contributions to the zaibatsu's petroleum enterprises.

Among the main enterprises of the Asano zaibatsu in 1930, Asano Dōzoku, the zaibatsu headquarters, had five directors but no salaried-manager directors, and Asano Cement had 11 directors but also no salaried-manager directors. Salaried-manager directors accounted for only two of 10 directors in Asano Zōsensho, two of eight directors in Asano Kokura Seikōsho (steelmaking, not included among the big enterprises), and one of five directors in Asano Bussan (trading, not included among the big enterprises). Tōyō Kisen went bankrupt after World War I and handed over the largest part of its shipping business to Nihon Yūsen.

One reason for the low degree of advancement of salaried managers in the Asano zaibatsu was that Asano depended on the joint stockholding of others because of its wide-ranging businesses and its insufficient funds, and therefore had to give the directorial positions to these big stockholders. The main reason, however, was Sōichirō's dictatorship and his superhuman energy. As the president of Tōyō Kisen, for example, he even kept track of the menus of third-class passengers.[25] His son-in-law Shiraishi Motojirō criticized his dictatorship and reliance on only his own experience and intuition, but could do nothing. Shiraishi established Nihon Kōkan in 1912 by collecting funds from a number of wealthy investors, including Sōichirō—as stated above, Shiraishi failed to bring in funds from Yasuda—and then concentrated on his role as president of Nihon Kōkan, keeping a certain distance from the Asano zaibatsu.[26]

Nihon Yūsen: The most interesting retreat $(Z_2 \rightarrow Y)$ was that of Nihon Yūsen (NYK); this was also derived from human factors. From the fall of 1915 to the spring of 1916 the two biggest stockholders, Iwasaki (owner of the Mitsubishi zaibatsu) and Mitsui Ginkō, sold a large part of their NYK stock to procure funds for expansion of their own zaibatsu by taking advantage of rising stock prices.[27] These NYK shares were bought by professional investors, who thereby strengthened their voices as big stockholders of NYK, while Iwasaki and Mitsui lost some influence. These investors then called upon NYK to greatly increase its capital and dividends. The board of directors, composed of salaried managers (at that time NYK was classified as Z_2) opposed these demands. Trouble arose as a result, but it was mediated by leading figures of the business world (*zaikai*) and settled in the form of an agreement to make moderate increases in NYK's capital and dividends.[28]

However, the investors also demanded an increase in the number of directors and the assignment of the increase to representatives of the big stockholders. Furthermore, because the senior executive director and the leading top salaried manager, Hayashi Tamio, resigned in 1917, the relative power of salaried managers in top management quickly dropped. Hayashi's resignation stemmed from personal conflicts that developed among the three top salaried managers—President Kondō Rempei, Vice-President Katō Masayoshi, and Hayashi—during Kondō's long presidency, which had begun in 1895. Katō played the role of mediator after his resignation in 1915, joining forces with the big stockholders, while Hayashi resigned as a result of Kondō's disapproval of Hayashi's active hostility toward the big stockholders and mediators.[29]

After Kondō's death in 1921 and the resignation of Katō and Hayashi, NYK's top management was greatly weakened. In this vacuum the Dōkōkai jiken (Dōkōkai affair) occurred in the autumn of 1924. The affair began with conflict between marine officers and shore officers within NYK and escalated, leading to the resignation of about 700 shore officers who had organized themselves into the Dōkōkai.[30] This affair was settled through the intervention of the big stockholders, but all the directors resigned, accepting responsibility for the incident. The stockholders who served as mediators increased the ratio of big stockholders on the board of directors and stopped the promotion of salaried managers to the post of director.[31] Consequently, the ratio of salaried managers in top management dwindled to only two of nine directors. In 1930 this increased to five of 12 directors, but by then NYK was classified as type Y.

Tokyo Gas: Tokyo Gas's paid-up capital in 1930 was ¥100 million, following Tokyo Dentō (¥400 million), Mitsui Gōmei (¥300 million), Sumitomo Gōshi (¥150 million), Daidō Denryoku (¥130 million), Mitsubishi Gōshi (¥120 million), and Tōhō Denryoku (¥120 million). Tokyo Dentō, Daidō, and Tōhō were electric power companies, while Mitsui, Sumitomo, and Mitsubishi were the headquarters of three big zaibatsu.

Unlike the zaibatsu enterprises, Tokyo Gas was a joint-stock company whose shares were offered to the public and widely dispersed. There were about 7,500 stockholders in 1928, including some powerful big stockholders, such as Watanabe Katsusaburō, Kume Ryōsaku, Iwasaki Seishichi (no relation to the Iwasaki of Mitsubishi), and Wakao Kōtarō, each of whom held around 1% of the shares and used them to scramble for the post of president or director.[32] They joined forces in factional alliances, dividing up the positions within the board of directors and leaving nothing for salaried managers.[33] In 1930 there was only one salaried manager (a chemical engineer) among the nine directors of Tokyo Gas. This situation paralleled that of Tokyo Dentō, but Tokyo Dentō had six salaried managers (two former high-level bureaucrats) among 15 directors.

In selecting four big enterprises in which salaried managers found it especially difficult to participate in top management, I have tried to study the factors preventing the development of managerial enterprises. In the case of family enterprises, these factors included founders' dictatorial methods (Yasuda, Asano), owners' lack of understanding of the value of education (Yasuda), and strong adherence to kinship ties (Asano). In the case of enterprises jointly established by a number of owners, conflicts among top salaried managers (NYK) and the struggle of big stockholders for the post of director (Tokyo Gas) were factors.

However, ultimately these factors could not stop the trend of the times toward managerial capitalism. The best proof of this is the fact that the above-mentioned four big enterprises eventually turned in the direction of managerial enterprise. The number of salaried managers, for example, had changed as follows by 1943: Yasuda Ginkō, nine of 13 directors, Z_2; Asano Cement, six of 11, Z_1; NYK, ten of 14, Z_2; and Tokyo Gas, five of 11, Y'. The same tendency can be pointed out in other cases. Many enterprises that had continued to maintain conservative behavior concerning the promotion of salaried managers eventually changed for such reasons as the death of a stubborn founder, the founding family's withdrawal from top management, and abandonment of the ridiculous struggle for directors' post.[34]

V

I emphasize the inevitability of managerial capitalism, in other words, the inevitability of the dominance of managerial enterprises, in every type of industry. But this inevitability does not mean that all enterprises move toward dominance by salaried managers. This is impossible. I refer only to the long-term trend.

Any enterprise within any industry can become a managerial enterprise according to changing circumstances and the willingness of owners to delegate top-level decisions to salaried managers. Any enterprise may face situations too difficult to be dealt with by a manager of ordinary talent, not occasionally but constantly. The reason is that when the enterprise becomes larger and adds more units, and when the industry within which it exists comes to the end of its own life cycle, the enterprise must adapt itself to the new circumstances. To succeed in this adjustment, the enterprise must reorganize its top management, and unless it can find an owner-manager of high ability, it must promote salaried managers to top management. Specifically, owners must delegate top decision-making authority to salaried managers.

Whether managerial enterprises can develop depends upon the progressiveness of owners (founders, founding families, joint stockholders). Progressiveness here means recognition of the indispensable role of salaried managers in the growth of the enterprise and reconsideration of owners' adherence to dominating top management. Of course high ability and solidarity among salaried managers must precede owners' progressiveness.

From a long-range viewpoint, although there may be temporary setbacks, the development of managerial capitalism and the
downfall of family enterprises and owner-dominated enterprises are
unavoidable. The development of big, technologically advanced,
multiunit enterprises always requires top management with a talent
for strategic leadership and administrative coordination. Aged
founders, "uninterested and incompetent" founding families (the
"Buddenbrooks effect"),[35] and high dividend-oriented and status-
oriented, part-time, big-stockholding top managers become increasingly unfit for top management. Although the possibility remains that competent full-time top managers may appear among
owners, it is much more likely that they will appear among the
multitude of salaried managers. Owners are obliged to rely upon the
wealth of experience and knowledge accumulated over a long
period within the hierarchy of salaried managers.

Yet not every owner of a big enterprise can always recognize the
inexorable trend toward managerial capitalism. The ability to
recognize this varies greatly according to the history of the enterprise and the background of the owner or owners. The personal
relationship between owner and salaried manager is also a factor.
As a result, the speed of the development of managerial enterprises
varies even among enterprises that belong to the same industry and
face the same situation.

Although I cannot draw any definite conclusion about the speed
of the development of managerial enterprises in Japan, since I have
never attempted an international comparison, it cannot have been
slower than it was in the United States and Europe. The advancement of salaried managers to the top management of big enterprises
in Japan was not the product of the development of big multiunit
enterprises in terms of the Chandler model. At least in prewar Japan,
when there was no large-scale and high-speed flow of goods from
mass production to mass marketing, the development of managerial
enterprises has to be explained outside the framework of the
Chandler model.

As seen in the above cases, the progressive attitude of owners
toward employing and promoting highly educated salaried managers was one of the most important factors. This progressiveness

brought about the formation of hierarchies of salaried managers in big enterprises and the accumulation of managerial know-how, and enabled salaried managers to be promoted to top management and hand on their posts to their juniors.

The progressiveness of owners in prewar Japan's big enterprises arose from their recognition of the severe situation of their enterprises in the face of the inflow of Western industrial goods and the scarcity of accumulated domestic managerial resources. At the same time, I should point out the influence of the owners' extraordinary faith in academic education. In developing prewar Japan, the institutions, technology, and science of the West, and the academic education necessary to transfer them to Japan, were extremely highly evaluated. Consequently, the talents of highly educated personnel were sometimes perceived as more precious than the real results that such an education produced. This illusion in regard to high education has played an unexpected important role in modern Japan in general. In addition, because of the chronic scarcity of highly educated personnel, the result of the speed of industrialization surpassing the development of educational institutions, owners of big enterprises offered highly educated personnel favorable treatment, including promotion to top management, in order to attract and keep them.[36]

NOTES

1. Alfred D. Chandler, Jr., "The United States: Seedbed of Managerial Capitalism," in Alfred D. Chandler, Jr. and Herman Daems, eds., *Managerial Hierarchies: Comparative Perspectives on the Rise of the Modern Industrial Enterprise*, Cambridge, Mass., 1980, p. 14.
2. *Ibid.*, p. 13.
3. For the managerial hierarchy, see Chandler and Daems, eds., *op. cit.*, and Alfred D. Chandler, Jr., *The Visible Hand: The Managerial Revolution in American Business*, Cambridge, Mass., 1978.
4. Data on the 65 big enterprises are drawn from Shōgyō Kōshinjo, *Nihon zenkoku sho kaisha yakuinroku* (Japanese directory of company directors), 1913, 1930. As a result of the choice of the years 1913 and 1930, this paper deals mainly with the 1910s and 1920s.

5. Yui Tsunehiko, "The Development of the Organizational Structure of Top Management in Meiji Japan," Nakagawa Keiichirō and Morikawa Hidemasa, eds., *Japanese Year Book on Business History: 1984*, Tokyo, 1984.

6. *Ibid.*, p. 1.

7. *Tokyo Kaijō Hoken Kabushiki Kaisha 100 nen shi* (One hundred years of Tokyo Marine Insurance Co.), Tokyo, 1979, pp. 232, 327.

8. *Ibid.*, p. 230.

9. Tekkō Shimbunsha, ed., *Tekkō kyojin den: Shiraishi Motojirō* (The life of Shiraishi Motojirō), Tokyo, 1967, pp. 536–38, 578–79, 605–7.

10. It may seem strange that some companies of the Mitsubishi zaibatsu suddenly appear in Table 3, since the only Mitsubishi companies listed in Table 1 are Mitsubishi Gōshi and Mitsubishi Sōko. This phenomenon is the result of differences in the way big enterprises of Mitsubishi were organized in 1913 and in 1930. In 1913 the diverse businesses of the Mitsubishi zaibatsu were organized as self-sustaining divisions of Mitsubishi Gōshi, not as independent companies. Mitsubishi Sōko was named Tokyo Sōko and was not directly managed by Mitsubishi. It was in the 1917–19 period that the diverse businesses of Mitsubishi (banking, mining, trading, shipbuilding) were organized into joint-stock companies and Mitsubishi Gōshi became a holding company, which controlled them through holding their stock.

11. Concerning Type III, for Jūgo Ginkō, see Mishima Yasuo, *Hanshin Zaibatsu*, Tokyo, 1984. For Kawasaki Zōsensho, see Mishima Yasuo, *ibid.*; Shiba Takao, "Kin'yū kyōkō ji ni okeru keiei senryaku no hatan to sono seiri: Kawasaki Zōsensho no baai" (The collapse of business strategy and its settlement during the monetary crisis: The case of Kawasaki Dockyard), *Keiei shigaku* (Japan business history review), Vol. 15, No. 1, 1980, pp. 39–41. For Teikoku Jinzō Kenshi, see Teijin Kabushiki Kaisha, *Teijin no ayumi* (History of Teijin), Vols. 2–4, 1968, 1969.

12. I define a zaibatsu as a diversified business group owned and controlled exclusively by a rich family. Whether each business took the form of a joint-stock company and whether a central headquarters to control diversified businesses functioned as a holding company are of secondary importance. This is because before the zaibatsu were reorganized as groups of joint-stock companies controlled by a holding company-style headquarters, each zaibatsu had its own development process.

13. Morikawa Hidemasa, "The Development of Management by Salaried Top Executives in Modern Japan—1868 to 1930," in Leslie Hannah, ed., *From Family Firm to Professional Management: Structure and Performance of Business Enterprise*, Budapest, 1982.

14. For Kōnoike, see Miyamoto Matao and Hiroyama Kensuke, "The Retreat from Diversification and the Desire for Specialization in Kōnoike: Late Meiji to Early Shōwa," in *Japanese Year Book on Business History: 1984*, Tokyo, 1984.

15. For the Ōkura zaibatsu, see Kakuyūkai, *Ōkura Tsuruhiko-ō* (Biography of Ōkura Kihachirō), 1924.

16. Kinugawa Taichi, *Honpō menshi bōseki shi* (The history of the Japanese cotton-spinning industry), Vol. 4, 1939, pp. 134–36, 148–49.

17. Abe Takeshi et al., eds., *Asakura Tsuneto nikki: Taishō 15 nen–Shōwa 8 nen* (The diary of Asakura Tsuneto: 1926–1933), 1983, pp. 177, 185–86, 205, 219–20.

18. There are some other X and Y companies that are not listed in Table 1. The X companies are five in number: Asano Dōzoku, Ogura Sekiyu, Nihon Kisen, Katakura Seishi Bōseki, and Noda Shōyu. The Y companies total 11: Tōshin Denki, Hokkaido Dentō, Keisei Denki Kidō, Aichi Denki Tetsudō, Sangū Kyūkō Dentetsu, Ajigawa Tochi, Ōsaka Hokkō, Okinoyama Tankō, Tōyō Seitetsu, Kawasaki Sharyō, and Tokyo Denki. Except for Kawasaki Sharyō, (rolling stock), a subsidiary of Kawasaki Zōsensho, and Tokyo Denki (electric power), partly owned by General Electric, these Y companies shared the characteristic of leading big stockholders fighting one another over their status as directors.

19. For the business history of the Yasuda zaibatsu, see Yui Tsunehiko, *Yasuda Zaibatsu*, Tokyo, 1985.

20. Tekkō Shimbunsha, ed., *op. cit.*, pp. 347, 356.

21. Yasuda Fudōsan, ed., *Yasuda Hozensha to sono kankei jigyō shi* (The history of Yasuda Hozensha and its affiliated companies), 1974, pp. 443–45.

22. *Ibid.*, pp. 531–41, 672–76. The year after Yuki left the Yasuda zaibatsu, he assumed the presidency of Nihon Kōgyō Ginkō. The relationship between Yuki and Nihon Kōkan, which borrowed money from Nihon Kōgyō Ginkō, was mentioned earlier in this paper.

23. For the Asano zaibatsu, see Kohayagawa Yōichi, "Strategy and Structure of the Asano Zaibatsu," *Keiei shigaku* (Japan business history review), Vol. 16, No. 1, 1981.

24. Tōyō Kisen Kabushiki Kaisha, *64 Nen no ayumi* (Sixty-four years of Tōyō Kisen), 1964, pp. 117–20; *Jitsugyō no Nihon* (Business Japan), Vol. 20, No. 2, 1918, p. 35.

25. *Jitsugyō no Nihon* (Business Japan), Vol. 14, No. 5, 1911, p. 65.

26. Tekkō Shimbunsha, ed., *op cit.*, pp. 327, 469.

27. Sugiyama Kazuo, *Kaiungyō to kin'yū* (Shipping and finance), Tokyo, 1981, p. 20.

28. *Ibid.*, p. 26.

29. *Jitsugyō no Nihon* (Business Japan), Vol. 20, No. 10–11, 1917; Vol. 21, No. 13–14, 1918.

30. Sugiyama, *op. cit.*, p. 126. Sugiyama refers to a contemporary review: "Yonejirō Itō, the president after Kondō, was apt to be at the beck and call of the marine officers."

31. *Ibid.*, p. 129.

32. *Meiji Taishō shi* (History of the Meiji and Taishō periods), Vol. 11, 1928, p. 45.

33. *Jitsugyō no Nihon* (Business Japan), Vol. 28, No. 16, 1925, pp. 65–67.

34. A number of X and Y companies in 1930 changed to Z_1 and Z_2 in 1943. Examples were Fujita Gumi (later Fujita Kōgyō, nine salaried managers of ten directors), Nihon Sekiyu (ten of 15), and Nihon Chisso Hiryō (five of nine). Noda Shōyu was the only exception. It continued to be a purely family enterprise that promoted no salaried managers to the board of directors.

35. Hannah, *op. cit.*, p. 3.

36. Morikawa Hidemasa, *Nihon keiei shi* (Japanese business history), Tokyo, 1981.

Comment

Hiroaki Yamasaki
University of Tokyo

In the first part of his paper Professor Morikawa emphasizes the inevitable trend toward managerial capitalism in Japan before World War II. He defines managerial capitalism as a capitalist economy in which managerial enterprises dominate and managerial enterprises as, in Professor Chandler's words, "firms in which representatives of the founding families or of financial interests no longer make top-level management decisions—where such decisions are made by salaried managers who own little of companies' stock." Professor Morikawa traces this trend through surveying statistically the relationship between the members of boards of directors and the ownership of company stock in 65 big businesses in 1913 and again in 1930. Here he notes the relationship between management and ownership of company stock.

In the second part of his paper Professor Morikawa observes the reasons salaried managers became dominant in the top management of many big businesses and concludes that the progressiveness of owners or of salaried managers who themselves already controlled top management was the most important factor behind this trend. By progressiveness he means recognition of the indispensable role of salaried managers in the growth of the enterprise. Here he no longer pays attention to the relationship between management and ownership of company stock.

Professor Morikawa's paper must be praised for its rigorous fact-finding, which makes it valuable as an empirical study of the development of managerial enterprises in Japan, and for its unique and challenging hypothesis concerning this development. Nevertheless, it seems to me that some questions still remain to be answered.

First of all, it is necessary to question the differences in approach to the relationship between management and ownership of company stock between the first and second parts of the paper. It is not clear to what extent this factor is taken into account in the final explanation of the development of managerial enterprises.

My second question concerns the so-called type Z_2 companies, which are shown in Table 3. In type Z_2 enterprises salaried managers dominate the board of directors. This type is further classified into three categories. Category I companies belong to zaibatsu, and Category II companies are independent of zaibatsu. Category III includes companies in the process of reconstruction after collapse during the financial crisis of 1927. Here I would like to focus on Category II. When we note the relationship between the members of the board of directors of each company and the company's major stockholders, we can further divide the companies that belong to Category II into two types.

The first type includes companies whose management is basically separated from large stockholders; Daiichi Ginkō, Tōyō Bōseki, Nissin Bōseki, Naigai Wata, Dai Nihon Seitō, and Meiji Seitō belong to this type. The second type includes companies whose large stockholders control the boards of directors; Nihon Menka, Gōshō, Yamashita Kisen, Osaka Gōdō Bōseki, Dai Nihon Beer, and Tōhō Gas belong to this type. Needless to say, companies of the first type are typical managerial enterprises. In the second type, a founder of the company occupies the position of president and at the same time holds a controlling share of the company's stock. These companies require separation from the first type.

In relation to the reason for the appearance of these types of managerial enterprises, the trend toward both large-scale and complex business management is most important. Complexity arises from diversification, integration, and multinationalization in the case of cotton spinning and sugar manufacturing. In addition, in the case of cotton spinning, cotton mixing operations made business management more complicated in Japan than in other countries. In the case of banking, the involvement in industrial finance made business management more complicated than in other countries. To return to Professor Morikawa's explanation in relation to this context: He criticizes Professor Chandler's thesis, stating that "the

advancement of salaried managers to top management of big enterprises in Japan is not the product of the development of big, multiunit enterprises in terms of the Chandler model." However, when
describing owner progressiveness, he declares that the development
of big, technologically advanced, multiunit enterprises always requires top management with a talent for strategic leadership and
administrative coordination. My second question regards typical
managerial enterprises and the economic conditions that oblige
owners to promote salaried managers to top management.

My third and last question concerns the factors that caused owner
progressiveness. Professor Morikawa emphasizes the scarcity of
salaried managers as one of the main factors. Nevertheless, according to Professor Daitō, the supply of salaried managers began to
surpass the demand for them at the turn of the century. If this is
true, it is necessary to examine Professor Morikawa's explanation
of the inevitable trend toward managerial enterprises in relation
to the disappearance of a scarcity of salaried managers in this
century.

Response

Hidemasa Morikawa

I do not think there is any difference between the first and second
parts of my paper. On the one hand, owners become willing to delegate top authority to salaried managers within the company; on the
other hand, salaried managers try to take the place of owners.
These two directions, which arise from the relationship between
ownership and management, are linked managerial enterprises.
But in my paper I stress the former direction, that is, the progressiveness of owners, because the realization of the latter direction depends
more or less on the progressiveness of owners, as I show in the
example of Fuji Gas Bōseki.

Although I stress the progressiveness of owners, I do not neglect the relationship between ownership and management or the upward movement of salaried managers to top management.

Professor Yamasaki's second question consists of two parts. In regard to the first part, if I had had room to expand my subject, I would have separated the second type of Category II managerial enterprise from the first type that Professor Yamasaki mentioned. But of the six companies that he classifies as belonging to the second type, in only two companies did a founder occupy the position of president and hold the major share of the company's stock: Yamashita Kisen and Osaka Gōdō Bōseki. The other four companies, Nihon Menka, Gōshō, Dai Nihon Beer, and Tōhō Gas, belonged to the first type.

As for the second part of the question, my reply is simple. Although I think that managerial enterprises can develop in every industrial sector, this does not mean that they can develop without major situational changes, especially technological progress. And I would like to add that while "the development of big, technologically advanced, multiunit enterprises always requires top management with a talent for strategic leadership and administrative coordination," such managerial talent does not always come from salaried managers, and "the development of big, technologically advanced, multiunit enterprises" is not the sole cause of the advancement of salaried managers to top management.

In regard to the third question, I will limit my reply to stating that I do not think that the scarcity of salaried managers was the decisive factor that caused owners' progressiveness or that this scarcity, *one* of the factors, disappeared in prewar Japan. Professor Daitō does not conclude in his paper that the scarcity of salaried managers disappeared in prewar Japan.

Finally, I would like to take this opportunity to add some necessary quantitative data to my paper. I emphasized the advancement of highly educated, salaried managers into the top management of prewar Japanese big enterprises. But I abridged the explanation of data on the education and careers of these top salaried managers. Please refer to Tables 1 and 2 here.

I compared the top salaried managers of 69 and 65 Japanese big

TABLE 1 Careers of Top Salaried Managers.

		1913		1930	
		Number	% of total	Number	% of total
Salaried-Manager Directors	I	27	28.4	145	49.2
	II	44	46.3	106	35.9
	III	24	25.3	44	14.9
	Total (A)	95	100.0	295	100.0
	Total No. of directors (B)	420		588	
	A/B		22.6		50.2

Source: Same as Table 1 in the paper.

TABLE 2 Academic Background of Top Salaried Managers.

	1913		1930	
Imperial universities (Law)	15		49	
Imperial universities[1] (Technology)	16	(16.8%)	73	(24.7%)
National Colleges of Commerce	7		49	
National Colleges of Technology[2]	2		17	
Other national colleges	0		5	
Keio University	13		29	
Other private universities	3		19	
Military Academy (Army and Navy)	1		4	
Engineering[3]	(0)		(3)	
Overseas study	8		7	
Technology[4]	(3)		(2)	
Subtotal (Higher education)	65	68.4%	252	85.4%
(of which Technology) (1+2+3+4)	(21)	(22.1%)	(95)	(32.2%)
Below middle-level education	30		43	
Total	95		295	

Source: Morikawa Hidemasa, *Nihon keiei shi*, Tokyo, 1981.

companies in 1913 and 1930, respectively, in my paper. Table 1 shows these managers' business careers.

I signifies the advancement to director of people who entered the company fresh from school. II signifies the advancement to director of people who entered the company in midcareer. III signifies the direct recruiting of people to the position of director from outside.

We can conclude that there was a tendency for the number and ratio of salaried managers on boards of directors of prewar Japanese big companies to increase and for advancement from within the company among salaried managers to dominate.

Table 2 shows top salaried managers' educational backgrounds. As a whole, top managers in prewar Japanese big businesses were highly educated, and the level of education rose over the years. The high ratio of graduates of the Faculty of Technology of the Imperial Universities is especially significant.

Managers, Families, and Financiers

Alfred D. Chandler, Jr.
Harvard University

One of the most significant economic phenomena of modern times has been the transformation of business enterprises from small, personally managed partnerships to giant corporations administered through extensive hierarchies of lower, middle, and top managers. This bureaucratization of business came later than that in the military and in government; but when it came, it came much more quickly. As late as the mid-nineteenth century no business enterprise was administered through a managerial hierarchy comparable to that depicted in Figure 1. Within a century such managerial enterprises had come to dominate the major sectors of all industrial, urban, technologically advanced economies.

The sudden appearance and rapid growth of the new bureaucracies reflected fundamental changes in the technology of production and distribution and in the size, nature, and location of markets. Because these new hierarchies were created to manage new and rapidly changing technologies whose output went to growing and ever-changing markets, the middle and top managers in these hierarchies acquired new specialized, product-specific skills. These skills could only be acquired through continuing experience in managing the new processes of production and distribution. The more complex the technology and the more extensive the market, the more critical were such skills to the profitability and continuing growth of the enterprise. Very few families, even extended kinship groups, were numerous enough or experienced enough to manage personally the new high-volume production for national and international markets. The founding families had to rely on nonfamily managers if they were to retain a profitable share of these markets.

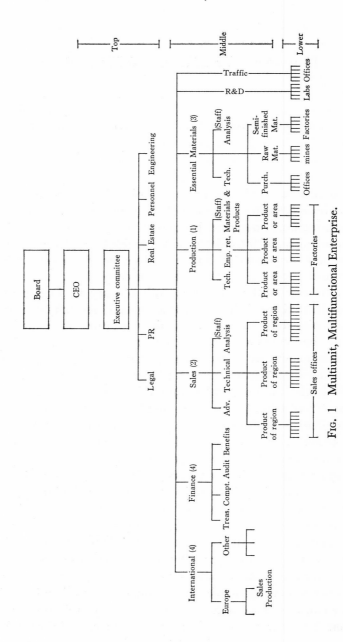

Fig. 1 Multiunit, Multifunctional Enterprise.

And if members of the family were not full-time managers, they were rarely able to acquire and maintain essential product-specific knowledge and skills.

Moreover, the founders of these new enterprises and their families often did not have the necessary capital to build such national and international organizations. They had to turn to outside investors and financial institutions for funds. These outside investors, who thus became part-owners of the new hierarchical enterprises, usually had far less knowledge than the founding families of the complexities of production and distribution, particularly in the new technologically advanced industries. However, like family members who were not full-time managers, they or their representatives sat on the governing boards of the enterprises and participated in top management decisions, especially those involving the investment of capital and the recruitment of personnel for future production and distribution.

As a firm grew and as its operations became more complex, the representatives of the stockholders who were not full-time managers had less and less to say in top management decisions, at least as long as the full-time managers kept the enterprise healthy and profitable. The governing board of the new large enterprise that was legally responsible for the affairs of the firm came to be made up of "inside" directors, who were senior full-time executives, and "outside" directors, the representatives of the investors. In all countries these outside directors found it increasingly difficult to get a full understanding at their monthly or often only quarterly meetings of the current and future developments in production and distribution, of changing markets at home and abroad, of changing sources of supplies of raw and intermediate materials, of progress made in research and development of new and improved products and processes, of the moves of competitors in all these functional areas, and of other operating concerns of the full-time managers. Moreover, the discussions at these board meetings were guided by inside directors. They set the agenda, and they provided the information on which the board was to decide and act. Only they could implement any action taken at a meeting. In time, too, the inside managers came to select not only the outside directors but their own successors. By then the firm had become what I have termed a managerial enterprise.

To understand this transformation of the relationship between ownership and management requires an understanding of why managerial hierarchies appeared at the time that they did and in the industries that they did, and why they grew in the way that they did. For it was only the appearance of such hierarchies that brought a separation between ownership and management. However, the timing, location, and processes of growth of these hierarchies and the resulting relationships between managers and representatives of the owners, that is, between inside and outside directors, did vary with time and place. Such historical variations in "the development of managerial enterprise in different countries" (Morikawa Hidemasa's definition of one major theme of this conference) reveal much about "the causes and inevitability of the development of the managerial enterprise" (his definition of its other basic theme). Let me begin, then, by reviewing in a highly condensed form what I have been writing about the coming of managerial enterprises and then consider variations in the evolution of such enterprises in three leading Western economies—those of Britain, Germany, and the United States.

I. The Growth of Modern Hierarchical Business Enterprise

As is now well known, the first managerial hierarchies appeared during the 1850s and 1860s to coordinate the movements of trains and the flow of goods over the new railroad networks and of messages over the new telegraph system.[1] They then quickly came into use to manage the new mass retailing establishments—the department stores, mail-order houses, and chains or multiple shops— whose existence the railroad and the telegraph made possible. Such administrative hierarchies grew to a still greater size in industrial enterprises that, again on the basis of modern transportation and communication, integrated new processes of mass production and mass distribution within a single business enterprise.

One way to review the emergence of managerial enterprises is, then, to focus on the evolution of the largest and most complex of managerial hierarchies, those of integrated industrial enterprises. These integrated enterprises had much in common. They appeared at almost exactly the same moment in history in the United States and Europe; they clustered in much the same types of industries; and finally, they grew in much the same manner. In nearly all cases they became large first by integrating forward, that is, investing in marketing and distribution facilities and personnel; next by moving backward into purchasing and often into the control of raw and semifinished materials; finally, though much less often, by investing in research and development. In this way they created the multifunctional organization that is depicted in Figure 1. They soon became multinational by investing abroad, first in marketing and then in production. Finally, they continued to expand their activities by investing in product lines related to their existing businesses, thus creating the organization depicted in Figure 2.

Tables 1–5 show where—that is, in what industries—the large and increasingly managerial enterprise appeared. Table 1 indicates the location by country and by industry of all industrial corporations in the world that in 1973 employed more than 20,000 workers. (The industries are those defined as two-digit industrial groups by the U.S. Census Standard Industrial Classification [S.I.C.].) In 1973, 263 (65%) of the 401 companies were clustered in food, chemicals, oil, machinery, and primary metals. Just under 30% were in three-digit categories of other two-digit groups—subcategories that had the same industrial characteristics as those in which the 65% clustered, such as cigarettes in tobacco; tires in rubber; newsprint in paper; plate glass in stone, glass, and clay; cans and razor blades in fabricated metals; and mass-produced cameras in instruments. Only 21 companies (5.2%) were in remaining two-digit categories—apparel, lumber, furniture, leather, publishing and printing, instruments, and miscellaneous.

A second point that Table 1 reveals is the predominance of American firms among the world's largest industrial corporations. Of the total of 401 companies employing more than 20,000 people, more than half (212, or 52.6%) were American. The United Kingdom followed with 50 (12.5%), Germany with 29 (7.3%), Japan

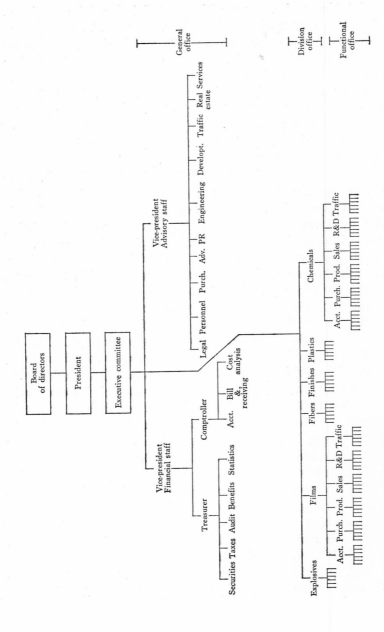

FIG. 2 The Multidivisional Structure.

TABLE 1 The Distribution of Manufacturing Firms with more than 20,000 Employees, by Industry and Nationality, 1973.

S.I.C.		U.S.	Outside the U.S.	U.K.	Germany	Japan	France	Others	Total
20	Food	22	17	13	0	1	1	2	39
21	Tobacco	3	4	3	1	0	0	0	7
22	Textiles	7	6	3	0	2	1	0	13
23	Apparel	6	0	0	0	0	0	0	6
24	Lumber	4	2	0	0	0	0	2	6
25	Furniture	0	0	0	0	0	0	0	0
26	Paper	7	3	3	0	0	0	0	10
27	Printing & publishing	0	0	0	0	0	0	0	0
28	Chemical	24	28	4	5	3	6	10	52
29	Petroleum	14	12	2	0	0	2	8	26
30	Rubber	5	5	1	1	1	1	1	10
31	Leather	2	0	0	0	0	0	0	2
32	Stone, clay & glass	7	8	3	0	0	3	2	15
33	Primary metal	13	35	2	9	5	4	15	48
34	Fabricated metal	8	6	5	1	0	0	0	14
35	Machinery	22	12	2	3	2	0	5	34
36	Electrical machinery	20	25	4	5	7	2	7	45
37	Transportation equipment	22	23	3	3	7	4	6	45
38	Instruments	4	1	0	0	0	0	0	5
39	Miscellaneous	2	0	0	0	0	0	0	2
	Diversified/conglomerate	19	3	2	1	0	0	0	22
	Total	211	190	50	29	28	24	59	401

Note: In 1970 the 100 largest industrials accounted for more than one-third of net manufacturing output in the United States and more than 45% in the United Kingdom. In 1930 they accounted for about 25% of total net output in both countries.

Source: *Fortune*, May 1974 and August 1974.

with 28, and France with 24. Only in chemicals, metals, and electrical machinery were there as many as four or five more firms outside the United States than there were within it.

Table 2 shows that throughout the twentieth century large industrial corporations clustered in the United States in the same industries in which they were concentrated in 1973. The pattern depicted in Tables 3, 4, and 5 is much the same for Britain, Germany, and also Japan. Other data document what is indicated here, that the American firms were larger, as well as more numerous, than those in other countries. For example, in 1948 only 50 to 55 of the British firms had assets comparable to those of the top 200 in the United States. In 1930 the number was about the same. For Germany and

TABLE 2 The Distribution of the 200 Largest Manufacturing Firms in the United States, by Industry.

	S.I.C.	1917	1930	1948	1973
20	Food	30	32	26	22
21	Tobacco	6	5	5	3
22	Textiles	5	3	6	3
23	Apparel	3	0	0	0
24	Lumber	3	4	1	4
25	Furniture	0	1	1	0
26	Paper	5	7	6	9
27	Printing & publishing	2	3	2	1
28	Chemical	20	18	24	27
29	Petroleum	22	26	24	22
30	Rubber	5	5	5	5
31	Leather	4	2	2	0
32	Stone, clay & glass	5	9	5	7
33	Primary metal	29	25	24	19
34	Fabricated metal	8	10	7	5
35	Machinery	20	22	24	17
36	Electrical machinery	5	5	8	13
37	Transportation equipment	26	21	26	19
38	Instruments	1	2	3	4
39	Miscellaneous	1	1	1	1
	Diversified/conglomerate	0	0	0	19
	Total	200	200	200	200

Note: Industries are ranked by assets.

TABLE 3 The Distribution of the 200 Largest Manufacturing Firms in the
United Kingdom, by Industry.

	S.I.C.	1919	1930	1948	1973
20	Food	63	64	52	33
21	Tobacco	3	4	8	4
22	Textiles	26	24	18	10
23	Apparel	1	3	3	0
24	Lumber	0	0	0	2
25	Furniture	0	0	0	0
26	Paper	4	5	6	7
27	Printing & publishing	5	10	7	7
28	Chemical	11	9	15	21
29	Petroleum	3	3	3	8
30	Rubber	3	3	2	6
31	Leather	0	0	0	3
32	Stone, clay & glass	2	6	5	16
33	Primary metal	35	18	28	14
34	Fabricated metal	2	7	8	7
35	Machinery	8	7	7	26
36	Electrical machinery	11	18	13	14
37	Transportation equipment	20	14	22	16
38	Instruments	0	1	4	3
39	Miscellaneous	3	4	3	1
	Diversified/conglomerate	0	0	0	2
	Total	200	200	204	200

Note: Industries are ranked by sales for 1973 and by market value of quoted capital
for the other years.

Japan it was smaller. Well before World War II the United States
had many more and much larger managerial hierarchies than did
other nations—underlining the fact that managerial capitalism first
emerged in that nation.

These tables also suggest (though only barely) basic differences
within the broad pattern of evolution. For example, in the United
States large enterprises were to be found throughout the twentieth
century in the production of both consumer and industrial goods.
Britain had proportionately more large firms in consumer goods
than the United States, while the largest industrials in Germany and
Japan concentrated much more on producer's goods. Even as late
as 1973 (as Table 1 shows) 13 of the United Kingdom's 50 firms

TABLE 4   The Distribution of the 200 Largest Manufacturing Firms in Germany, by Industry.

	S.I.C.	1913	1928	1953	1973
20	Food	23	28	23	24
21	Tobacco	1	0	0	6
22	Textiles	13	15	19	4
23	Apparel	0	0	0	0
24	Lumber	1	1	2	0
25	Furniture	0	0	0	0
26	Paper	1	2	3	2
27	Printing & publishing	0	1	0	6
28	Chemical	26	27	32	30
29	Petroleum	5	5	3	8
30	Rubber	1	1	3	3
31	Leather	2	3	2	1
32	Stone, clay & glass	10	9	9	15
33	Primary metal	49	47	45	19
34	Fabricated metal	8	7	8	14
35	Machinery	21	19	19	29
36	Electrical machinery	18	16	13	21
37	Transportation equipment	19	16	14	14
38	Instruments	1	2	4	2
39	Miscellaneous	1	1	1	1
	Diversified/conglomerate	0	0	0	1
	Total	200	200	200	200

Note: Industries are ranked by sales for 1973 and by assets for the other years.

employing more than 20,000 people were in the production and distribution of food and tobacco products, whereas France and Japan had only one each and Germany none. Before World War II Germany had many more firms in chemicals and heavy machinery than did Britain, while Japan, the late industrializer, still had a greater number of textile firms in its top 200 than did the other nations. As Japan's economy grew, the number of chemical and machinery enterprises on that list increased substantially.

Why did these large integrated hierarchial enterprises appear in some industries but rarely in others? And why did they appear at almost the same historical moment in the United States and Europe? Why did these industrial enterprises in advanced economies grow in the same manner, first integrating forward into volume

TABLE 5   The Distribution of the 200 Largest Manufacturing Firms in Japan by Industry.

	S.I.C.	1918	1930	1954	1973
20	Food	31	30	26	18
21	Tobacco	1	1	0	0
22	Textiles	54	62	23	11
23	Apparel	2	2	1	0
24	Lumber	3	1	0	1
25	Furniture	0	0	0	0
26	Paper	12	6	12	10
27	Printing	1	1	0	2
28	Chemical	23	22	38	34
29	Petroleum	6	5	11	13
30	Rubber	0	1	1	5
31	Leather	4	1	0	0
32	Stone, clay & glass	16	14	8	14
33	Primary metal	21	22	28	27
34	Fabricated metal	4	3	6	5
35	Machinery	4	4	10	16
36	Electrical machinery	7	12	15	18
37	Transportation equipment	9	11	18	20
38	Instruments	1	1	3	5
39	Miscellaneous	1	1	0	1
	Diversified/conglomerate	0	0	0	0
	Total	200	200	200	200

Note: Industries are ranked by assets.

distribution, then taking on other functions, then becoming multinational and finally multiproduct?

Because these enterprises initially grew larger by integrating mass production with volume distribution, answers to these critical questions require a careful look at both these processes. Mass production is an attribute of specific technologies. In some industries the primary way to increase output was adding more workers and machines. In others it was improving and rearranging the inputs; improving the machinery, furnaces, stills, and other equipment; reorienting the process of production within the plant; placing the several intermediate processes of production required for a finished product within a single works; or increasing the application of energy (particularly fossil fuel energy). The first set of industries remained labor intensive; the second set became capital intensive. In this second set of industries the technology of production permitted much larger economies of scale than were possible in the first. That is, it permitted much greater reduction in cost per unit of output as volume increased. So in these capital-intensive industries with large-batch or continuous-process technologies, large works operating at minimum efficient scale (the scale of operation that brought the lowest unit costs) had a much greater cost advantage over small works than was true with labor-intensive technologies. Conversely, cost per unit rose much more rapidly when production fell below minimum efficient scale (say, 80% to 90% of rated capacity) than was true in labor-intensive industries.

What is of basic importance for an understanding of the coming of the modern managerial industrial enterprise is that the cost advantage of a large plant cannot be fully realized unless a constant flow of materials through the plant or factory is maintained to assure effective capacity utilization. The decisive figure in determining costs and profits is, then, not rated capacity but throughput —that is, the amount of output processed during a single day or other unit of time. The throughput needed to maintain minimum efficient scale requires careful coordination not only of flow through the processes of production but also of the flow of inputs from the suppliers and the flow of outputs to the distributors and final consumers. Such coordination cannot happen automatically. It demands the constant attention of a managerial team or hierarchy. Thus scale is only a technological characteristic. The economies of scale measured by throughput are organizational. They depend on knowledge, skills, and teamwork—on the human organization essential to exploit the potential of technological processes.

In the S.I.C. classifications in Tables 1–5 where the large firms clustered, the economies of scale as measured by throughput provided substantial cost advantages—advantages that could only be exploited if the founders of an enterprise recruited an effective managerial team. On the other hand, in those classifications where few large firms appeared, that is, in the older, technologically simple, labor-intensive industries, such as apparel, textiles, leather, lumber, and publishing and printing, neither technological nor organizational innovation substantially increased minimum efficient scale. In these industries large plants did not offer significant cost advantages over small ones. In these industries the opportunities for cost reduction through material coordination of high volume throughput by managerial teams remained limited.

The differentials in potential scale economies of different production technologies not only indicate why the large hierarchical firms appeared in some industries and not in others, that is, why they appeared *where* they did. They also explain why these firms appeared *when* they did, that is, why they appeared so suddenly in the last decades of the nineteenth century. Only with the completion of the modern transportation and communication networks—those of the railroad, telegraph, steamship, and cable—could materials flow into a factory or processing plant and the finished goods move out at a rate of speed and volume required to achieve substantial economies of throughput. Transportation that depended on the power of animals, wind, and currents was too slow, too irregular, and too uncertain to maintain a level of throughput necessary to achieve modern economies of scale.

However, such scale and throughput economies do not in themselves explain why the new technologies made possible by the new transportation and communication systems caused the new mass producers to grow in the way they did, that is, why they became large and managerial by integrating forward into mass distribution. Coordination between producers and distributors might have been achieved through contractual agreement with intermediaries—both buyers and sellers. Such an explanation requires a more precise understanding of the process of volume distribution, particularly of why the wholesaler, retailer, and other commercial intermediaries lost their cost advantage vis-à-vis the volume producer.

The intermediaries' cost advantage lay in exploiting both the economies of scale and what has been termed "the economies of scope." Because they handled the products of many manufacturers, they achieved a greater volume and lower unit cost than any one manufacturer in the marketing and distribution of a *single* line of products. Moreover, they increased this advantage by the broader scope of their operation, that is, by handling a number of *related*

product lines through a single set of facilities. This was true of the
new volume wholesalers in apparel, dry goods, groceries, hardware,
and the like and even more true of the new mass retailers—the
department store, the mail order house, and the chain or multiple
shop enterprise.

The commercial intermediaries lost their cost advantage when
manufacturers' output reached a comparable scale. As one economist has pointed out, "The intermediary will have a cost advantage over [his] customers and suppliers only as long as the volume
of transactions in which he engages comes closer to that [minimum
efficient] scale than do the transactions volumes of his customers or
suppliers."[2] This rarely happened in retailing, except in heavily
concentrated urban markets, but it often occurred in wholesaling.
In addition, the advantage of scope was sharply reduced when
marketing and distribution required specialized, costly facilities and
skills that could not be used to handle other product lines. By
investing in such product-specific personnel and facilities, the intermediary not only lost the advantage of scope but also became dependent on what was usually a small number of producers to provide
those supplies.

All these new volume-producing enterprises created their own
sales organizations to advertise and market their products national-
ly and often internationally. From the start they preferred to rely
on a sales force of their own to advertise and market their goods
rather than to depend on the salesmen of wholesalers and other
intermediaries, who sold the products of many manufacturers,
including those of their competitors. Of more importance, mass
distribution of these products—many of them quite new—often
required extensive investment in specialized, product-specific facilities and personnel. Because the existing wholesalers and mass
retailers made their profits from handling related products of many
manufacturers, they had little incentive to make large investments
in facilities and personnel that could only be useful for a handful of
specialized products processed by a handful of producers on which
they would become dependent for supplies essential to make that
investment pay.

For these reasons, then, the large industrial firm that integrated mass production and mass distribution appeared in industries with two characteristics. The first and most essential was a technology of production in which the realization of potential scale economies and the maintenance of quality control demanded close and constant coordination and supervision of materials flows by trained managerial teams. The second was volume marketing and distribution of products, which required investment in specialized, product-specific human and physical capital.

Where this was *not* the case, that is, in industries where technology did *not* have a potentially high minimum efficient scale, where coordination was *not* technically complex, and where mass distribution did *not* require specialized skills and facilities, there was little incentive for the manufacturer to integrate forward into distribution. In such industries as publishing and printing, lumber, furniture, leather, apparel and textiles, and specialized instruments and machines, the large integrated firm had few competitive advantages. In these industries the small, single-function firm continued to prosper and to compete vigorously.

But where this was the case, that is, in those industries that had the two critical characteristics, the most important entrepreneurial act of the founders of an enterprise was the creation of an administrative organization. That is, it was first the recruiting of a team to supervise the process of production, then the building of a national and very often international sales network, and finally the setting up of a corporate office of middle and top managers to integrate and coordinate the two. Only then did the enterprise become multinational. Investment in production abroad followed, almost never preceded, the building of an overseas marketing network. So, too, in the technologically advanced industries, investment in research and development followed the creation of a marketing network. In such a firm this linkage between trained sales engineers, production engineers, product designers, and the research laboratory became a major impetus to continuing innovation in the industries in which it operated. The result of such growth was an enterprise whose organization is depicted in Figure 1. The continuing growth of the firm rested on the ability of its managers to transfer resources in marketing, research and development, and production (usually those that were not fully utilized) into new and more profitable related product lines, a move that carried the organization shown in Figure 1 to that illustrated in Figure 2. If the first step—that of integrating production and distribution—was not taken, the rest did not follow. The firm remained a small, personally managed producing enterprise buying its materials and selling its products through intermediaries.

II. National Comparisons

This review of the coming of the large industrial enterprise in the West emphasizes that personal and family management had little difficulty maintaining itself in labor-intensive, fragmented industries, but that in the capital-intensive, concentrated industries the recruitment of managerial hierarchies was essential for an enterprise to enter and then to maintain and expand market share. The review also suggests that differences in the processes of production and distribution demand different product-specific facilities and skills. Enterprises in industries using less complex processes of production and needing less extensive investment in distribution required smaller hierarchies than did those in industries using complex technologies of production and needing highly product-specific distribution networks. By the same token, the capital requirements were smaller in the former than in the latter industries. Therefore, this explanatory theory suggests that members of the founder's family were able to have a continuing say in top-management decision making, as either inside or outside directors, in less technological, less capital-using industries, and that representatives of banks, other financial institutions, and large investors had more influence as outside directors in the more complex and more capital-using industries.

The historical evolution of the relationship between managers and owners in Britain, Germany, and the United States appears to support these hypotheses. In Britain, where the large firms concentrated more in light consumer industries, requiring relatively small hierarchies and relatively little capital, particularly branded, packaged products, the family continued to play a larger role for a longer period of time than in the other two countries. In Germany, where the large firms clustered in the more capital-using metals, industrial machinery and chemical industries, hierarchies were much larger and banks played a more important role in the funding of the new enterprises. Therefore their representatives shared top-management decisions with members of the founding family and senior full-time salaried managers. In the United States the large firms clustered in those industries mass-producing branded, packaged products, light machinery, metals, and chemicals—industries that had the greatest potential for scale economies—for the world's largest and fastest-growing market. Their founders had to recruit even larger hierarchies than did their British and German counterparts. At the same time the cost advantages of scale provided funds for continued growth, so that American entrepreneurs had far less need of external financial aid than did those in Germany. As a result the senior full-time managers came, as inside directors, to dominate top-level decision making more quickly than they did in either Britain or Germany.

III. Britain: The Persistence of the Family Enterprise

The family firm persisted in Britain longer than elsewhere primarily because British entrepreneurs were reluctant to make a substantial investment in new and other untried processes of production; to invest heavily in marketing, distribution, and research personnel and facilities; and above all, to turn the administration of at least part of the enterprise over to nonfamily, salaried managers. Thus, although Britain was the world's first industrial nation, by the second decade of the twentieth century its largest industrial firms were producers of branded, packaged consumer products. During the interwar years five of the seven largest firms in terms of the market value of their securities were Imperial Tobacco, Distillers' Corporation (Scotch whisky), Lever Brothers (soap), Guinness (ale), and Anglo-Iranian Oil (kerosene and gasoline). As was pointed out earlier, in 1973 Britain had 13 food companies employing more than 20,000 employees, while Germany and Japan had only one each.

As late as 1948 all but a small number of the largest firms were operated through two types of organizational structures that had all but disappeared among the top 200 American companies. Either

they were personally, usually family, managed enterprises whose
stockholders made the coordinating, monitoring, and allocating
decisions, or they were federations of such family firms legally
unified under the control of a holding company with almost no
central administrative staff or organization. The large British firms
had integrated high-volume production with high-volume distribution, but it was usually the founder, and then members of his
family with one or two close associates, who administered the production, sales, and operating departments. These firms rarely com-
peted vigorously with one another, relying instead on contractual
agreements to determine price and production schedules and to
allocate markets. However, because British common law forbade
combinations in restraint of trade, such agreements could not be
legally enforced in courts of law. Therefore competitors formed a
holding company, with the constituent companies exchanging
shares of their stock for that of the new holding company. Its central
office was then able to legally enforce the decisions as to price and
production determined by the heads of the constituent companies.

In these federations each firm continued to operate much as it
had before the merger.[3] It continued to handle its own production
and its own distribution. This was true of Imperial Tobacco, Lever
Brothers, and Distillers and in very large mergers in the textile
industries, such as the Calico Printers' Association, the Bleachers'
Association, and British Cotton and Wool Dyers. It was also true of
much smaller mergers (in terms of the number of firms involved)
between industry leaders, such as British Cocoa and Chocolate (a
merger of Cadbury and Fry), Associated Biscuit Manufacturers (a
merger of Peak Frean and Huntley & Palmer), and Cross & Blackwell (a merger of three jam and confectionery companies), and comparable mergers in the brewing industry. In such mergers family
firms were able to continue to compete with one another in a gentle-
manly manner for two or three generations. Of these federations only
Lever Brothers began to create a corporate office with an extensive
managerial staff before World War II.

There were exceptions. In the few industries where British entrepreneurs did make the investment in production and distribution
and did recruit the essential managerial hierarchies, they were able

to compete at home and abroad in the new global oligopolies. They did so in oil, rubber, plate and flat glass, rayon, explosives, and synthetic alkalies. In each industry, the first firm to make the investment and recruit the managers quickly dominated the industry at home and became the British representative in the global oligopoly abroad. In glass, rayon, and synthetic alkalies (Pilkington, Courtaulds, and Brunner, Mond) the members of the founding family continued to be recruited into the firm. As full-time managers these family members continued to dominate the board. In rubber (Dunlop) the family was removed after a financial crisis and the firm was reorganized in 1921–22. The restructured firm became one of the earliest of British managerial enterprises, along with Anglo-Iranian Oil and Nobel Explosives. In the oil company (later British Petroleum) there never was a founding family. Two years after its first refinery went into operation in 1912, the British government took 51% of the company's voting shares. The founders of Nobel Explosives, the inventor Alfred Nobel and large investors, such as Charles Tennant, were deeply involved in other business activities and so relied from the start on salaried managers to administer their enterprise.

In other basic new industries, however, British entrepreneurs failed to make the essential investment in production, sales, and purchasing and failed to recruit the necessary managerial hierarchies. In these industries they lost not only the global market but the British home market as well. Such entrepreneurial failure was particularly devastating in the production and distribution of light mass-produced machinery, more specialized heavy machinery, and industrial chemicals. American firms quickly overpowered British competitors in the production and distribution of light mass-produced machines, including sewing, office, and agricultural machinery; household appliances; and until the 1920s automobiles. The Germans and Americans quickly took over the electrical machinery industry, the producers of light and of the energy so critical to increased productivity in manufacturing and increased efficiency in urban transportation. In 1912, for example, two-thirds of the electrical manufacturing output within Britain was produced by three companies, the subsidiaries of the American General Electric and Westinghouse and of the German Siemens.[4] The dye story is even more dramatic.[5] An Englishman, William H. Perkin, invented the first synthetic dyes. Dyes were made of coal tar, of which Britain had an inexhaustible supply. The huge British textile industry was the largest market in the world for dyes. And in 1870 the chemists who would head the industrial laboratories of the great German dye firms were all working in Britain. Yet within a very brief period German enterprises completely dominated the new industry. By 1913, of the 160,000 tons of dyes produced the Germans made 140,000 tons and their Swiss neighbors another 10,000, while British producers made only 4,000, most of which were of low quality.

The British entrepreneurs were not held back in these industries because of the lack of funds. London was the largest and most sophisticated money market in the world. Americans and Germans had no difficulty raising money in Britain for British and European plants and distribution facilities, nor did the successful British companies like Anglo-Iranian Oil and Dunlop. Nor was labor a handicap, since nearly all the workers in the American and German factories in Britain were British. The British failure resulted from the inability or unwillingness of British entrepreneurs to make the necessary investment and to recruit the management organization necessary to exploit the cost advantage of large-scale production in these industries. The price paid for the persistence of the family enterprise was that Britain's entrepreneurs and the British economy as a whole failed to harvest many of the fruits of the second industrial revolution, which was made possible by the advent of modern transportation and communication.

IV. Germany: The Importance of the Banks

Before World War II German entrepreneurs were never as effective as their British and American counterparts in branded, packaged products or as effective as the Americans in mass-produced light machinery. One reason may have been that in both broad sets of industries foreign firms were the first in Germany to build plants with scale economies and to set up national sales forces. Thus, the German subsidiaries of Lever, Nestlé, Quaker Oats, and Corn

Products came to dominate the market in their industries, as did the subsidiaries of Singer Sewing Machine, International Harvester, National Cash Register, American Radiator, Ford, and Otis Elevator in theirs. Nevertheless, the success of the Stollwerck family in creating a much larger cocoa and chocolate multinational empire than any British or American competitors suggests that where the German entrepreneurs were the first movers in branded, packaged products, they could perform effectively.

German entrepreneurs, like British ones, did create at least one major company to represent their nation in the global oligopolies in oil (European Petroleum Union, founded in 1905 under the aegis of the Deutsche Bank), in rubber (Continental), in rayon (Vereinigte Glanzastoff Fabriken), and in explosives and synthetic alkalies (members of the Nobel and Solvay alliances).[6] It was, however, in metals, both ferrous and nonferrous, and even more in complex industrial machinery and chemicals that the Germans excelled. In the last two, the managerial hierarchies were needed to exploit the economies of scope even more than those of scale. (The economies of scope in manufacturing can be defined as those resulting from making several end products from the same set of materials and intermediate processes.) Some management teams in production were even greater in size than those in American firms. In the 1880s and 1890s these enterprises also built extended networks of branch offices throughout the world to market products, most of which were technologically new, to demonstrate their use, to install them when necessary, to provide continuing after-sales service, and to give customers the financial credit they often needed to make such purchases. Once abroad, these enterprises built and acquired branch factories. Finally, they invested far more heavily than any British and most American enterprises in research and development.

The founders of these new industrial giants relied much more heavily on banks to fund their operations than did their counterparts in either Britain or the United States. Their production processes and product development required much more initial capital than did the production of branded, packaged products or mass-produced light machinery. Moreover, in Germany in the 1870s and 1880s there were no capital markets of the size and sophistication of those of London and New York. As a result, the entrepreneurs turned to the German all-purpose "great" banks that had come into being to finance the railroad networks of Germany and eastern Europe. These banks not only marketed the securities of the new corporations but, as was not true of British or American financial institutions, held their shares on their own account and normally voted the proxies of the investors to whom they sold the securities. They also appear to have had more direct supervision over the internal finances of their clients than British or American banks ever had. At the turn of the century representatives of these banks had joined those of founding families and occasionally wealthy investors on supervisory boards of most large German industrial enterprises. (Germany with its two-tiered board was the only country to make a legal distinction between the inside directors who made up the *Vorstand*, or managing board, and the outside directors who made up the *Aufsichtsrat*, or supervisory board.)

Nevertheless, after the initial investment was made in production and distribution at home and abroad, the companies that prospered —and most of them did—came to rely primarily on retained earnings to finance continued growth. So the bankers' influence waned. By the turn of the century banks and bankers had little to say on the strategic decisions in the chemical industry. By World War I their influence had also lessened in metals and machinery. Leading historians of German industry—Gerald Feldman, Hans Pohl, Wilfred Feldenkirchen, and Norbert Horn—all agree with Jürgen Kocka that Rudolph Helferding's famous "theory of the dominance of banks over industry was basically outdated when it was formulated," that is, in 1910.[7] However, the losses in both world wars meant that the industrialists had to continue to rely on banks for financing far more than they did in other Western countries.

If the influence of banks declined, that of founders and their families continued. But whereas in Britain many families continued to manage their firms personally, in Germany they stood at the head of extensive, well-organized managerial hierarchies. The Siemenses, Thyssens, Krupps, Haniels, Klöckners, and, later, Quandts and Flicks continued to have a major say in the affairs of their concerns. Nevertheless, even before the turn of the century salaried general directors, such as Emil Kirdof and Wilhelm Beukenberg in steel, Paul Reusch in machinery, and Carl Duisberg, Karl Bosch, and Heinrich von Brunk in chemicals, ruled their enterprises even more completely than the Siemenses and Krupps did theirs. As time passed the strength of the managers increased and that of the families lessened. In Feldman's words, "The tension between the continued effort at personal rule by the owner and the progress of bureaucratized management was being decided painfully but fatefully in favor of the latter."[8] Yet as late as the 1930s and indeed in the years after World War II, representatives of families, like those of banks, had a far greater influence on the boards of large industrial firms in Germany than they did in the United States.

V. The United States: The Dominance of the Managers

In the United States, where large enterprises came more quickly and in greater numbers and appeared in a wider range of industries, banks played a much less important role in the initial financing than they did in Germany, and families remained less influential in top management than they were in Britain. In other words, managerial enterprises appeared more quickly and in a purer form in America than they did in Europe. These differences reflect not only the much larger and much faster growing domestic market that provided many more opportunities to exploit economies of scale. They can also be traced to the massive turn-of-the-century merger movement in that country. The financing of mergers and, much more important, the financing of the rationalization of production and distribution that followed the mergers for the first time brought representatives of financial institutions on to the boards of American industrials. In many, that same rationalization also lessened family control by bringing a reorganization of management in which nonfamily managers replaced owners of constituent companies in the administration of large sectors of an industry.

In the United States, the initial financing of the large new industrial enterprises (as differentiated from financing of the rationalization after mergers) was personal rather than institutional. The funds came from local investors who had made their money in railroads, banking, and land. Soon, too, the most successful of the new industrialists—the Rockefellers, the Armours, the Bordens, the Dukes of American Tobacco, the Clarks of Singer Sewing Machine, the Havemayers of American Sugar, and a little later the du Ponts —provided capital for new ventures in other industries. They were joined by traction magnates like the Wideners, Whitneys, Elkinses, and Bradys. The continuing high rate of return resulting from the exploitation of the new technologies meant that the leaders had little need to go to the New York or Chicago money markets. Growth was financed by retained earnings.

Investment bankers and brokers first became deeply involved in American industry when they helped finance consolidations during the mergers of the 1890s, which reached a crescendo between 1898 and 1901. First these financiers helped facilitate the funding of the mergers. Because this usually involved little more than exchanging the stock of a new holding company for that of the many small personally managed firms coming into the merger, the cash involved was minimal. However, these bankers and brokers were then committed to raising the funds needed to centralize the administration and then to rationalizing the production and distribution facilities of the new consolidated enterprise so that it might take more effective advantage of the economies of scale and scope. In production the management of the plants of the constituent companies was centralized under a single production department. Some factories were disbanded, others combined, and new ones built to assure continuous operation at close to minimum efficient scale. The different sales forces were consolidated into a single unit with a multitude of regional offices. Purchasing was also centralized, and corporate research laboratories were set up. In this way mergers led to the creation of extensive managerial hierarchies in industries in which up to that time enterprises had been personally managed. At the same time the stock issued by a new consolidated enterprise to finance the resulting rationalization was widely marketed, and the number of stockholders was greatly enlarged.

As I have indicated, such rationalization, recruitment of managers, and an increased scattering of ownership did not occur in

Britain. There a merger remained a federation of family firms whose activities continued to be personally managed in the same way as they had been before the merger. Since there was no rationalization to be financed, much of the stockholding of the enterprise usually remained in the hands of the owners of the constituent companies. In Germany, where cartels were legal and industry-wide agreements could be enforced in courts of law, far fewer industry-wide mergers occurred than in the United States and Britain.

In the United States bankers' influence in top-level decision making that resulted from mergers remained short-lived. Once the managers in the newly created hierarchies had learned their trade and once continued growth was funded through retained earnings, the influence of these outside directors on top-level decisions waned even more quickly than that of bankers on German supervisory boards. Moreover, unlike their German counterparts, American financial institutions rarely held the securities of the companies they helped finance or voted the proxies of the investors who purchased those securities. In the United States proxies were voted by the inside directors, by managers, not bankers. Also, the staffs of American banking and brokerage houses were much smaller than those of the German "great" banks. In Germany the bankers on company boards could rely on these staffs for information about a company and the industry in which it operated. In the United States they had to rely almost entirely on the inside directors for such information. As a result in American firms these banking representatives soon became little more than financial advisers to the inside directors.

In American companies that did not come into being through merger, or in industry-wide mergers that were engineered by one or two enterprises, bankers rarely became directors. And in such companies personal management had all but disappeared by the 1930s. The dismal performance of the Ford Motor Company, one of the rare examples of an entrepreneur and his son operating a large firm with a small, lean management staff in the British manner, suggests the weakness of such control. Ford's share of the market dropped from 55% in 1921 to 16% in 1937, while the share of General Motors, with its massive managerial hierarchy, rose from

11.5% to 45% in the same period. Between 1927 and 1937 Ford's losses were well over $100 million.[9] In the same decade General Motors' profits after taxes were $ 2 billion.

By the 1920s industrial families still involved in the enterprises they or their forebears had founded were far fewer than they were in Germany or in Britain. By the 1920s there were no Rockefellers in oil, no Carnegies in steel, no Armours in meatpacking, no Dukes in tobacco, no Procters or Gambles in soap, no Otises in elevators, no Babcocks or Wilcoxes in industrial machinery, no Worthingtons in pumps, no Havemayers in sugar, no Westinghouses in electrical equipment, and no Pullmans in transportation equipment. Where du Ponts, Swifts, McCormicks, Deeres, Wrigleys, and Heinzes still influenced their enterprises, they did so as full-time inside directors sharing the decisions and responsibilities with the other inside directors, who stood at the head of extended managerial hierarchies. By the 1930s very few of their competitors had representatives of the founding families or major investors as inside directors. By then, in probably a majority of the 200 largest industrial enterprises outside directors were selected by the full-time inside directors, who together rarely held as much as 5% of the stock outstanding. By the approach of World War II the separation between ownership and management had become clearly defined in the dominant firms of the leading American industries.

VI. Conclusion: The Inevitability of Managerial Enterprise

One point this paper stresses is that managerial enterprise was not inevitable. Indeed, before the mid-nineteenth century it was unnecessary. In nearly all industries the technical skills required by the processes of production and distribution were simple enough and the capital need was small enough to be met by one or two entrepreneurs, their families, and a small number of investors. (Such industries continued to flourish throughout the twentieth century.) Then in the 1870s and 1880s the completion of the new transportation and communication systems, and the coming of the new source of energy, electricity, created in some, but certainly not all, industries a potential for cost savings through economies of scale and scope. These savings could only be fully exploited by building large plants, by recruiting management teams to coordinate flows through the processes of production, and in most cases by making an extensive investment in marketing and distribution facilities. In such industries those entrepreneurs who failed to recruit the essential management teams and to make investment quickly lost out to those who did, as the British experience so dramatically attests. Where these entrepreneurs did both and where they were able to personally raise initial funding, they and their families managed their enterprises. They continued to do so, however, only if the members of their families were trained in the necessary product-specific functional and administrative skills and remained full-time managers of the enterprises. If the family members did not receive such training and did not make a career of the family business but instead became part-time outside directors, the family influence rapidly waned.

Where the founders required institutional financing or where mergers brought reorganization and rationalization of the plants and facilities of the constituent firms, representatives of financial institutions came on the boards of these industrial combinations. But because they had little knowledge of the firms' product-specific processes of production and distribution, they probably had less influence on top-level decision making than did the outside directors representing family and other large investors.

As long as an enterprise remained solvent and as long as it was able to finance growth largely through retained earnings (as was indeed the general rule in the three economies studied, at least up to World War II), the full-time managers on the governing board dominated top-level decision making. They did so because they knew the business better than any outsider. They had developed the critical functional and administrative skills essential if their firm was to continue to compete in national and international markets. Even if a firm encountered financial difficulties that made it necessary for outside directors to remove inside ones, their replacements needed to have comparable training and experience if the enterprise was to maintain market share on which profits were based. Such an enterprise could not be effectively managed by untrained, inexperienced part-time outside directors. In industries where complex product-specific technical and managerial skills were essential to maintain market share in national and international markets, managerial enterprise became inevitable.

NOTES

1. The following paragraphs closely follow what I have written in "The Emergence of Managerial Capitalism," *Business History Review*, Vol. 59, Winter 1984. Because they present my views on the beginning of modern, multiunit industrial enterprise as concisely as I can define them, some paragraphs are taken verbatim from that article.
2. Scott J. Moss, *An Economic Theory of Business Strategy*, Oxford, 1981, pp. 110–11.
3. These brief statements on British firms are based on archival materials, journal articles, and company histories, including works by such distinguished writers as Charles Wilson on Unilever, Theodore Barker on Pilkington, Donald Coleman on Courtaulds, Ronald Ferrier on British Petroleum, and William Reader on Nobel Explosives and Brunner, Mond. The story will be told in detail in my forthcoming *Global Enterprise*.
4. I. C. R. Byatt, *The British Electrical Industry, 1875–1914: The Economic Returns of a New Technology*, Oxford, 1979, p. 150.
5. John J. Beer, *The Emergence of the German Dye Industry*, Urbana, Ill., 1959, chaps. 5–6, 8–9.
6. As in the case of the statements on the British firms, these are based on published histories, journal articles, and archival information and will be presented in detail in my forthcoming study.
7. Jürgen Kocka, "Entrepreneurs and Managers in German Industrialization," in Peter Mathias and M. M. Postan, eds., *The Cambridge Economic History of Europe*, Vol. VII, Cambridge, 1978, p. 570; Gerald D. Feldman, *Iron and Steel in the German Inflation, 1916–1923*, Princeton, N.J., 1977, pp. 19–20; Norbert Horn, "Company Law and the Organization of Large Enterprises 1860–1920—Germany, Great Britain, France and U.S. in Comparative Perspective," in Norbert Horn and Jürgen Kocka, eds., *Law and the Formation of the Big Enterprise in the 19th and 20th Centuries*, Göttingen, 1979, pp. 183–84; Hans Pohl, "On the History of Organization and Management in Large Enterprises Since the Nineteenth Century," *German Yearbook on Business History 1982*, Berlin, 1982, p. 111; Wilfred Felden-

kirchen, "The Banks and the Steel Industry in the Ruhr," *German Yearbook on Business History 1981*, Berlin, 1981, pp. 34–51.

8. Feldman, *op. cit.*, p. 25.

9. Alfred D. Chandler, Jr., *Giant Enterprise: Ford, General Motors and the Automobile Industry*, New York, 1963, pp. 3–7.

Comment

Jurō Hashimoto
University of Electro-Communications

As is well known, Professor Chandler has created the most influential theory of the growth of modern hierarchical business enterprise, generally called the Chandler model. His theory is persuasive and has universal validity, and I agree with him in principle.

The heart of his model, as I interpret it, lies in the concept of "throughput," which is a word borrowed from the petroleum industry. Throughput is the amount of output, processed during a single day or other unit of time, required to maintain a minimum efficient scale. Professor Chandler points out in his paper that "what is of basic importance for an understanding of the coming of the modern managerial industrial enterprise is that the cost advantage of a large plant cannot be fully realized unless a constant flow of materials through the plant or factory is maintained to assure effective capacity utilization." This statement indicates that he believes that modern managerial enterprise appeared only in restricted fields of industry.

He stresses, therefore, that the modern managerial industrial enterprise appeared at the same moment in history in the United States and Europe and in the same types of industries. According to his model, these industries have one characteristic in common, the integration of mass production with volume distribution. Modern managerial enterprises have appeared in the capital-intensive industries.

Throughput with cost advantages "requires careful coordination not only of flow through the processes of production but also of the flow of inputs from the suppliers and the flow of outputs to the distributors and final consumers." Such coordination and supervision demand the constant attention of managerial teams and require adjustment and control over managerial teams by senior officers. To assert these requirements, the mass-producing enterprises created a managerial hierarchy for "the realization of potential scale economies and the maintenance of quality control." For such industries, which adopted advanced, complex technology, investment in specialized human capital with high-level training was required. As a consequence, inside directors came to play a major role in top-management decision making and "came to select not only the outside directors but their own successors." Chandler concludes that by then the firm had become what he has termed a managerial enterprise.

I would like to raise a few questions regarding the Chandler model. The first point concerns the standards by which we can recognize a modern managerial enterprise. At the beginning of his paper Professor Chandler indicates the location of all industrial corporations in the world that in 1973 employed more than 20,000 workers. He also points out the industrial characteristics and differences among the largest industrial corporations according to their location by country. Though he takes into consideration basic differences within the broad pattern of evolution, he emphasizes that large industrial corporations have clustered in the same industries throughout the twentieth century. I mention again his assertion that these industries have one characteristic in common, the integration of mass production with volume distribution. This being the case, large industrial corporations with more than 20,000 workers are virtually identical with modern managerial enterprises.

However, being a large industrial corporation with more than 20,000 workers is a sufficient but not a necessary condition to be a managerial enterprise. We can find a large number of managerial enterprises, in Chandler's terms, among industrial corporations with fewer than 20,000 workers. This being the case, I think it is necessary to clarify the distinction between large industrial corporations and managerial enterprises.

If one accepts this objection, the location of managerial enterprises by industry must be done differently. Although it is difficult to adopt an adequate procedure for this purpose, it is important for the formation of a growth theory of managerial enterprises. Managerial skills can also be essential in industries where complex product-specific technology (Professor Chandler's term) is not adopted.

This brings me to my second objection. The definitions of some basic terms concerning production, distribution, and integration in this model are too specific for the general theory of the development of managerial enterprise, making it impossible to fit Chandler's model to the Japanese historical experience, as Professor Morikawa has indicated. Although I disagree with Professor Morikawa where he excessively stresses the importance of owner progressiveness, I agree with his assertion that the Chandler model cannot adequately explain the Japanese historical experience.

We must examine further the matter of arriving at more adequate definitions. I would like to suggest defining some basic terms in a different way. For example, it seems safe to assume that the terms "complex" and "specific," used in relation to technology, have the same meaning, namely, high or advanced. Complexity and specificity are attributes of technology itself in the model. These terms can be defined more generally. In a similar way, the term "integration" is not restricted to forward integration into mass distribution but also involves backward or horizontal integration and conglomeration. These forms of integration require technically complex coordination. For the unification of a corporation, maintaining the efficiency of the organization's control over several processes and divisions requires a number of middle managers. Only well-trained full-time managers can adequately fill these positions. If the number of employees of the company is more than the owner's family can control directly and the company has several divisions, the company will inevitably become a managerial enterprise in the long run. But by the time this transformation is complete, the company may be influenced partly by owner progressiveness.

Third, it is necessary to address the issue of organizational inefficiency in big business. I would like to end my comment with the following. I would like to ask Professor Chandler to explain in detail the peculiarities of the evolution of managerial enterprise in Germany. He indicates that the reason industrial giants relied more heavily on banks there than in other countries was partly that in

Germany there were no capital markets of adequate size and sophistication, such as those in London and New York. But most Japanese scholars have a different image of the Berlin capital market. It is generally understood that it functioned efficiently and that industrial giants and banks formed close relationships that were without parallel in history.

Response

A. D. Chandler, Jr.

I very much agree with Professor Hashimoto's central point about the need "to clarify the distinction between large industrial corporations and managerial enterprises." Such a clarification is needed not only to understand the argument in my paper but also to relate my concepts to those developed by Professor Morikawa in his very significant paper. The critical distinction is really not that between the terms "managerial enterprise" and "large industrial corporation" but between the terms "managerial enterprise" and "managerial hierarchy." All corporations that employ a number of managers create a hierarchy. The largest—those with more than 20,000 workers—obviously employ the most extensive hierarchies, but much smaller corporations also have sizeable ones.

The only difference between Professor Morikawa and myself is that we describe managerial hierarchies at different levels of the enterprise. In this paper (and also in *The Visible Hand*, pp. 1–3) the hierarchies I describe are ones that coordinate, monitor, and allocate resources to a number of operating units—factories, offices, mines, and the like. Such hierarchies include middle and top salaried managers who are senior to the executives in charge of the factories, sales offices, and other operating units and whom I have defined as lower-level managers. Professor Morikawa's managerial hierarchies include managers *within* the operating units, that is, those that are subordinate to the managers of factories, offices, mines, and other operating units. In Japan, as was not the case in Britain, Germany, and the United States, many salaried managers —college graduates who expected to make their careers by moving up the hierarchy—were employed within such operating units as heads and members of sections (see Professor Daitō's paper). Indeed, in Japan before World War II, except in the large multiunit, diversified zaibatsu, probably more managers worked *below* the plant- and office-manager level than *above* it. The reason was that early in this century Japanese businessmen and industrialists were learning to use brand-new technologies and business procedures and therefore had to rely on educated salaried managers to a much greater extent than was ever the case in the West.

I use the term "managerial enterprise" to define an enterprise in which salaried managers—the senior members of a managerial hierarchy—and not representatives of its owners made the top-level decisions. Adjectives that modify the term "enterprise"—personal, family, financial, and managerial—are used to indicate the relationship between the owners and managers of a business enterprise. In a *personal* enterprise the owners managed. They employed few salaried managers, if any. They made the long-term policy and allocating decisions as well as the day-to-day operating decisions. In an *entrepreneurial* or *family* firm (entrepreneurial in the first generation and family in later ones) a number of middle and top managers were employed, but the founder and then his family continued to participate with salaried managers in making top-management coordinating and allocating decisions. In a *financially oriented* enterprise, representatives of large nonfamily investors, particularly banks, participated with senior salaried managers in such decisions; while in a *managerial* enterprise neither representatives of such investors nor representatives of the founding family participated in top-management decision making. Table A defines these types of enterprises in terms of the position of salaried managers and owners on the board of directors, which in all modern economies remains the senior legal and administrative body.

Such a definition of the relationship between owners and managers is valid for managerial hierarchies that appear *within* operating

TABLE A Types of Enterprises

Personal: Directors are owners.
Little or no hierarchy exists.

Entrepreneurial/family: Inside directors include family and salaried managers.

Financial: Outside directors are primarily representatives of large non-family investors. Inside directors are salaried managers.

Managerial: Outside directors are selected by inside directors, who are salaried managers.

FIG. A   The Basic Hierarchical Structure of Modern Business Enterprise.

Note: Each box represents an office.

Source: A. D. Chandler, Jr., *The Visible Hand: The Managerial Revolution in American Business*, Cambridge, Mass., 1977, p. 2.

units as well as those that are created *above* such units. In Japan hierarchies with middle and top salaried managers above the operating units began to appear in enterprises other than the zaibatsu after World War I and only in large numbers after World War II, and did so in the same industries as in the West.

As to other points raised by Professor Hashimoto: Figure A indicates that the hierarchies above the operating units resulted from both vertical and horizontal integration. The Essential Materials Department resulted from vertical integration, while the large number of plants and offices often came from horizontal combination. It seems to me that the close relationship between the industrial giants and banks that was unparalleled in history came in Germany, not in the United States and the United Kingdom, precisely because industrials in the latter two countries had access to larger and more sophisticated capital markets than did the German industrials.

The Rise of the Managerial Enterprise in Germany, c. 1870 to c. 1930

Hartmut Kaelble
Freie Universität Berlin

Research on the rise of the professional manager implies in fact two different debates with different topics, definitions, and questions. One is a debate on innovations in management techniques and business structure. With this topic in mind, Alfred D. Chandler, Jr., has introduced a range of terms and hypotheses that are widely used. His main argument is, roughly, that the rise of the most efficient form of big business, the multidivisional diversified enterprise, was accompanied by the rise of the managerial enterprise, in which managers made the strategic decisions. The managerial enterprise replaced the personal enterprise, which lacked managerial hierarchies, as well as the entrepreneurial and the financial enterprise, which had managerial hierarchies but were still under the control of business families and banks, respectively. Though Chandler himself is careful not to overrate the links between the change of business structure and the change of ownership, this is how his argument is usually understood.

The other debate, on the rise of the professional manager, is a debate on the social and political modernization of the business elite. Sociologists have argued that the secular step from ownership to control of enterprises, that is, from owners to managers, led not only to a fundamental change in the economic attitudes of the business elite but also to a more open and more meritocratic access to top business positions and to changing attitudes in industrial relations and in politics. Though the goals of these two debates are different—innovation and economic performance on the one hand, modernization and social change on the other hand—the two

71

debates deal with the same topic, the rise of professional management, and hence overlap.[1]

Both debates also propose general historical models for all industrializing and modernizing societies. This is why the models are
discussed so widely. This general approach has led to two questions,
which in fact were proposed by Professor Morikawa as the leading
questions of the conference. On the one hand, one might ask to
what degree the managerial enterprise in fact has become or seems
to have become the predominant structure of business firms, at least
in Western societies, and to what degree the traditional family
enterprise persists. On the other hand, one might ask whether these
general theories apply to all industrializing societies in the same
way or whether they are generalizations from particular countries
and do not help us as much in the historical interpretation of other
countries.

With these questions in mind, I shall consider the two topics
proposed by the organizers of the conference. I shall first give an
account of the rise of professional managers in German big business, touching upon the comparative perspective. Then I shall
discuss several causes of the rise of professional managers in Germany. With some short remarks at the end of the paper, I shall
return to my introductory questions.[2]

I. The Rise of the Managerial Enterprise

There is no doubt that we have much difficulty in tracing the
change of business structure in Germany for reasons that are well
known in other countries, too: a thorough study would have to be
based on hundreds of studies of individual firms and would have
to check in each case whether families, banks, or independent
managers made the strategic investment decisions and appointments in the enterprise. Since we do not have this type of extensive
research in German business history, we have to use three approximate approaches.

First, we can follow the rise of anonymous societies, especially
the *Aktiengesellschaften* (joint-stock companies), which include a
certain, though probably changing, proportion of managerial enterprises besides a substantial number of de facto family firms. The

distinct rise of joint-stock companies should carry with it the rise of managerial enterprises. Hence the rise of joint-stock companies can be used as an approximate though inflated indicator. For Germany we have to rely in this respect on the work of contemporary economists rather than upon recent studies. We add to the joint-stock companies two other types of enterprises that consist almost exclusively of managerial enterprises: the public firms (*öffentliche Unternehmen*) and the cooperatives (*Genossenschaften*).

Second, we can trace the rise of managerial enterprises by concentrating on the top firms. This has been done by Jürgen Kocka and Hannes Siegrist in a very valuable study of the hundred largest industrial firms in Germany between 1887 and 1927.[3] To be sure, this study can neither yield a total description of the German development nor provide exact data on the proportion of managerial enterprises, since even for this restricted number of firms the decision-making process cannot be thoroughly investigated for each individual enterprise. Nevertheless, the estimates of this study are reliable, as business archives have been used extensively.

Finally, we can trace the rise of the managerial enterprise by following the rise of managers, that is, in the German case the *Direktoren* and *Vorstandsvorsitzende*. Once again, we do not know the exact business role of individual managers. It is often unclear whether they were confined to routine decisions or made the strategic decisions in the firm that they headed. But we can assume that the distinct rise of managers in the business elite also indicates the rise of powerful managers. Taken together, these more or less soft indicators give us a certain, though somewhat overrated, impression of the timing of the general rise of managerial enterprises, of the concentration of managers in specific parts of the German economy, and of the German situation compared with that of other countries. So far, these indicators have not been looked at in combination. Following are the main conclusions.

First of all, the available indicators corroborate the timing that has often been described: the period from the 1870s until the 1930s was the major period of the rise of the managerial enterprise. The development of joint-stock companies clearly supports this idea in various respects.[4] The *capital* of German joint-stock companies remained more or less constant during the 1850s and 1860s and rose distinctly from the 1870s on. In 1913 it amounted to about 1500% of the total capital of 1870, remaining rather stable after 1925. The *number* of joint-stock companies also grew very slowly during the period of classical capitalism in Germany. It also increased distinctly only from the 1870s on. In 1886–87 contemporary economists in Germany counted 2,143 joint-stock companies. In 1909 the number had more than doubled, the late 1880s and the 1890s being the period of the most distinct expansion. After 1920 the number leveled off. The *work force* employed in joint-stock companies also rose clearly throughout the entire period between 1882 and 1923, especially from the 1890s on. Growth was even more marked in those types of enterprises that were exclusively managerial. The share of the labor force employed in public enterprises was 6% in 1907, the most dramatic period of growth being the 30 years or so before World War I. Cooperatives grew from 0.1% of all firms in 1895 to 1.1% in 1925, with the early Weimar Republic as the period of the most marked increase. The proportion of the labor force employed in all three types of enterprises increased from somewhat over 10% in 1882 to around 30% in 1925. No doubt, not all these firms were under the full control of managers. However, these data indicate that managerial enterprises had become an important part of the German economy.

The development of the number of *Direktoren* was similar. Before the 1870s very few members of the business elite were directors. The proportion of managers rose distinctly among those appointed between 1870 and 1900. Just before World War I a third or more members of the business elite were *Direktoren* (see Table 1). Even among the 500 richest businessmen at that time, around 20% were categorized as managers rather than owners of firms. The proportion of managers in the business elite continued to increase in the interwar period. In 1935 managers were more numerous than owners of firms (Table 1). No doubt problems of definition lie behind these series (see the annotation to Table 1 in the appendix). Still, a distinct rise of managers in the German business elite can be taken for granted.

Finally, Kocka and Siegrist show that the personal enterprise virtually disappeared among the 100 largest industrial enterprises between 1887 and 1937. They estimate that at the same time managerial enterprises became distinctly more numerous in this top group of German industry.[5]

The second conclusion that we can draw from the available research covers the limits and the uneven distribution of managers and managerial enterprises in the German economy. It is no surprise that most managerial enterprises seem to have been large firms. The average number of personnel in joint-stock companies and public enterprises was far higher than that in personal enterprises (in 1895 the numbers were 166 and 179, respectively, compared with 3 in German firms as a whole). In joint-stock companies the average number of employees grew rapidly until 1929. In public enterprises the number decreased but still remained far above the level for the average family firm. Except for the cooperatives, which were small but managerial (eight people per firm on the average in 1895, with a tendency to decrease), size was crucial.[6]

What is more important, however, is the restriction of the managerial enterprise to specific branches of industry and services. Once again, our soft indicators coincide clearly in this respect. The concentration of joint-stock companies was very strong in mining, iron and steel, chemicals, electronics, brewing, and insurance, and less so in banking and engineering. One can estimate that in 1880 two-thirds of all anonymous societies, which amounted to less than 5% of all German firms, were active in these few branches. In 1910 this concentration had become less strong. But still more than one-third of joint-stock companies were active in this small sector of German industry.[7]

The same is true for the *Direktoren*. The proportion of managers in the business elite (outside public enterprises and cooperatives) was especially high in the heavy industries, the chemical and electronics industries, and insurance, and less high though still remarkable in banking and engineering. In 1914 about 60% of managers were active in these branches, in which only about 10%–15% of the total nonagrarian German work force was employed. In contrast, managers were rare in important areas of German industry

TABLE 1 Managers in the German Business Elite, 1800–1935 (%).

	Business elite (NDB sample)			
	1840–1872ᶜ (1)	1873–1905ᶜ (2)	1906–1939ᶜ (3)	1918–1933ᵈ (4)
All businesses	8	26	58	43 .
All industries	11	31	62	45
Heavy industries	26	46	90	86
Metal and engineering	3	19	49	20
Textiles	(15)ᵇ	(7)ᵇ	(0)ᵇ	10
Chemicals	—	24	83	53
Electronics	. . .	. . .	. . .	68
Building	(25)ᵇ	(17)ᵇ	—	(0)ᵇ
Commerce	—	—	—	25ᵇ
Banking	—	20	(60)ᵇ	36
Insurance	—	(100)ᵇ	—	—
Transportᵉ	—	(14)ᵇ	(100)ᵇ	66ᵇ
Total (N)	155	243	112	232

a=Cases with sufficient information only; cases with insufficient information=251.
b=Fewer than ten managers and owners in this category.
c=Estimated year of appointment.
d=Businessmen active at this time.
e=Railway directors not included.
—=No case in this category; . . . =Category not used; 0=Below 0.5%.
Note: This table is preliminary, since it still contains some inconsistencies.
Notes and Sources:
All available surveys are combined in this table even if they are not strictly comparable.
The surveys differ in two respects. First, there are differences of timing. In one part of the
table businessmen are broken down by year of appointment (columns 1–4), in another
part by the time of activity (columns 5–9). In general, year of appointment shows changes
more clearly. Second, the table contains different samples. The first sample (the NDB
sample) includes not only the business elite proper but also businessmen from middle-
sized firms. The second sample (the *Wer ist's* sample) is restricted to large enterprises.
The third sample covers only very rich businessmen (multimillionaires) before World
War I. Each sample has specific strong points and shortcomings and throws a somewhat
different light on German managers.

Columns 1–3 are calculated from W. Stahl, *Der Elitekreislauf der Unternehmerschaft:
Eine empirische Untersuchung im deutschsprachigen Raum*, Frankfurt, 1973, p. 100f. Stahl's
data are based on a recent biographical dictionary, *Neue Deutsche Biographie*, Berlin, 1953
and after. No exact criteria for the entries of this dictionary exist. General reputation
and merit as an innovative entrepreneur but also as an inventor, patron, or politician
are the main criteria. A certain number of Swiss and Austrian businessmen are included.
Column 3 must be used with special care, since the number of cases is small (the NDB
does not accept articles on people still alive). Stahl organized the table from which the

Business elite (*Wer ist's* sample)					Multi-millionaires 1911–1914[d]
1907[d]	1914[d]	1922[d]	1928[d]	1935[d]	
(5)	(6)	(7)	(8)	(9)	(10)
46	36	39	55	54	20
24	26	...	55	58	25
...	...	...	...	69	37
...	...	...	...	44	16
...	...	...	...	12	2
...	...	...	...	82	...
...	...	...	...	86	28
...	...	...	...	(25)[b]	20
6	6	...	52	9	5
86	69	...	77	52	24
90	89	...	100	100	60
56	72	...	81	60	...
381	793	670	596	890	322[a]

calculations are made according to birth cohorts of 1801 through 1833, 1834 through 1866, and 1867 through 1900. Years of appointment were calculated from the median age of appointment of 39 that Stahl found for the managers in the sample (Stahl, *Der Elitekreislauf*, p. 245).

Column 4 is also based on *Neue Deutsche Biographie*. Swiss and Austrian businessmen are excluded. All businessmen active in the Weimar period are included. These data are from an unpublished study.

Columns 5–9 are based on different editions of a contemporary biographical dictionary, *Wer ist's*. No exact definition of the entries is given. However, the business biographies seem to concentrate on large enterprises. Information on entrepreneurial positions are not detailed. Directors, heads of the *Vorstand*, are classified as managers (provided that no information on ownership of enterprises is given). A certain proportion of the managers may in fact have been owners of the firms that they directed or of other firms. Hence the proportion of managers may be somewhat too large. An additional problem of this source is that it does not yield a very consistent series. The number of the entries is relatively small, especially for 1907 and 1928. A higher proportion of managers seems indicated. For historical change, one would do better to compare only pairs of editions of this dictionary, for example, 1907 and 1928 or 1914 and 1935. This is another reason that an additional study of a clearly defined group, managers of the 100 largest industrial enterprises, is in progress. Data based on the 1922 edition of *Wer ist's* is from *Sozialer Aufstieg und Abstieg im deutschen Volke*, Munich, 1930, p. 137.

Column 10 is based on a manual of German millionaires in the last years before World War I: R. Martin, *Handbuch der Millionäre*, Berlin, 1911 and after. For the most part, only millionaires who owned taxable property worth 6 million marks or more are given short biographies. The data are preliminary, since the information is limited to Martin's manual. Other published and unpublished sources will be used later.

and services: In the textile and building industries, in commerce, and in other branches the personal enterprise predominated. Even among the very rich businessmen, the multimillionaires, around 1910 the same pattern appeared though at lower general rates (Table 1). Therefore one can speak of a dual economy: a small, highly managerialized sector that included the growth industries and services of the late nineteenth and early twentieth centuries and a large, more traditional stronghold of the personal or family enterprise.

Third, it is difficult to draw reliable conclusions from the available research on whether the rise of professional management in the German economy before World War II was more rapid than in other developed economies. Nevertheless, the available research allows some preliminary conclusions that are not mere speculation. Taken together, the conclusions give an ambiguous impression.

On the one hand, some strong evidence points to a rather advanced business structure among German enterprises. This is especially true in regard to the degree of diversification and integration of German enterprises. Kocka and Siegrist demonstrate in their study of the 100 largest enterprises in Germany in 1887, 1907, and 1927 that diversification and integration in German big business was more advanced than in British big business and probably also than in French big business. In the early twentieth century diversification in German industry was even more distinct than in American industry. So in this respect the structure of large German enterprises was one of the most modern in the world and ahead of that in the other large European countries. Kocka and Siegrist argue that a major reason for the rapid rise of diversified and integrated enterprises in Germany was late industrialization, which forced German firms to develop the exploitation of resources, transport, and the marketing of products in the form of integrated and diversified enterprises rather than rely upon a developed economic network as did British firms.[8]

On the other hand, in various respects German business structure clearly was less developed than the structure of American enterprises. Germany was in an intermediate position between the United States and the other large European countries—in other words, it was a quite ordinary European country. This applies to the rise of managers in the German business elite, to the size of German industrial firms, and to the persistence of family control in large enterprises. One must add, however, that in all these respects the evidence is much less clear than that for diversification and integration. Further research is needed, especially on the differences among Germany, Britain, and France, which are still unclear.

The proportion of managers in the German business elite is difficult to compare with the proportion in other countries because of the many problems of definition. If we use the available data as a rough approximation, we find that almost half of American businessmen were managers on the eve of World War I (Table 2). In Germany about a third of the members of the business elite were managers at that time, rising to half only in the interwar period. We know from a study by Maurice Lévy-Leboyer that in France about a third of the businessmen in the 30 largest enterprises were managers, on the average, in the period from 1912 to 1939. To Lévy-Leboyer's thinking France was a generation behind the Anglo-Saxon countries.[9] Probably the proportion in France was below 30% in 1912 and hence at that time perhaps somewhat lower than that in Germany, too (Table 2). But this is only an estimate. For Britain we have reliable data only for the iron and steel industry. Among the businessmen active in this industry between 1905 and 1925, about a third were managers. In Germany, about two-thirds of the leaders of the same industry appointed between 1906 and 1939 were managers—a much higher proportion. However, the data are biased in various respects and must be interpreted with great care (Table 2).[10] In sum, it seems quite clear that managers rose more rapidly in the United States than in Europe, whereas differences within Europe have not yet been sufficiently explored.

The size of enterprises is also difficult to compare, since reliable lists of the largest firms are not abundant. Once again, it seems that German enterprises were clearly smaller than American enterprises in the late nineteenth and early twentieth centuries. It is perhaps more important that German firms were not so clearly larger than British firms as has often been assumed. For the period

TABLE 2   The Rise of Professional Managers in Comparative Perspective (%).

	Founders	Owners	Salaried businessmen	Heirs
U.S. I				
1870[a]	36[b]	68[c]	32[d]	32[k]
1900–1910[a]	21[b]	56[c]	44[d]	35[k]
1950[a]	6[b]	17[c]	81[d]	11[k]
U.S. II				
1928	...	11	89[i]	19[f]
France				
1912[a]	ca.20			...
1929[a]	...	}58	}32[g]	...
1939[a]	13			...
Britain				
(iron and steel)				
1875–1895[a]	35	72	28[e]	37
1905–1925[a]	15	66	34[e]	51
1935–1947[a]	5	46	54[e]	41
Germany				
(national sample)				
1914[a]	9–39[h]	64	36	22–52
1929[a]	7–28[h]	45	55	15–36
1935[a]	5–20[h]	46	54	26–41
Germany				
(iron and steel)				
1840–1972[l]	...	12	88	...
1873–1905[l]	...	32	68	...
1906–1939[l]	...	12	88	...

a=Years of activity.
b="Self-made men."
c="Self-made men" plus "family-made men."
d="Bureaucratically made men" plus "professionally made men."
e="Salaried administrators" plus professionals.
f=Inheritance as well as transfer of salaried top positions between relatives.
g=Measured against the labor force in the enterprise.
h=Minimum and maximum rates. For a substantial number of owners, it is unclear
   whether they inherited, purchased, or founded the firm they headed (1914: 30%;
   1919: 21%; 1935: 15%). Preliminary data.
i=Presidents or chairmen of the board: 53%; vice-presidents: 21%; other: 15%.
k="Family-made men."
l=Estimated year of appointment.
...=Category not used.
Sources: U. S. I: S. I. Keller, *The Social Origins and Career Lines of Three Generations
   of American Business Leaders*, High Wycomb, 1953, p. 82. U.S. II: W. L.

around 1905, Helga Nussbaum has found no difference in the capital of the 50 largest joint-stock companies in Germany and Britain.[11] For the interwar period, the new list of the 20 largest enterprises in Britain in 1936 compared with the list compiled by Siegrist for 1927 shows that only the top five firms were larger—in fact much larger—in Germany than in Britain in terms of number of employees. For the rest of the 15 big firms the reverse is true. British firms were as large as or even larger than the German ones (Table 3). This situation is too complicated to permit us to talk generally of a more advanced German business structure, especially if one takes into account that British enterprises should have been even larger in 1927, before the Great Depression. There are no published lists for other European countries and other periods before 1945. But Britain is a crucial case.

Finally, there is no clear evidence that the family enterprise declined more rapidly in Germany than elsewhere in Europe. Chandler and Herman Daems have made the assessment that the decline of entrepreneurial and family enterprises was much slower in prewar and interwar Europe in general than in America. More recently, Herman van der Wee has reviewed the evidence and arguments for this view. For Britain, Peter L. Payne has reinforced this view in a recent article based on earlier research by Charlotte Erickson and Leslie Hannah. Payne shows that even after World War II, most large British enterprises had some characteristics of family control. Only in the 1960s and 1970s could a clear decline of family control be observed.[12]

There is a consensus among German economic historians that family control was also strong in German big business. The decline of business families is considered to have been much slower than in

Warner and J. C. Abegglen, *Occupational Mobility in American Business and Industry, 1928–1952*, Minneapolis, 1955, p. 169 (survey of 8,000 American business leaders in 1928). France: M. Lévy-Leboyer, "Le patronat français, 1919–1973," in M. Lévy-Leboyer, ed., *Le patronat de la seconde industrialisation*, Paris, 1979, pp. 171, 173–74 (all numbers taken from the text rather than from homogeneous tables). Britain (iron and steel): C. Erickson, *British Industrialists: Steel and Hosiery 1850–1950*, Cambridge, 1959, p. 51. Germany (national sample): Unpublished survey based on *Wer ist's* (this source described in the appendix). Germany (iron and steel): Calculated from W. Stahl, *Der Elitekreislauf der Unternehmerschaft*, Frankfurt, 1973, p. 100f.

TABLE 3   The Largest Manufacturing Firms in Interwar Britain and Germany.

Britain (1935)		Germany (1927)	
Firm	No. of employees	Firm	No. of employees
1. Unilever	60,000	1. Vereinigte Stahlwerke	198,000
2. GKN	50,000	2. Siemens	116,000
3. ICI	49,706	3. IG Farben	101,000
4. Vickers	44,162	4. Krupp	76,750
5. London Midland & Scottish Railway	41,301	5. AEG	65,000
6. Cooperative Whole- sale Society	36,831	6. Kokswerke & Chem. Fabriken	33,529
7. London North Eastern Railway	36,789	7. Klöchkner-Werke	26,300
8. Naval Dockyards	31,680	8. Harpener Bergbau	25,548
9. Imperial Tobacco	30,000	9. Mansfeld	24,026
10. Fine Cotton Spinners	30,000	10. Kammgarnspinnerei Bremen	24,500
11. Harland & Wolff	30,000	11. Mannesmannröhren-Werke	23,323
12. AEI	30,000	12. Eisen- und Stahlwerk Hoesch	19,312
13. Textile Machinery Manufactory	24,300	13. Daimler-Benz	17,220
14. General Electric	24,000	14. Vereinigte Glanzstoff-AG	13,400
15. Courtaulds	22,506	15. Bergmann	12,000
16. Lucas	20,000	16. Deutsche Erdöl AG	16,590
17. United Steel	19,229	17. Dt. Schiff- und Maschi- nenbau	12,000
18. Austin Motor	19,000	18. Gutehoffnungshütte	11,139
19. Great Western Railway	18,766	19. Mitteldeutsche Stahlwerke	10,832
20. Dorman Long	18,028	20. Continental	10,750

Note: This comparative list is preliminary, since the full British list with the exact definitions of the enterprises included will only be published in 1985 and since estimates for several big German enterprises, such as Stinnes, Opel, and Henschel, are lacking.

Sources: Britain: "100 largest British Manufacturing Employers in 1935," *Business History Newsletter*, No. 8, 1984, pp. 14–15. Germany: H. Siegrist, "Deutsche Grossunternehmen vom späten 19. Jahrhundert biz zur Weimarer Republik," *Geschichte und Gesellschaft*, Vol. 6, 1980, pp. 93–99.

America. In contrast to Britain, however, statistical studies do not exist even for the post-1945 period. Reliable estimates come from Siegrist, who thinks that in 1907 the majority of large German enterprises were still under family control, mostly as entrepreneurial enterprises.[13] Therefore it seems that the size of firms, family control, and the rise of managers were clearly less advanced in big German firms than in U.S. firms and even may have differed little in these respects from firms in other European countries, whereas in diversification and integration German firms were very modern and "American." What is special about Germany seems to be the combination of modern management methods and traditional power structures in business—a combination that we also find often in German politics and that hence should come as no surprise.

II.   The Reasons for the Rise of the Managerial Enterprise

What are the reasons for the rise of the professional manager and the parallel decline of the family enterprise between the 1880s and the 1930s? Four possible explanations are discussed by economic historians: the educational and professional superiority of professional managers, the decay of entrepreneurial talent in the second and third generations of business families, the weakening of family control because of the rise of big business, and several more specific German preconditions for the decline of the family enterprise, such as the role of big banks, the law, and cartelization. I shall discuss these explanations in turn.

1.   The first reason given for the rise of professional managers is their superior training compared with that of members of business families. Managers had much more often attended universities and had concentrated their studies on fields that were related to business activities, such as economics, natural sciences, engineering, and law. Hence managers are considered to have been much better prepared to run large enterprises, especially in the period of the growing impact of university research on business.

At first glance, the training of owners compared with that of managers in Germany seems to corroborate this view. In fact, owners of firms were qualified in the formal sense of university training much less often than managers. In 1907, only 35% of the owners of firms had attended universities compared with 77% of managers.[14] More scattered evidence gives the impression that the fields of studies of owners of firms were less directly related to business than those of managers.

Nevertheless, there are several doubts about the validity of this view. First, the qualification gap between managers and owners was much smaller if businessmen in the *same* branch of activity are compared. Owners of firms in those branches of industry in which managers were concentrated—the heavy industries, the electronics industry, the chemical industry, and banking—were much more highly qualified than owners in general. Thus, in the pre-1914 Ruhr 50% of the (former) owners of heavy-industry firms were university graduates, compared with 78% of the managers.[15]

Moreover, business families seem to have adapted quite rapidly to the new need for higher qualifications. The gap in higher education between managers and owners narrowed distinctly. In 1935, 54% of the owners of firms had graduated from universities, compared with 71% of the managers.[16] In addition, one can show that even before 1914 there were large reserves of highly qualified young members of business families in Germany (Table 4). Thousands of sons of businessmen attended universities. For the most part, their fields of study were closely related to business. They seem to have outnumbered the openings in top managerial positions (Table 4). All openings for the top positions in anonymous societies (entrepreneurial or managerial ones) could have been filled by young members of business families. If in fact only about 40% of the managers were sons of businessmen, this was probably because these men were not the best choice rather than because highly qualified young members of business families were scarce. Hence the lack of high qualifications in business families is not a convincing explanation for the rise of managers in Germany. I would even hesitate to argue that professional managers increased in number because of a short-term lack of university graduates in business families during the late nineteenth and early twentieth centuries, the very period of the rise of the managerial enterprise. If education had been a crucial factor during such a short period, there should have been a corresponding renaissance of the family firm in big business when business families had filled the education gap. We know of no such renaissance.

Finally, these doubts are reinforced by international comparison, which does not corroborate the implicit assumption that a university education necessarily improved the economic performance of business leaders in the late nineteenth and early twentieth centuries. The comparison between France and the United States is most striking in this respect. In the prewar and interwar period French business leaders were much more highly qualified than their American counterparts. Lévy-Leboyer shows that in 1912 three out of four top business leaders in France had graduated from universities, and the proportion tended to increase in the interwar period. In the United States only about one out of three top businessmen had attended college at that time.[17] Despite the far lower rate of university education among American businessmen, the economic performance of the American economy was far superior to that of the French economy even before 1914, when such external factors as wars had not yet undermined French economic growth. Moreover, in contrast to Germany, American managers and owners of enterprises did not differ much in educational qualifications.[18] Owners of firms had not attended universities less frequently than managers. Still, the family enterprise declined in the United States at least as rapidly as in Germany. These are further reasons why severe doubts exist about education as a crucial factor for the decline of family enterprises in big business.

2. A second reason given for the decline of the family firm and the rise of the professional manager is the demise of the entrepreneurial spirit in late-nineteenth-century European business families. Sons or grandsons of the big founders are considered to have taken the "Buddenbrooks way" or to have become feudalized. They retreated into the arts, lived the unproductive life of the *rentier*, or chose the more prestigious life of the landed aristocracy. The late nineteenth and early twentieth centuries, the period of the rise of the managerial enterprise, are often seen as the time of crisis of business families in Europe. Germany is an important case in this debate. Not only is the notion of the "Buddenbrooks effect" derived from a German novel, but the German bourgeoisie is often con-

TABLE 4   The Reservoir of Highly Qualified Managers among Sons of Business Families in Germany.

Supply from business families			Demand from anonymous societies[a]		
Method of calculation	c. 1885	c. 1910	Method of calculation	c. 1885	c. 1910
Number of students (including technical and other higher education)	31,418	68,000	Number of anonymous societies[a]	2,143	5,222
Sons of businessmen receiving higher education (15%)	4,700 (approx.)	10,200 (approx.)	Number of managerial enterprises (rough maximal approximation) 1885: 70%; 1910: 88%	1,500	4,200
Sons of businessmen studying fields related to business (economics, natural sciences, engineering, law) 1885: 79%; 1910: 67%	3,700 (approx.)	6,800 (approx.)			
Estimated number of graduates each year (sons of businessmen in fields mentioned above: dropout rate 30%; length of studies 5 years)	520 (approx.)	950 (approx.)	Demand for managers each year (two managers per society, 30 years of activity)	100 (approx.)	280 (approx.)

Sons of businessmen becoming businessmen but not going into their fathers' firms per year (approx. 30%)	Demand for managers graduated from institutions of higher education per year (70%)
160 (approx.)	80 (approx.)
290 (approx.)	230 (approx.)

a = *Aktiengesellschaften* only. Public enterprises and nonprofit private enterprises are not included, since they are not part of the debate on the demise of the family enterprise.

Sources: Number of students: G. Hohorst, J. Kocka, and G. A. Ritter, *Sozialgeschichtliches Arbeitsbuch*, Munich, 1975, p. 161. Students from business families: H. Kaelble, *Soziale Mobilität und Chancengleichheit*, Göttingen, 1983, p. 130 (Germany in 1910 also applied to 1885 for lack of better data). Fields of study of businessmen's sons: *Preussische Statistik*, Vol. 236, 1911–12, p. 140ff (students in law, chemistry, natural sciences, and mathematics at *Technische Hochschulen* and *Bergakademien*). Proportion of businessmen's sons not entering their fathers' firms (approx. 30%): estimate from an unpublished study of the German business elite in 1907 and 1914 (source: *Wer ist's*). Number of anonymous societies (*Aktiengesellschaften and Gewerkschaften*): *Handwörterbuch der Staatswissenschaften*, ser. 4, Vol. 1, 1923, p. 149. Average year of appointment of managers (about 40 years of age or over, about 30 years of activity): W. Stahl, *Der Eliteskreislauf der Unternehmerschaft*, Frankfurt, 1973, p. 245. Proportion of university graduates among managers: rate for 1914 from an unpublished study of the German business elite in 1907 and 1914 (sources: *Wer ist's*). All assumptions are to the disadvantage of our argument. This is especially true for the rate of managerial enterprises, years of activity, and dropout rate of students from business families.

sidered to have been a prominent case of feudalization and of sub-
mission to the aristocratic lifestyle and values.

However, it does not seem that a massive alienation from business
existed among the sons of German businessmen in the form of
Buddenbrooks decay or in the form of the feudalized bourgeoisie.
Quite to the contrary, there is clear evidence that businessmen's
sons had a strong interest in business careers. In this respect, the
crucial layer of the German business elite was the richest business
families, who usually were the most sensitive to aristocratic values
and who could also most easily finance an aristocratic lifestyle.
Hence it is striking that in the 400 wealthiest non-noble German
business families around 1914, only one out of ten sons entered
careers that would have been aristocratic in the pre-1914 German
context, that is, became large landowners, army officers, or diplo-
mats. It is even more important that three out of four sons became
businessmen like their fathers—a high rate of occupational heredity
compared with the pattern in other parts of the pre-1914 German
middle class. Business careers were so attractive that a substantial
number of sons of the richest businessmen who could not or would
not inherit their fathers' businesses founded enterprises on their
own. One out of four sons did this.[19]

If few sons of businessmen took up aristocratic activities, this
does not mean that the aristocratic model was weak in Germany.
It was undoubtedly strong, as the aristocracy still had privileged
access to top positions in the army, in administration, and in the
large estates.[20] The impact of the aristocratic model in Germany
can be seen clearly among the daughters in business families. In the
400 richest non-noble business families, daughters married into
aristocratic milieus almost as often as into middle-class milieus.
Businessmen's sons' interest in business must have been very strong,
as they rarely followed the attractive model. Whatever feudalization means, German businessmen seem to have remained much
more business-oriented than has been assumed. There is no clear
evidence that many members of the pre-1914 business families left
business and thus made room for professional managers.

This does not mean that the history of the business family did not
contribute to the rise of the professional manager. But it seems to

have done so in ways other than those often presumed. Two changes seem to have been important. First, the demographic structure of the German business family changed. The number of children in business families shrank distinctly, as was the case in other European countries. Most of the multimillionaires around 1914 still had (as had businessmen in general) around five children on the average. The strategy of controlling large enterprises through family members could still work, especially if cousins, nephews, and sons-in-law were included. Business families were still numerous enough to fill the main top positions even if some family members had no business talent. But even before 1914 the number of children in business families began to shrink. In the 1930s, the average number of children in business families in general had fallen to three or even two.[21] Hence business families had to rely more and more on managers who did not belong to the family. The traditional family enterprise in which the top positions were held by family members had run into demographic difficulties.

Furthermore, the cohesion of the classical nineteenth-century business family seems to have lost some of its strength. In the nineteenth-century business family strong links existed among most family members. The family intervened massively in the major personal decisions of its individual members. The resulting strong cohesion of the business family was based partly on the strong patriarchal authority of the head of the family and partly on the vital role of kinship in capital formation and business contacts, training after school in the firms of fathers or relatives, and the use of kinship to build up loyalties among the top men in the enterprise in a period in which other management models did not yet exist and in which communication between plants in different locations was still difficult.[22]

From the end of the nineteenth century on, the cohesion of the business family may have weakened for various reasons that can only be touched on here. Capital formation did depend less upon the family when modern banking developed and when the size of the capital concerned became too large for kin to provide. Training was provided less by family enterprises when university training became more crucial. Kinship loyalties were less needed when

modern management methods had been tested and when more
advanced communication techniques (rapid railway connections,
telegraph, telephone) had been established, opening up close routine
contacts and much stricter control of top executives in other locations. The patriarchal authority of the head of the business family
was weakened by the generation conflict, which intensified in
central Europe around the turn of the century and which also
affected business families. No doubt the business family remained
important in the crucial individual decisions of its offspring, such
as training and career. But for all these reasons it was less involved
in the actual management and decision making of individual enterprises. In this way it contributed to the rise of the professional
manager.

3.   There is a consensus among economic historians in Germany
(as among historians in other countries) that big business is an
important precondition for the rise of managerial enterprises,
though big firms did not automatically become managerial enterprises.[23] Large size had various consequences, all of which tended
to work in favor of the rise of managers. I shall mention the most
important ones very briefly for lack of space. Large size implied
a much more complex top management structure than had existed
in the early industrial firms, because more plants in more locations in more industrial branches with more personnel were to be
controlled. Large, diversified, integrated enterprises could not be
run without managers, though not necessarily without being managerial enterprises. Large size also led to larger amounts of investment capital and to new forms of capital formation. Moreover,
large size led to new forms of growth. Growth in competition was
gradually replaced by growth for market control and by managers'
business policies that were often more aggressive than those of
more traditional family enterprises.

The impact of firms' large size on the rise of managers in Germany is usually demonstrated by tracing the histories of individual
enterprises as they grew from middle-sized to large firms. Two cases
that are often discussed by German economic historians are those
of the two largest enterprises in the German electrical engineering
industry, Siemens and AEG. These companies are especially inter-

esting because one was a family firm and the other one was largely a managerial enterprise (though with some elements of family control). Thus they demonstrate the historical interplay between the two types of enterprises. Business growth was much more rapid in AEG, the managerial enterprise, and the Siemens enterprise was forced to adapt to the pace and methods of growth of its managerial competitor.[24]

4. Skepticism and reservations rather than strong assessments in regard to the impact of the specifically German characteristics of big business on the rise of the professional manager prevail among historians. Once again, for lack of space I shall just touch upon these questions. Most economic historians are careful not to overrate the impact of particular legal regulations, especially the impact of the German joint-stock company. Though in theory the German joint-stock company may have reinforced the rise of managerial enterprises for various reasons, most historians do not hold that such an impact can be proved.[25]

Another special German characteristic, the strong influence of big banks on German large industrial firms, especially in the 1880s and 1890s, is also not regarded as having clearly paved the way for the rise of the managerial enterprise. No doubt the banks could exert strong pressure on family enterprises to expand more rapidly than the family businessmen would otherwise have done, being afraid of losing control over the firm. However, control could be retained even in this situation. Once again, Siemens is an interesting example. Pressed by the Deutsche Bank, upon which Siemens depended, the firm was forced to diversify by buying up other firms and to resist the aggressive managerial competition of AEG much more than Siemens had originally intended. Nevertheless, the Siemens family did not lose control over the firm even under rapid growth. The influence of the banks sometimes may have even strengthened the flexibility of family firms and their adaptation to the methods of the managerial enterprise rather than diminished family control.[26]

Finally, the impact of the cartels, which were frequent in Germany, did not work simply in favor of the rise of managers, either. No doubt cartelization in its most developed form, the *Syndikate*, did enhance the power of the managers in the central agency of the cartel, to the detriment of the member enterprises. On the other hand, cartelization was also a shelter for family firms, which as cartel members were less threatened by the more aggressive managerial enterprises. So this German characteristic was also ambivalent in its impact on the decline of family control in big business. In general, these and other particular German characteristics of big business did not necessarily work in favor of the rise of the managerial enterprise. Hence it would be not astonishing if future, more exact, comparative research should demonstrate that the entrepreneurial or family enterprise retained its position in the prewar and interwar period in Germany about as well as in other European countries.

III. Concluding Remarks

I wish to close with some short general remarks that return to my introductory questions. Research on the history of business has demonstrated that for at least two reasons we should be careful with historical models that assume a general trend from the family enterprise to the managerial enterprise in all societies. First, many business historians now seem to take the view that the family enterprise remained much stronger and more important than had originally been assumed. The overwhelming majority of firms in Western industrial societies are still run by owners, and there is no indication that this will change in the future. Hannah has summarized this predominant view among economic historians very well.[27] Therefore the historical model of the shift from the family enterprise to the managerial enterprise applies to a limited though important sphere of the economy and perhaps also to a limited period of time. There is, however, no doubt that the ownership of enterprises and the owners have changed dramatically since the nineteenth century, partly under the influence of the success of the managerial enterprise. The nineteenth-century business family has almost disappeared in our societies. Thus there has been a shift not only from family enterprise to managerial enterprise but also from the nineteenth-century family enterprise to the postwar business family. As this dramatic change is not included in the models under debate, it has largely been neglected. I think much more research on this change in the family enterprise and the business family from the industrial revolution to the postwar period is needed.

Second, in my view research has shown that the historical models mentioned at the beginning of my paper are to be applied to European history with great care. This is especially true of the models of the social consequences of the rise of managers, which we did not discuss here. In a much more limited sense, this is also true of the Chandler model. No doubt this model has many merits and strong points, which clearly prevail. For the period covered here, however, one point is difficult to see: the distinction between the entrepreneurial or family enterprise and the financial enterprise on the one hand and between the entrepreneurial or family enterprise and the managerial enterprise on the other hand is used to distinguish between more backward and more modern firms. Hence it is argued that European enterprises were more backward, since family or bank control in our period was still stronger than in the United States. This European "backwardness" seems to be a purely formal one, however, since the economic performance of entrepreneurial or family enterprises and of financial enterprises was not necessarily worse than that of European managerial enterprises. Kocka has demonstrated this, at least for entrepreneurial enterprises, in a case study of the Siemens firm.[28] The persistence of entrepreneurial and financial enterprises seems, rather, to have been the answer to specific European circumstances. Therefore I think we should allow for the peculiarities of business history in Europe.

NOTES

1. A. D. Chandler, Jr., *The Visible Hand: The Managerial Revolution in American Business*, Cambridge, Mass., 1977. A. D. Chandler, Jr., and H. Daems, "The Rise of Managerial Capitalism and Its Impact on Investment Strategy in the Western World and Japan," in H. Daems and H. van der Wee, eds., *The Rise of Managerial Capitalism*, The Hague, 1974. J. Burnham, *Das Regime der Manager*, Stuttgart, 1948. R. Dahrendorf, *Class and Class Conflict in Industrial Society*, Stanford, 1959. J. Galbraith, *The New Industrial State*, Boston, 1967.
2. I shall not deal with the social and political consequences of the rise of professional managers in Germany, since this is not a topic of

the conference, but research on Germany has probably centered most on that topic. See the excellent summary by J. Kocka, "Les entrepreneurs salariés dans l'industrie allemande à la fin du XIXe et au début du XXe siècle," in M. Lévy-Leboyer, ed., *Le patronat de la seconde industrialisation*, Paris, 1979. See also H. Kaelble, "From the Family Enterprise to the Professional Manager: the German Case," in L. Hannah, ed., *From Family Firm to Professional Management: Structure and Performance of Business Enterprise*, Budapest, 1982, pp. 50–59.

3. J. Kocka and H. Siegrist, "Die hundert deutschen Industrieunternehmen im späten 19. und frühen 20. Jahrhundert," in N. Horn and J. Kocka, eds., *Law and the Formation of the Big Enterprises in the 19th and Early 20th Centuries*, Göttingen, 1979. H. Siegrist, "Deutsche Grossunternehmen vom späten 19. Jahrhundert bis zur Weimarer Republik," *Geschichte und Gesellschaft*, Vol. 6, 1980, pp. 60–102.

4. For a good summary see J. Brockstedt, "Family Enterprise and the Rise of Large-Scale Enterprise in Germany (1871–1914): Ownership and Management," in A. Okochi and S. Yasuoka, eds., *Family Business in the Era of Industrial Growth*, Tokyo, 1984, p. 138ff.

5. For the increase in number of *Aktiengesellschaften* see *Handwörterbuch für Staatswissenschaften*, ser. 4, Vol. 1, 1923, article on *Aktiengesellschaften*; H. van der Borght, *Statistische Studien über die Bewährung der Aktiengesellschaften*, Jena, 1983, p. 222ff. (for the period before the 1880s); E. Moll, *Das Problem der amtlichen Statistik der deutschen Aktiengesellschaften*, Berlin, 1907; *Handwörterbuch der Sozialwissenschaften*, Vol. 1, Tübingen, 1956, p. 153ff. For the capital of the *Aktiengesellschaften* see W. G. Hoffmann, *Das Wachstum der deutschen Wirtschaft seit der Mitte des 19. Jahrhunderts*, Berlin, 1965, p. 772 (railway companies are excluded from the series). For the work force employed in the *Aktiengesellschaften*, in public enterprises, and in cooperatives see R. Stockmann, G. Dahm, and K. Zeifang, "Konzentration und Reorganisation von Unternehmen und Betrieben: Empirische Analysen zur Entwicklung der nichtlandwirtschaftlichen Arbeitsstätten und Unternehmen in Deutschland, 1875–1970," in M. Haller and W. Müller, eds., *Beschäftigungssystem im gesellschaftlichen Wandel*, Frankfurt, 1983, p. 104ff. For detailed figures see G. Ambrosius, *Der Staat als Unternehmer: Öffentliche Wirtschaft und Kapitalismus seit dem 19. Jahrhundert*, Göttingen, 1984, pp. 22ff., 64ff. For the 100 largest firms see Kocka and Siegrist, "Industrieunternehmen," p. 89.

6. Stockmann, Dahm, and Zeifang, "Konzentration," p. 115f.

7. For 1880 see van der Borght, *Aktiengesellschaften*, p. 215ff. The figure for 1910 is calculated from the detailed list of industrial joint-stock companies in W. Sombart, *Die deutsche Volkswirtschaft im 19. Jahrhundert und im Anfang des 20. Jahrhunderts*, 5th ed., Berlin, 1921, p. 501ff.

8. Kocka and Siegrist, "Industrieunternehmen," pp. 84–96. Siegrist, "Grossunternehmen." See also J. Kocka, "Grossunternehmer und der Aufstieg des Managerkapitalismus im späten 19. und frühen 20. Jahrhundert: Deutschland im internationalen Vergleich," *Historische Zeitschrift* 232, Munich, 1981, pp. 39–60.

9. M. Lévy-Leboyer, ed., "Le patronat français 1912–1973," in Lévy-Leboyer, ed., *Le patronat de la seconde industrialisation*, p. 173.

10. The German figures are inflated compared with the British ones because they cover only the businessmen appointed to managerial posts in this period rather than all active businessmen, because they cover a longer and later period, and because they include only some businessmen—probably those belonging to the largest firms—rather than all businessmen like the British study.

11. H. Nussbaum, "Cartels and Syndicates in the Process of Transition from Family to Large-Scale Enterprises (Germany and Britain)," in Hannah, ed., *From Family Firm to Professional Management*, p. 94f.

12. A. D. Chandler, Jr., and H. Daems, "The Rise of Managerial Capitalism and Its Impact on Investment Strategy in the Western World and Japan," in Daems and van der Wee, eds., *The Rise of Managerial Capitalism*, pp. 9f., 14, 23ff. H. van der Wee, *Der gebremste Wohlstand*, Munich, 1984, chap. 5. P. L. Payne, "Family Business in Britain: A Historical and Analytical Survey," in Okochi and Yasuoka, eds., *Family Business*, p. 186ff.

13. Siegrist, "Grossunternehmen," p. 88. Brockstedt, "Family Enterprise," p. 258. H. Pohl, "Zur Geschichte und Leitung deutscher Grossunternehmen seit dem 19. Jahrhundert," *Zeitschrift für Unternehmensgeschichte*, Vol. 26, Wiesbaden, 1981, p. 158ff. (English version in *German Yearbook on Business History 1982*, Berlin, 1982, pp. 91–122). R. Tilly, "The Growth of Large-Scale Enterprise in Germany since the Middle of the 19th Century," in Daems and van der Wee, eds., *The Rise of Managerial Capitalism*, p. 155ff.

14. Data from an unpublished study based on the biographical dictionary *Wer ist's*. For details see footnote to Table 1.

15. T. Pierenkemper, *Die westfälischen Schwerindustriellen, 1852–1913*, Göttingen, 1979, p. 60.

16. Data from an unpublished study based on the biographical dic-

tionary *Wer ist's*. For details see footnote to Table 1. For a comparison of fields of study of sons of owners and sons of managers see C. Lorenz, *Zehnjahresstatistik des Hochschulbesuchs und der Abschlussprüfungen*, Berlin, 1943, p. 362ff.

17. See the data on the university and college training of businessmen in H. Kaelble, "Long-Term Changes in the Recruitment of the Business Elite: Germany Compared to the U.S., Great Britain, and France since the Industrial Revolution," *Journal of Social History*, Vol. 13, 1979–80, p. 417; another version appears in H. Kaelble, *Social Mobility in Comparative Perspective*, Leamington Spa, in press.

18. W. L. Warner and J. C. Abegglen, *Occupational Mobility in American Business and Industry, 1928–1952*, Minneapolis, 1955, p. 280.

19. All data from D. L. Augustine Pérez, "Heiratsverhalten und Berufswahl in den nichtagrarischen Multimillionärsfamilien in Deutschland vor 1914," M.A. thesis, Freie Universität Berlin, 1983, p. 55ff. For similar evidence for the business elite in general see W. Stahl, *Der Elitekreislauf der Unternehmerschaft: Eine empirische Untersuchung im deutschsprachigen Raum*, Frankfurt, 1973, p. 174ff.; H. Kaelble, "Wie feudal waren die Unternehmer im Kaiserreich?" in R. Tilly, ed., *Beiträge zur quantitativen Vergleichenden Unternehmensgeschichte*, Stuttgart, 1985.

20. A. J. Mayer, *The Persistence of the Old Regime: Europe to the Great War*, London, 1981. D. Spring, ed., *European Landed Elites in the 19th Century*, Baltimore, 1977. B. Moore, *Social Origins of Dictatorship and Democracy*, London, 1967, p. 418ff.

21. A. von Nell, "Die Entwicklung der generativen Strukturen bürgerlicher und bäuerlicher Familien von 1750 bis zur Gegenwart, Dissertation, Bochum, 1973, p. 29 (the dramatic decline in marriages from 1900 on is discussed; for our problem this work is important only in the interwar period, when the children of these marriages became adults).

22. Most important for the nineteenth-century German business family: J. Kocka, "Familie, Unternehmer und Kapitalismus: An Beispielen aus der frühen deutschen Industrialisierung," *Zeitschrift für Unternehmergeschichte*, Vol. 24, Wiesbaden, 1979, pp. 99–135 (English version in *German Yearbook of Business History 1981*, pp. 53–82). See also H. Rosenbaum, *Formen der Familie*, Frankfurt, 1982, pp. 336ff., 353ff.

23. For the following remarks see J. Kocka, *Unternehmer in der deutschen Industrialisierung*, Göttingen, 1975, p. 155ff.; Tilly, "Large-Scale Enterprise"; Pierenkemper, *Schwerindustrielle*.

24. Pohl, "Grossunternehmen," p. 160f., Kocka, "Les entrepreneurs salariés," p. 90ff., and "Siemens und der aufhaltsame Aufstieg der AEG," in *Tradition*, Munich, 1972, pp. 125–42.

25. Kocka and Siegrist, "Industrieunternehmen," p. 95f. Tilly, "Large-Scale Enterprise," p. 153ff. Pohl, *Grossunternehmen*, pp. 157, 163.

26. W. Feldenkirchen, "The Banks and the Steel Industry in the Ruhr: Developments in Relations from 1873 to 1914," *German Yearbook on Business History 1981*, Berlin, 1981, p. 32ff. J. Kocka, *Unternehmer*, p. 100ff. P. von Strandmann, *Unternehmenspolitik und Unternehmensführung: Der Dialog zwischen Aufsichtsrat und Vorstand bei Mannesmann, 1900–1919*, Düsseldorf, 1978, p. 27ff.

27. L. Hannah, "Introduction," in Hannah, ed., *From Family Firm to Professional Management*, pp. 1–8.

28. For the social consequences of the rise of managers see Kocka, "Familie, Unternehmer und Kapitalismus" and "Les entrepreneurs salariés."

Comment

Takeo Kikkawa
Aoyama Gakuin University

Professor Kaelble's paper is extremely significant because it refutes the commonly accepted theory on many points. Therefore it is rather easy to indicate the points in his paper that I would like to question. I wish to pose three problems.

The first problem concerns the continuance of family enterprise in Germany. Professor Kaelble states that "there has been a shift not only from family enterprise to managerial enterprise but also from the nineteenth-century family enterprise to the postwar business family." This conclusion emphasizes the continuance of family enterprise, in contrast to the commonly accepted theory. But I think this conclusion is somewhat contradictory. Why does the postwar business family survive in spite of the shift from family enterprise to managerial enterprise? What is the difference between the nineteenth-century family enterprise and the postwar business family? What is the definitive condition that determines whether an enterprise shifts to a form of managerial enterprise or to a new type of business family? To what degree has managerial enterprise become predominant and to what degree does the business family persist in postwar Germany? The first problem consists of these questions. Perhaps a detailed explanation of the development of Siemens holds the key to the answers to these questions.

The second problem concerns the role of banks. Professor Chandler in his paper emphasizes the role of German banks. In his introduction to *Managerial Hierarchies* he also writes that "industrial sectors dominated by big business in Germany are therefore examples of financial capitalism."[1] He thereby clearly distinguishes Germany as an example of financial capitalism as opposed to Britain, which exemplifies family capitalism. Professor Kaelble, by contrast, does not necessarily emphasize the role of German banks. As a result he seems to make much of the common characteristics of European countries, that is, the persistence of entrepreneurial enterprise. There seems to be a clear difference of opinion between Professors Chandler and Kaelble as to the role of banks in Germany. I think this difference is not only a matter of degree but also a question of theoretical framework. Professor Chandler categorizes financial capitalism separately from family capitalism and managerial capitalism. Professor Kaelble, however, only distinguishes between family enterprise and managerial enterprise. He mentions the role of banks only in terms of their effect on the shift from family enterprise to managerial enterprise. It is obvious that there is a notable difference of opinion between Professors Chandler and Kaelble.

The third problem concerns the relationship between the *Aufsichtsrat* as a supervisory board and the *Vorstand* as an executive board. This problem is closely related to the second problem. According to Jürgen Kocka, "German corporation law after 1870 prescribed a dual board structure. Thus firms had not just one 'board of directors' at the top of the corporation, but a supervisory board (*Aufsichtsrat*), on the one hand, and an executive board (*Vorstand*), on the other." The members of the supervisory board "made the most basic decisions, particularly those about investments and top-level appointments. The supervisory board appointed the members of the executive board, who made the day-to-day decisions and actually ran the company." Moreover, "before 1914, bank directors made up the largest single group among the supervisory board members of German joint-stock companies." Therefore "the supervisory board was the most important channel through which the large banks exercised direct and continuous influence over industrial firms." But "in the long run, the executive board became more influential than the supervisory board, whatever the law; this shift gradually reduced the banks' control of industry and increased the power of salaried managers."[2] If Kocka's interpretation is correct, it is necessary to clarify the relationship between the *Aufsichtsrat* and the *Vorstand* in order to comprehend the role of banks and the development of managerial capitalism in Germany. Nevertheless, Professor Kaelble's paper for this conference hardly mentions this dual board structure at the top level of German corporations.

NOTES

1. Alfred D. Chandler, Jr., and Herman Daems, "Introduction", in Alfred D. Chandler, Jr., and Herman Daems, eds., *Managerial Hierarchies: Comparative Perspectives on the Rise of the Modern Industrial Enterprise*, Cambridge, Mass., 1980, pp. 6–7.
2. Jürgen Kocka, "The Rise of the Modern Industrial Enterprise in Germany," in Chandler and Daems, eds., *Managerial Hierarchies*, pp. 91–92.

Strategy, Structure, and Management Development in the United States and Britain*

William Lazonick
Harvard University

I. Specialization and Coordination

The dominant institutional feature of twentieth-century capitalist development has been the evolution of the bureaucratic business corporation. Using social organizations rather than impersonal markets to pursue expansionary strategies, corporations based in the United States, Germany, and Japan have brought their economies to the forefront in international competitiveness. In contrast, an important cause of the relative decline of the once-powerful British economy has been the failure of its enterprises to keep pace with international developments in business organization.[1]

There is nothing inevitable about the success of large-scale business organizations. Many corporations that have sought to become too big too fast have stumbled under their own weight, while some once-dominant corporations have found old modes of bureaucratic organization and administration to be formidable obstacles to adaptation to new competitive conditions. The successful implementation of a strategy of corporate expansion requires the development of a managerial structure that permits top management to integrate and coordinate a specialized division of labor to achieve enterprise goals.

Influenced mainly by the persistence of the small family firm in Britain, neoclassical economists have long stressed the limitations that managerial capability places on the growth of the firm.[2] Alternatively, influenced by the ongoing administrative problems of

*Leslie Hannah and the participants at the Fuji International Conference on Business History provided useful comments on an earlier draft of this paper, and Heidi Willmann supplied excellent research assistance.

large-scale organizations in the United States, organizational theorists such as Herbert Simon have used the term "bounded rationality" to describe the managerial constraints on enterprise growth.[3] From either perspective, the limitation on the growth of the firm is that an individual can only absorb so much knowledge and oversee the activities of so many people and processes before the marginal return to his or her managerial capacity becomes negative.

The tremendous expansion of the scale and scope of the enterprise since the late nineteenth century suggests, however, a considerable unbounding of organizational rationality that stands in need of explanation. In his classic work, *The Functions of the Executive*, Chester Barnard made a valuable theoretical start by emphasizing the relationship between the collective rationality of the organization and the individual rationality of the various participants in its bureaucratic structure.[4] The "functions of the executive" are to develop sources of information, lines of communication, and structures of authority to render, as far as possible, the goals of individuals consistent with organizational objectives.

How is the collectivization of rationality achieved? At any point in time, an industrial bureaucracy will be made up of generalists who coordinate and specialists who carry out detailed technical (including legal and commercial) tasks. But as a dynamic social process, the unbounding—or collectivization—of rationality involves a more or less continuous transformation of a proportion of specialists into generalists. As specialists attain more responsibility for process and product development within their own functional areas, they will need a broader understanding of overall enterprise potential and goals in order to determine what types of information to supply to coordinators, whose tasks are to make and implement policy. Similarly, general managers must be capable of evaluating what types of information to accept from specialists.

As an organizational process in the modern industrial corporation, therefore, successful management development not only trains competent specialists but also selects the best of these specialists and turns them into generalists as they climb the corporate hierarchy. The more complex and far-flung the enterprise, the more must the process of transformation of specialists into generalists take place more or less continuously over the careers of upwardly mobile managers. Hence the periodic rotation of promising specialists to new functional areas outside their specialties in order to give them a broader perspective on overall operations. An assumption underlying such firm-level practices is the long-term attachment of particular individuals to particular organizations—attachment that is typically secured by offering vertical mobility within the firm.

Getting desired performance from the specialized division of labor is not, however, simply a technical matter of training, information, and lines of communication. The performance of individuals and groups in a bureaucracy depends not only on their productive capabilities but also on their willingness to exert those capabilities in ways that are consistent with the overall goals of the firm. Conflict and cooperation among interested parties impart a social dimension to the problem of coordination. Specialists will be much more likely to cooperate with generalists if they see successful specialist performance as a means to upward mobility within the firm—mobility to positions where the coordination of specialists and the possession of generalist training and attitudes will be increasingly important.

In a modern industrial bureaucracy, successful management development results in the *bureaucratic integration* of specialists and generalists, making functional specialists amenable to managerial coordination and developing general managers who can effectively coordinate the specialized division of labor. From the point of view of the firm's strategy makers, bureaucratic integration permits the unbounding of rationality by harnessing the individual efforts of managerial personnel to the goals of the enterprise.

In the absence of movement of individuals around and up the corporate organization, *bureaucratic segmentation* will set in. General managers will have to be recruited from outside the firm. By not promoting from within, the firm will forgo the use of a powerful incentive mechanism to elicit work effort from subordinate managerial personnel. Specialists, moreover, will owe no particular loyalty to these outsiders, who may in fact know little about the firm's specialist activities or personalities. With avenues of upward mobility blocked, the best of the specialists will be likely to leave the firm, while the rest will pursue their careers within a narrow specialty, rendering functional departments self-serving entities, impervious to effective coordination from above.

The advantages of the multidivisional form of managerial organization that became increasingly dominant among U.S. corporations in the twentieth century derived less from the flexibility of decentralized management per se, which if not adequately coordinated could lead top management to lose control, than from the scope that this organizational structure provided for bureaucratic integration. What decentralized decision making demanded was the integration of specialist knowledge and generalist capabilities on the part of middle managers. And what helped to ensure that the decisions of competent middle managers would conform to the overall goals of the firm was the promise of promotion within the organization, with the central office as the limit to vertical mobility. Without a process of management development that ensured bureaucratic integration, higher-level management would not have been able to coordinate divisional activities in the interests of long-term enterprise goals.

For the business organization, management development occurs externally, primarily in the system of higher education, as well as internally in accordance with policies of management training and promotion. We can expect a dynamic interaction between these two realms of management development: the demands placed by business organizations on the educational system to supply certain types of management personnel will depend in part on the types of internal policies these organizations seek to pursue, which will in turn depend in part on the types of personnel they find ready at hand. As we shall see, in the first half of this century there occurred in the United States, but not in Britain, a simultaneous transformation of traditional education and traditional structures of bureaucratic organization that brought management development in line with expansionary corporate goals.

In both the United States and Britain, the collectivization of rationality confronted a similar problem of deeply entrenched individualism. If anything the ideal of independent as opposed to corporate employment was stronger in the land of Thomas Jefferson than in the land of Adam Smith. Yet in the United States the confrontation of social organization and individualism resulted in bureaucratic integration, whereas in Britain it resulted in bureaucratic segmentation. The arguments made above suggest that a comparative analysis of the historical evolution of management development in the two countries will provide considerable insight into the relations among bureaucratic integration, organizational form, and business performance.

In the next section of this paper, I outline how management development resulted in bureaucratic integration in the United States in roughly the first half of the twentieth century. To American-style management development I then contrast the mode of management development that generally prevailed in Britain well into the second half of the twentieth century—a mode in which technical specialization and general management were highly segmented in terms of both training and careers, underdeveloping and undermining the ability of general managers to coordinate the specialized division of labor. In the final section, I consider the relationship between management development and the multidivisional enterprise in the light of the U.S.–British comparison.

II. Bureaucratic Integration in the United States

The integration of U.S. higher education with business has provided a model that other capitalist societies have sought to replicate in the post-World War II period. As the foundation of the management development process, the U.S. educational system has provided industrial corporations with large supplies of managerial and technical personnel. Through the liberal-arts orientation of undergraduate education in the United States, potential managers can develop social values, communicative skills, and a general understanding of social process that are basic for cooperative participation and generalist training within the firm. As technical preparation for specialist roles, in which recruits to the bureaucracy must almost always begin their careers, higher education is structured to provide familiarity with basic principles in science, technology, commerce, and human relations. In addition, the professional orientation of graduate as well as some undergraduate education can equip the potential manager with specialized knowledge in fields as diverse as accounting, marketing, and chemical engineering.

With this system of higher education in place, corporate employers have been able to take for granted that recruits to the managerial bureaucracy will possess a level of competency in social and technical skills necessary for effective performance. Within the corporate structures, management development programs that are designed to shape social attitudes and cognitive abilities to meet firm-specific needs can build upon pre-employment educational foundations.

The fit between the U.S. system of higher education and business has never been perfect. In the 1950s, for example, there were complaints that university graduates were too specialized to become top managers.[5] Besides, as a social institution, higher education does serve nonbusiness purposes and respond to nonbusiness pressures. Nevertheless, comparative perspective makes it clear that the U.S. educational system has been very business-oriented since the turn of the century. As we shall see, the system of higher education had not been brought into the service of business in Britain even by the 1960s as it had been in the United States some 40 or 50 years earlier. Why was this the case? Why was there a successful integration of higher education with business in the one country but not in the other?

In the mid-nineteenth century the form and content of higher education in the United States and Britain were not markedly different. Harvard and Yale had been modeled after Oxford and Cambridge and, along with a few other colleges established in the colonial period, set the standards for the 261 colleges and universities founded between 1776 and 1865. Until the post-bellum period (and beyond in many institutions) the basis of the college curriculum was classical—Latin, Greek, mathematics, moral philosophy, a little Hebrew, and very elementary physics and astronomy—and reflected Oxbridge tradition in methods of teaching and academic ritual as well as subject matter.[6]

The early American college ostensibly provided a stepping-stone to careers in the "learned professions" (law, medicine, and theology) as well as politics. But a college education was by no means necessary to enter these callings. It was only later in the nineteenth century that the professional schools in law and medicine became part of the system of higher education. Until that time, a college degree had little value as an occupational credential but considerable value as a symbol of elite status.

From the late nineteenth century onward, the American system of higher education—including the most elite colleges, such as Harvard and Yale—underwent a dramatic transformation away from the classical model with its aristocratic creed to a utilitarian model designed to ready large numbers of people for professional and business careers. Two social forces—one ideological and the other practical in nature—were present in the United States that brought about the integration of higher education into economic activity.

First, there was the ideology of equal opportunity that prevailed in the United States, an ideology that flourished in the absence of a traditional aristocratic class on the one hand and the presence of considerable social mobility on the other. In the first half of the nineteenth century the aristocratic pretensions of the existing institutions of higher learning were in conflict with the dominant Jeffersonian ideology, which viewed independent farmers and artisans as the warp and weft of the American social fabric. In the 1820s representatives of these social groups began to argue for the establishment of higher education that would be of relevance to the so-called industrial classes. The outcome of these movements was the passage in 1862 of the Morrill Land Grant College Act, which gave each of the states an endowment for a college that could serve the intellectual needs of the sons and daughters of America's yeomanry.

To some extent the land-grant colleges adapted their curricula and rituals (including the awarding of Bachelor of Arts degrees) to the classical model in an attempt to reap the cultural prestige of the older institutions. But a distinguishing feature of the new colleges was the goal of offering instruction of practical relevance to farmers and artisans. Nevertheless, with the notable exception of Cornell University, the land-grant colleges had difficulty attracting students in the quarter-century after the Civil War, in part because secondary education was not well enough developed in the United States to supply the colleges with qualified students and in part because farmers and artisans simply did not perceive the net benefit to their sons and daughters of a four-year college degree.

It was only in the 1890s, when the U.S. Department of Agriculture and big business began to take an interest in higher education, that the land-grant colleges started to attract large numbers of students. With government funding and private support (mainly from the Rockefeller-endowed General Education Board, banks, large retailers such as Sears, Roebuck, and agricultural machinery manufacturers such as John Deere and International Harvester), the land-grant colleges began to be used for scientific experimentation as well as for the training of agents who could demonstrate new agricultural methods to the farmers. Of more significance for industry was the development of engineering education within the land-grant colleges, most notably at M.I.T., for the purpose of supplying trained personnel to the emerging bureaucratic structures of the large manufacturing corporations.

The integration of the land-grant colleges into the system of corporate production put great pressure on the classical colleges to adapt their curricula, often against the wishes of educators. Particularly after the turn of the century, large sums of money began to flow into higher learning from big business in order to shape the educational system in its own image and to supply its personnel and scientific needs. Bolstered by business support, land-grant colleges such as M.I.T. and Purdue began graduating large numbers of engineers. In 1870 only 100 engineering degrees were conferred in the United States, and these mostly in civil engineering. By 1914 the system of higher education was producing some 4,300 engineering graduates, mainly in industrial, chemical, and electrical engineering, to serve the needs of the new mass-production and science-based industries.

Prior to 1898 there was only one business school—Wharton—in the United States. In 1908 the Graduate School of Business Administration at Harvard University provided the first bona fide graduate education in business, admitting only students with bachelor's degrees. Between 1908 and 1930 more than 100 undergraduate and graduate business schools came into being. By 1952, 173 universities contained business schools, of which ten were exclusively for graduate study.[7]

The U.S. system of higher education underwent significant expansion in all its faculties in the first half of the twentieth century. In 1900 about 2% of 18- to 24-year-olds were enrolled in institutions of higher education; in 1930, over 7%; and in 1950, over 14%. Between 1900 and 1930 the number of bachelor's or first professional degrees per thousand 23-year-olds tripled from 19 to 57, and between 1930 and 1950 more than tripled again. The supply of graduate students also expanded rapidly: in 1900 there were six master's or second professional degrees awarded per 100 bachelor's degrees awarded two years earlier; by 1930 this figure had risen to 15, and by 1950, to 22.[8]

As both cause and effect of this transformation of the system of higher education was a change in attitude toward college graduates that seems to have appeared around the turn of the century. In the nineteenth century Andrew Carnegie argued the case against college education for business:

> In my own experience I can say that I have known few young men intended for business who were not injured by a collegiate education. Had they gone into active work in the years spent in college they would have been better educated in every true sense of the term.

Later Carnegie changed his mind, asserting that "the exceptional graduate should excel the exceptional nongraduate. He has more education, and education will always tell, the other qualities being equal."[9] In 1900 the author of an article entitled "College Education and Business" reiterated the common nineteenth-century view that "the graduate has not the slightest chance, entering [business] at twenty, against the boy who swept the office, or begins as a shipping clerk at fourteen." He went on to argue, however, that as the educational system forsook "culture for its own sake" and sought to bestow "culture for the sake of making the whole man active for the purposes of masterful reaction with an external world of affairs," a college education would become relevant for business.[10]

The rise of the corporate enterprise in the United States created great demands for bureaucratic personnel. The total number of salaried managers and administrators in the United States increased from 352,000 (1.3% of the paid labor force) in 1900 to 1,348,000 (3.0%) in 1930. Over the same period the number of employees with professional degrees rose from 913,000 (3.1% of the paid labor force) to 2,488,000 (5.7%). The number of engineers in the United States grew from 38,000 in 1900 to 217,000 in 1930. The number of chemical, metallurgical, and mining engineers increased from 3,000 to 14,000 over this period, and the number of industrial, mechanical, and electrical engineers rose from 14,000 to 116,000.[11]

Increasingly, the large corporations turned to the system of higher education to find fresh recruits to fill technical and administrative positions in the growing bureaucracies. For example, Procter & Gamble began to recruit technical and sales personnel from college campuses as early as 1918. Similarly, Goodyear began going to the colleges in 1917, and by the 1920s recruitment at engineering and business schools was a basic part of its management development program. In the mid-1920s Goodyear's rival, Firestone, was providing in-house management development to college graduates. By recruiting on the campuses every year, Harvey Firestone, Jr., argued, "we'll have a continuous complement of good men on hand acquiring the experience necessary for filling important posts. Their first jobs will merely be stepping-stones to their future responsibilities."[12]

Prior to 1928 Sears, Roebuck recruited managers for its rapidly growing mail-order and retail-store business from executive placement agencies in New York. In 1928, however, an increase in the number of stores in operation from 25 to 192 strained the limits of outside recruitment. The following year Robert Wood, Sears's chief executive, even considered a merger with J. C. Penney as a means of securing trained store managers. Instead, Sears began recruiting at colleges as a first step in a new policy of training and promoting managers from within (a policy that the company was already pursuing at nonmanagerial levels). By 1934, according to Boris Emmet and John Jeuck, "the company was recruiting from colleges on a systematic basis."[13]

By 1930 well over 90% of the stock of university-educated engineers were employed in technical and managerial positions in industrial firms. Certainly after World War II, if not before, large corporate employers simply assumed that technical and managerial personnel would be recruited from the ranks of college and university graduates. The growing predominance of college graduates in U.S. business is reflected in a number of studies carried out in the 1950s on the changing educational backgrounds of top business executives.[14] Thirty percent had degrees in both 1870 and 1900, but by 1925 the proportion had increased to 40% and by the early 1950s to over 60%. An increasing, but by no means predominant, proportion of these top executives had specialized degrees. In Mabel Newcomer's study, the proportion with engineering degrees rose from under 7% in 1900 to over 13% in 1925 to 20% in 1950, and the proportion with law degrees rose from over 8% in 1900 to 12% in 1925, then fell to slightly under 12% in 1950. In public utilities about 34% of top executives had engineering degrees in 1950, whereas in railroads this proportion was about 20% and in industrials about 16%. In the *Fortune* study of top executives in the early 1950s, 46% had educational backgrounds in science and engineering, 31% in business and economics, 15% in law, and 9% in arts.

The qualitative importance of the reshaping of higher education was that it provided pre-employment foundations for bureaucratic integration within the corporate organization. The relationship between the transformation of U.S. engineering education and the rise of the corporate economy as documented by David Noble is a case in point.[15] In the last decades of the nineteenth century, the prominence of mechanical engineers as owners and managers of growing manufacturing firms led to the professionalization of engineering (the American Society of Mechanical Engineers was formed in 1885) and a clear distinction between the engineer and the mechanic. Although not themselves college graduates, many of the early entrepreneur-engineers began to support the integration of engineering education into the college system as a further movement toward professionalization. Their prime concern was the development of standards of technical competence and social outlook among potential recruits to the growing bureaucracies. Thus, by the second decade of the twentieth century, "school culture" was rapidly replacing "shop culture" in the training of mechanical engineers. In the new, expanding chemical and electrical industries, where no strong shop-culture traditions existed, the training of engineers quickly developed within the system of higher education.

In the professionalization of engineering in the United States, the expectation was that engineers who demonstrated their technical worth to the corporation would climb the hierarchy to assume managerial responsibilities. As the president of the American Institute of Chemical Engineers told the first convention in 1908: "There must be a body of men supplied in increasing numbers who can take charge of [the science-based] industries, first as aides and ultimately as managers of the several works, qualified to continue the successful administration of the same and able to push them steadily to fuller development along safe and profitable lines."[16] From the 1920s onward, the engineering professions made systematic efforts to ensure that engineering education would be adapted to corporate bureaucratic needs. Management subjects became increasingly important in engineering curricula (by 1940 a minimum of 20% of the course work had to be in the social sciences, broadly defined). Many undergraduates with engineering degrees began to take advantage of the expanding facilities for graduate studies in business administration.

The influential Wickenden report on engineering education, published in 1930, stressed the social training of engineers to equip them not only for more immediate technical work but also for future managerial responsibilities. In the 1930s the Engineers Council for Professional Development, a body that combined engineering educators and corporate executives, took up the task of implementing the proposals of the Wickenden report. According to Noble, the efforts of the ECPD meant that "success in the profession now officially meant education for both subordinate technical employment in and responsible management of corporate industry."[17] In other words, U.S. engineering education was striving to produce a "bureaucratically integrated" product.

The business schools also sought to provide future managers with a general education while at the same time laying foundations for the development of technical competence in a particular specialty. At midcentury the typical undergraduate program was made up of at least 40% nonbusiness courses, core courses in economics, accounting, statistics, business law, finance, marketing, and management, and specialized courses in one or more of these subjects. At the graduate level, M.B.A. courses sought to provide specialized training in a chosen field, but not at the expense of a general approach to business administration.[18]

For large U.S. corporations, the system of higher education laid the foundations for management development policies designed not only to secure competent specialists but also to transform the best performers among these specialists into general managers. All new recruits were allocated to a specialist department. As Newcomer remarks in her study of big-business executives, "training for general administration [at lower managerial levels] is rare, and the demand for 'general administrators' just out of college is almost unheard of."[19] Engineering graduates went into production, law graduates into legal departments, and those with nonprofessional degrees into purchasing, marketing, finance, or lower-level line positions (where, in effect, specialist experience in human relations could be gained). The new employee then had to demonstrate his or (rarely) her worth to the firm as a specialized cog in the corporate machine if he or she expected career advancement.

By the 1920s, therefore, the system of higher education provided the foundations for bureaucratic integration. But many top executives still viewed the specialization of salaried personnel at earlier stages of their careers as problematic for the development of general managers by promotion from within. In 1936, for example, James O. McKinsey, chairman of the American Management Association, argued, "As activities become more specialized and routinized it becomes more difficult to develop ability in the ranks. . . . It may not be safe for us to rely upon securing a sufficient number from the ranks who will qualify for executive leadership." Or as Barnard put it, "We deliberately and more and more turn out specialists; but we do not develop general executives well by specific efforts, and we know very little about how to do it." Newcomer claims that her search of the management literature revealed a "consensus that the top executive needs broader training than the specialists are apt to get" but that most top executives were in fact being promoted from within the company.[20]

One way to resolve the problem would have been to create an elite group of general managers who would begin their careers as coordinators rather than as parts of the specialized division of labor. In Britain family management and elite education served precisely this role. But the separation of ownership from control in many large U.S. corporations after the turn of the century made it difficult for corporate leadership simply to be passed down from father to son. Nor was there an existing elite in American society whose members, quite apart from property ownership, possessed ascribed status that would have given them legitimacy as candidates for such generalist roles. The growth of the land-grant colleges, moreover, had had a leveling influence on the elite status of the older universities, diminishing greatly the extent to which a Harvard or Yale degree in itself brought its bearer a distinct social standing that could confer a claim to immediate generalist status. Even elite graduate programs in business administration did not create a class of generalist recruits. The route to top-management positions was surer and faster for M.B.A.s, but even they had to begin as specialists and work their way up the corporate hierarchy.[21]

In the early decades of this century the system of higher education was providing the corporations with personnel with a mix of specialist training and generalist outlook. Given the supportive educational environment, the internal promotion of specialists to generalist rank was sound corporate policy. The success of corporate expansionary strategies required the agglomeration of large amounts of specialized knowledge. Specialists were needed in abundance. But in a land of individualism, enterprise, and expectations of social mobility, the corporations had to offer a member of the newly educated elite more than just a job.[22] To retain good specialists and get the desired quantity and quality of work effort out of them, the corporations had to offer the specialist a career.

In 1931 the director of employment and training for the New York Telephone Company asserted that "large companies employ young men and promote to the more responsible places the men who are already in the organization. There usually must be some special reason, which can be stated with justification to those within the organization, when an outsider is brought in and placed in a high-salaried position."[23] To secure the attachment and loyalty of the individual, the corporation had to hold out the prospect of a career unfettered by inherent barriers to upward mobility, such as a rigid segmentation of bureaucratic personnel into lifelong specialists and lifelong generalists. Outstanding performance by lower-level and middle-level bureaucratic personnel would be suitably rewarded by social mobility within the corporation.

Upward mobility on a meritocratic basis also helped counteract tendencies for superiors to stifle the development of subordinates for fear of losing their own jobs. In the interwar period the head of Goodyear, Paul Litchfield (an M.I.T. graduate) was explicit in making dispensability in one's current position a precondition for promotion: "A man is ready for promotion only when he has his department so well organized that it will carry on just as efficiently after he has left it." Given this promotion structure, Litchfield could instruct his middle managers:

> Don't be afraid that the man under you will know more than you do, and so take your job away from you. Give your key men full information. Let them know the reasons for decisions. Put jobs up to them which will compel them to organize their work and make their own decisions—which you can review.

In a similar vein, in 1930 Walter Teagle, president of Standard Oil (New Jersey), warned the company's top operating officers that "no executive can be said to have done his full duty unless and until he has made available for promotion to his position a man or men capable of assuming and administering his office."[24]

Attachment, and presumably loyalty, to the organization could be well rewarded. Newcomer found that only 18% of the 1900 sample had reached higher management levels by working within the company, whereas this proportion was over 37% in 1925 and about 51% in 1950. In the 1950 sample, working from within was particularly important for those who started with high school diplomas (62%) as well as those who had professional and engineering degrees (53% and 54%, respectively), and less marked among those with some college or a college degree (46% and 42%, respectively). The average age of attaining top positions was about 50 years in 1900, 1925, and 1950. The proportion of the 1950 executives who had worked their way up within the company was almost identical in railroad, industrial, and public utility corporations, but increased markedly with the assets of the firm.[25]

Suzanne Keller found that only 10% of the top executives in her 1870 and 1900 samples had worked for only one company, as compared with 27% in the 1950 sample. The careers of 68% of the 1870 sample and 56% of the 1900 sample but only 17% of the 1950 sample were classified as "self-made" or "family-made," with the rest being either "bureaucratically made" or "professionally made." In 1870 only 12% of the business leaders, and in 1900 still only 23%, had spent 20 or more years in their current company before reaching the top. But by 1950, 46% had been with the company for 20 or more years. One-third of the 900 high-ranking executives in the *Fortune* study had spent their whole career with only one company, and another 26% with only one other company.[26]

A standard method for transforming specialists into generalists in large U.S. corporations was to move promising lower-level and middle-level managers around from region to region, department to department, and division to division. By the early 1920s many large industrial corporations gave college graduates a one- or two-year internship, sometimes even before placing them in specialist positions, moving them through the various functional departments of the firm with a view to creating integrated managers. For example, in 1933 Sears began its "reserve-group program" for training personnel who seemed capable of doing more than routine work. By the 1940s Sears was recruiting 200 or more college graduates per year who, through superior performance in initial job assignments, would try to make the reserve group. The basic training technique was four or five years of job rotation. As early as 1913, Goodyear had placed promising technical (and, beginning in 1927, sales) personnel in "flying squadrons," the members of which were moved around within the company in order to gain the broader understanding of operations necessary for the generalist. In developing these training schemes, management did not necessarily take existing job structures as given. As a top executive at Standard Oil (New Jersey) argued in 1949:

> Systematic job rotation is one method used for giving a broader understanding of the business as a whole. Sometimes it is necessary to create assistant or "assistant to" positions to make available some desired experience.[27]

Marshall Dimock contends that the coordination of skilled staff activity at general headquarters with line activity in its divisions was an important factor in the success of administrative decentralization at AT&T from the 1920s onward. "Indeed," he argued, "its staff work, its decentralization policy, and its careful selection of executives constitute what most outside observers consider the three most prominent features of the corporation's management." By the 1930s AT&T was bringing promising recruits from field units to the staff offices in New York, then sending them back to line positions in the field after three or four years. In addition, within its multidivisional structure AT&T elevated top staff positions in its central office to upper-management status. According to Dimock, these transfers between general headquarters and the divisions were used strategically over a person's career:

> At a certain point it may be discovered that a particular individual has an outstanding talent as a central office staff man; he has the necessary temperament plus a certain wisdom and levelheadedness, a philosophical cast of mind and a native diplomacy, that "go down well" with the field. Such a man may be kept in a top staff position for the rest of his official career. But if a man shows any inclination to become stale or to act remote, these being signs of boredom and bureaucracy, he is quickly transferred back to the field because action at that level [that is, on the line] keeps a man alert and discourages complacency and inertia.[28]

The multidivisional form of organization that was becoming more widespread in the corporate sector of U.S. industry from the 1920s onward required bureaucratic integration if it was to be an effective device for administrative decentralization. If middle managers were to be able to make profitable managerial decisions about processes and products, they had to be able to integrate into the decision-making process specialist information concerning market prices, the nature of product markets, the availability of resources, industrial relations, legal constraints on prospective activities, and technological potential. The key to successful bureaucratic integration on the basis of the multidivisional structure was not only the decentralization of line responsibility but also the company-wide coordination of staff activities to ensure that operational decision makers had knowledge of, as well as access to, relevant specialized information.

In 1945 Ralph Cordiner, himself a college graduate who had spent some 20 years climbing up the managerial hierarchy to become a General Electric vice-president (and future president), made the case for bureaucratic integration. He argued that a line type of organization was useful for "the clear definition of responsibility and authority, and ease of securing discipline," but that it would render managers incapable of taking full advantage of specialist knowledge generated by research and development, marketing, and production staffs. The functional form of organization, on the other hand, tended to create confusion in lines of authority and responsibility and "to develop narrowness through specialization." What a diversified company like G.E. needed, he argued, was an integration of line and staff types of organizations to preserve the advantages of each. Besides the decentralization of decision making in manufacturing operations in order to bring general management "as close as possible to the daily problems and daily decisions bearing on the individual transactions and the individual productive efforts," G.E. put into effect "a corresponding integration . . . on a company-wide basis . . . of the functional activities and developments in each technical field."[29]

The training and movement of managerial personnel within the company was critical to the success of the multidivisional structure.

According to Cordiner:

> A distinct line organization cannot properly arrange for the selection of technical and prospective executive talent, for the broad education of that talent, for the rotation of personnel to provide basic experience and determine real aptitude, and for the assuring of promotion on a company-wide merit basis, contrasted with a restricted department or division basis.

The integrated organizational structure made possible company-wide coordination of management development, a key component of which was, in Cordiner's words, "development, through integration, of management ability at an early date." At all levels in the organization, staff and line executives were accorded equal hierarchical stature, and the most competent operating executives were regularly appointed to head the staff functions where they had some prior expertise.[30]

As we have seen, Barnard, a past president of New Jersey Bell, did not believe that managerial practice as it existed in the late 1930s contained much knowledge about how to turn specialists into generalists. Nevertheless, in the interwar years large U.S. corporations were actively confronting the problem of how to implement management development policies that would aid in the coordination of the specialized division of labor. These efforts were in sharp contrast to the British situation, documented below. At a minimum, the transformation of the U.S. system of higher education to provide "organization men" to business created solid underpinnings for bureaucratic integration within the enterprise in the first half of this century. As we shall now argue, such a transformation did not occur in Britain, primarily because British business did not put pressure on the educational system to provide "integrated" corporate personnel.

III. Bureaucratic Segmentation in Britain

In the late nineteenth and early twentieth centuries, the persistence of a highly fragmented structure of industrial organization in Britain contrasted sharply with the rise of big business in the United States. After the turn of the century the largest British firms were

not only much smaller than the largest U.S. firms but also much
more under the control of family owners.[31] In many U.S. industries
the massive merger movement of the 1890s and 1900s created
oligopolistic market power by transferring ownership of existing
assets from the entrepreneurial industrialists who had built up the
firms to dispersed shareholders. The result was the separation of
capital ownership from managerial control. Top managers controlled the long-run destiny of the corporate entity. But as the
agents of property owners, they lost any inherent right to pass on
that control to their kin as inherited property.

The separation of ownership and control did not render nepotism
impossible. In many cases stock ownership of a public company was
so widely distributed that top managers could have appointed their
successors unchallenged. But given the size of the new oligopolies,
the expectations for social mobility prevalent in the United States,
and the growing availability of bureaucratic personnel produced
by the system of higher education, a nepotistic firm would have
been at a competitive disadvantage compared with an enterprise
that took up the opportunities for creating an integrated bureaucratic structure. In the American context, therefore, even when the
family remained dominant in the firm (as at Dupont and IBM),
there were strong pressures for family members to acquire professional credentials and work their way up from specialist to
generalist status.

In the British social context, the widespread persistence of the
practice of passing on managerial control of the firm to family
members from generation to generation had a far-reaching impact
on management development (or, more accurately, underdevelop-
ment). For the sake of maintaining control, the family firm often
adopted a nonexpansionary strategy in order to avoid becoming
dependent upon outside creditors and shareholders or an internal
bureaucracy of technical specialists and middle managers. The
widespread persistence of the *small* family firm in the early decades
of this century meant, therefore, that the industrial demand for
managerial and technical personnel was moderate when compared
with that in the United States. For many, if not most, British firms
a reluctance by owners to share managerial control dictated a low-

growth enterprise strategy, which in turn generated little pressure for the creation and expansion of social institutions for the development of professional managerial personnel.

Some British family firms, however, were willing and able to expand in the early twentieth century. In cases such as Pilkington Bros. and Imperial Tobacco, the existence of a large issue of offspring from whom to recruit top managers meant that the family could pursue an expansionary strategy without facing the danger of losing control over enterprise policy and operations. In other cases, such as Brunner, Mond and Courtaulds, the basis of family-firm expansion was a first-mover advantage secured by control over a key scientific or technological innovation. In still other cases, such as Lever Bros., the source of first-mover advantage was an aggressive entrepreneur who quickly established brand-name recognition for a household product.[32]

Whatever the factors that enabled the growth of the family firm (and, of course, where some succeeded others failed), in the middle of this century family control remained widespread and substantial in the largest British industrial firms, whereas it had already become almost nonexistent in the largest U.S. industrial corporations some four decades earlier. In those large British firms where one family maintained control, the growth of the firm had typically come from internal expansion. During the interwar period, however, an increasingly common route to growth of British firms was amalgamation rather than internal expansion. Competitive firms combined to control product prices rather than to rationalize operations, leaving previous family owners with their managerial autonomy intact within the amalgamated organization.[33]

The persistence of family control meant that at the higher managerial levels recruitment was from within a fairly closed circle. In 1927 Lyndall Urwick, then the organizing secretary for Rowntree, argued:

> Broadly speaking, in ninety-nine hundredths of British industry there is no system of promotion. Family connections, ownership of capital, toadyism, seniority, inertia, or luck decide which men shall be selected to rule their fellows. . . . It is a fact that in the majority of our great enterprises, there is no analysis of the factors which

constitute "fitness" for most of the managerial positions and no
methods of measuring or assessing those factors whatever.[34]

One observer in the 1920s told an industrial conference at Oxford
that the only principle of organization that he had been able to
discover in English industry was "myself, my father, my son, and
my wife's sister's nephew." In the mid-1920s an American visitor,
surveying the then-depressed British industrial scene, wrote that
"a tremendous drawback to effective business organization in
England is the habit of asking who you are, as opposed to the
American inquiry as to what you are."[35] In other words, the
professionalization of British industrial management had not yet
occurred.

The principle of asking "who you are" fit well with notions of
aristocratic privilege that remained entrenched in Britain well into
the twentieth century. British industrialists, however, did not themselves emerge from the ranks of the hereditary aristocracy. In the
nineteenth century their social status was at best middle class. The
upper class, living off parentage rather than achievement, frowned
upon the active pursuit of moneymaking through industry precisely
because it required education (whether formal or informal) in skills
that were not developed through an aristocratic upbringing or
appropriate social connections. Indeed, in nineteenth-century Britain it was skilled workers, even more than middle-class industrialists,
who possessed knowledge of, and control over, technology. The
aristocratic bias against technology was, if anything, strengthened
in the late nineteenth and early twentieth centuries by the fact that
material well-being was becoming ever more dependent on the
application of technical knowledge. Aristocratic antipathy to industry remained strong well into the twentieth century. In 1961, for
example, the deputy secretary of the Ministry of Education recalled
that when he left school (presumably in the 1920s), "trade was not
respectable. The City of London was all right, but manufacturing
industry was not. I believe the picture is changing *slightly and
recently.*"[36]

Rather than confront aristocratic ideology and values, British
industrialists sought to partake of them. Successful British business-

men aspired to use their newly acquired wealth to escape the middle class and become gentlemen.[37] In this goal they were accommodated by the distribution of peerages. If they did not actually put their fortunes into landed estates, they at least sent offspring to the elite public schools and perhaps to Oxford or Cambridge. Data collected in the mid-1950s on a cross section of managers indicate that over the first half of the twentieth century an increasing proportion were recruited from the public schools, and that by midcentury a highly disproportionate number of those from the major public schools had reached top management levels.[38]

Given the aristocratic aversion to industry and technology, therefore, affluent British businessmen who aspired to aristocratic status were loath to exert great pressure on the elite educational system to make it directly useful to business. As early as 1903, a British visitor noted the importance of a university education for rapid promotion within the firm in the United States, not because of the prestige but rather because of the knowledge that it provided. He chided, "In America you cannot waste four years more efficiently than by not going to university. The same is true in England, but for reasons of general culture, not of commercial success."[39] From the point of view of social mobility, the interests of British businessmen lay more in preserving than in transforming existing institutions.

The ultimate impact of the pursuit of aristocratic status by industrialists was to legitimize and reinforce the closed circle of managerial succession by constituting higher management as a social class apart within the enterprise. A powerful mechanism for implanting the existing class structure in the enterprise as well as reproducing it in society as a whole was the evolution of a highly segmented system of higher education. The prestige of the ancient universities, Oxford and Cambridge, could not be challenged by the civic universities that grew up in the early part of this century; and both these institutions stood above the technical colleges that arose out of governmental reform of higher education in the post-World War II period.

At the turn of the century attendance at Oxford or Cambridge was of immense value for achieving high position in the civil service. But there was little flow of these elite graduates to industry. Before

World War I, however, a number of business enterprises began to recruit managerial personnel on a regular basis from Cambridge, on a scale that, according to Michael Sanderson, was "totally new compared with the 1880s and 1890s." Most Oxford and Cambridge graduates who entered industry had arts degrees, a trend that remained true through the interwar period and into the post-World War II era. The study of managerial succession in the mid-1950s by the Acton Society Trust found that in terms of upward mobility in the business world the most advantageous educational background for a British manager was an arts degree from Oxford or Cambridge, and the second most advantageous was attendance at a major public school.[40]

Science graduates from Oxford and Cambridge were not ignored. In the early decades of the century some forward-looking, science-based firms, such as Brunner, Mond, Crosfield's, and British Petroleum, were eager to employ Oxbridge-trained chemists, engineers, and geologists. These companies needed people with scientific knowledge and analytical ability. Elite social credentials were also welcomed, however, as evidenced by Brunner, Mond, where membership in the Winnington Hall Club was "a carefully guarded privilege," and where "the whole structure [of hierarchical status] rested on class distinction." It also helped to become a member of the owning family. A promising Cambridge science graduate hired in 1911 by Pilkington's rose to a high position in the tightly knit family firm, his career aided immeasurably no doubt by marrying into the Pilkington family in 1922.[41]

The loss of potential managerial successors to family-dominated firms in World War I led these firms to approach the Cambridge Appointments Board in the interwar period, seeking Cambridge graduates as suitable substitutes who could rise to the higher levels very quickly.[42] In addition, and undoubtedly of more importance, British firms, constrained in many cases by family size, came to see the products of public schools and Oxbridge as trustworthy family surrogates who would make possible a strategy of growth. These educational institutions continued to stress aristocratic values and social class status, and insofar as British industry recruited from them, the social structure of the firm tended to display the hierarchical social distinctions that were deeply embedded in British society.

The relatively closed ranks at the higher management levels segmented general management from specialists and lower-level line managers (often drawn from the ranks of specialists). As British firms grew in size in the interwar period, bureaucratic segmentation became the norm, and it appears to have remained characteristic of British managerial structures even into the 1960s and 1970s.[43] Again we see a sharp contrast with the United States. Although U.S. managerial personnel were an elite relative to white-collar and blue-collar workers, higher education and internal-promotion policies integrated specialists and lower-level managers into this elite instead of excluding them as was the case in Britain.

The creation of the civic universities in the early decades of this century both reflected and reinforced the bureaucratic segmentation of specialists from generalists. As a practical matter, the main interest of businessmen in the expansion of the system of higher education was the need for technical specialists in the new science-based industries, and particularly in chemicals. Some early science-based firms secured the necessary expertise abroad, typically in Germany. But with the growth of competition for these relatively scarce personnel (who might take trade secrets back with them to Germany), British firms were willing to employ home-grown scientists if they could be found in the slowly growing chemistry departments of British universities.

After the turn of the century some of Britain's wealthier industrialists began to donate large sums for the expansion of higher education through provincial civic universities, such as Manchester, Birmingham, and Bristol. Sanderson suggests that the act of gift giving may have been motivated by unwritten philanthropic prerequisites for knighthood.[44] In any case, the best-off of the new institutions were decently, if not extravagantly, endowed when compared with U.S. land-grant colleges. In 1913 the endowment income of Manchester, the richest of the civic universities, was $112,000, only 15% less than that of M.I.T. But the increasing integration of U.S. higher education into the affairs of a dynamic economy meant that there were sources of income for colleges and universities in the

United States that were not so readily available in Britain. At M.I.T. in 1913 income from students was three times endowment income. Cornell, another land-grant college, had investment income in excess of $450,000 in 1913, and tuition income of about the same amount. In the United States, moreover, the interest of federal and state governments as well as of private foundations and alumni in funding higher education was on the rise. In the late 1930s the total income of the U.S. system of higher education was five times greater per capita than that of the British system, and this ratio may well have been even higher earlier in the century.[45]

To be of practical relevance to industry, the civic universities tended to adopt a more favorable view of instruction in science and technology than did Oxford and Cambridge. By the same token, however, the new institutions became less capable of challenging the ancient universities as purveyors of social standing. Given the aristocratic bias against industrial pursuits, the more the civic universities produced specialists for industry, the more they could be depicted as second-rate institutions. As a 1914 Oxford broadsheet jibed:

> He gets degrees in making jam
> At Liverpool and Birmingham.[46]

The Cambridge University Appointments Board found that many firms that were favorable to technically trained university graduates in the late 1930s were of the opinion that equally good technical knowledge could be acquired at provincial universities or technical colleges "but that the Cambridge man of the right sort gets something beyond his technical training that is useful to him in industry." Quoting from firm responses, the report went on to say that " 'provided the individual has time for social activities,' a Cambridge course is good for technical posts in industry. It prevents a man from becoming 'too much a specialist and tends to develop his character.' " The Acton Society Trust study in the mid-1950s found that in terms of promotion within the firm, a degree from a civic university was inferior not only to attendance at Oxford, Cambridge, or a major public school but also to the possession of a nontechnical qualification or direct entry into the firm as a managerial trainee (presumably on the basis of personal connections). Even among civic-university graduates, those with arts degrees (less than one-sixth of the total) did significantly better than did those with science degrees.[47]

The failure of the civic universities to force change upon the elite institutions contrasts sharply with the way many of the land-grant colleges in the United States imposed their standards of useful knowledge and training on older colleges that had originally adopted the classical Oxbridge model of education. The result was that Britain developed a highly segmented university system that produced bureaucratic personnel for highly segmented managerial structures. The ancient universities supplied men thought to be suited for quick advancement to higher-level managerial positions, while the civic universities produced specialists tailored for lower-level salaried positions.

By the 1920s bureaucratic integration of specialized knowledge for the development, diffusion, and utilization of technology was already well underway in the U.S. corporate sector. Not so in Britain. Bureaucratic segmentation in British industry was, if anything, reinforced by the fact that the determination and control of technological standards and professional accreditation remained largely in the hands of people who did not see themselves as part of the "management team." The widespread persistence of highly competitive industry in Britain meant that many scientists and technologists were not even salaried employees of the industrial firms to which they provided specialist knowledge and advice. In British industries characterized by large numbers of relatively small firms, research and development was provided by separate, government-aided research associations rather than by in-house staff departments of industrial firms as was the practice in the United States.[48] Firms that were unwilling or unable to employ technical specialists directly could not even begin to implement a policy of management development designed to facilitate the coordination of the specialized division of labor.

But even technical specialists in the direct employ of larger British industrial firms could be resistant to coordination and control. Particularly in the mechanical technologies derivative of the first industrial revolution, much of the knowledge and decision making concerning the use of technology remained the prerogative of skilled blue-collar workers. As a result, in Britain the term "engineer" continued to connote a skilled craft worker well into the twentieth century, whereas in U.S. industry it had long since come to mean a college-educated member of a managerial team. In 1913 there were only 1,129 students in engineering in all the universities of England and Wales, none of them at the graduate level. In 1950 only 10% of the mechanical engineers in Britain were university educated. The engineering associations controlled access to the various branches of engineering, and even required university graduates to undergo apprenticeship. In some cases, as in the municipally run electricity supply industry, British electrical engineers maintained strong craftlike unions.[49]

Along with the very different socialization processes involved in apprenticeship as opposed to university education, a very different intellectual outlook distinguished the shop-culture from the school-culture engineer. To use the language of a British university-trained engineer visiting the United States in 1903, the distinction was between engineers who "could . . . apply rules, but not the principles upon which the rules were founded" and those who had had the opportunity for "the development of intellect—grasp, judgment, and ability to apply general principles to details."[50] The remarks of the editor of a British engineering journal confirm that shop culture so defined remained strong in British mechanical engineering in the late 1920s, well past the time when it had been superseded by school culture in the United States:

> In these days of organized college courses it is well to remember that in the last analysis the leaders in our industry are produced from one source—they are the products of the workshops or factories. . . . [I]t may be said that they are scientific without being scientists. A list of past presidents of our senior engineering institutions would include many names of distinguished leaders whose unique merit consisted in a highly developed mechanical instinct which was sufficient to guide them to the right point of view on any problem connected with their work. Without anything more than this valuable intuition many of our great engineers of the past would

continue to be eminent in these days. . . . A perusal of the correspondence and inquiry columns of engineering journals and the proceedings of institution meetings makes manifest the fact that the real difficulties of engineers are principally those of a practical character.[51]

As the heads of their own successful undertakings, some of the most outstanding shop-culture engineers sought unsuccessfully to continue to manage in the manner of the "practical man." For example, Charles Wilson and William Reader recount how, from the early nineteenth-century on, "three generations of a family each nobly endowed with engineering and inventive talent" permitted D. Napier & Son to remain a force in the British mechanical engineering industry. The Napiers, however, had "a dislike for the mass market and everything to do with it," an aversion that got them into periodic financial difficulties from the 1890s on. Struggling to stay in the game in the 1930s on the basis of past successes, financial setbacks thwarted any new engineering innovation, in part because "the best of [their] rising talent had been allowed to go."[52] In 1942 Napier's came under the control of English Electric.

The experience of a university-trained electrical engineer at Standard Telephones and Cables in the 1950s illustrates the persistence of shop-culture attitudes in Britain. The higher management of STC (the British subsidiary of ITT) was made up of shop-culture engineers "who in their time had made undeniable contributions to the progress and success of the company but who had now grown old together in a virtually closed society." Gordon Duddridge joined the firm in the early 1950s (he had been employed at ICI. before the war and then ran government factories) as "one of the first of the new breed of division managers [in charge of undersea cables] to have full responsibility embracing engineering, marketing, and manufacturing." But he had difficulty getting along with the chief engineer of the telephone cable division, who told him, "The whole trouble is you're a damned traitor, Gordon. You're working in manufacturing with a university degree. You're a traitor to the engineering cause."[53]

The family firm, aristocratic values, and control of technology by the "practical man" meant, therefore, that even by midcentury

British higher education did not as a rule provide a general technical and social training to future managers upon which firm-specific management development policies could build as was the case in the United States. By the 1940s, however, many British businessmen, consultants, and statesmen had come to recognize the economic superiority of American modes of management. Inspired by the success of technical and managerial education in the United States, the British sought to make their own system of higher education more relevant to business needs in the post-World War II period.

Active British interest in U.S. higher education goes back at least to the turn of the century, when the Moseley Educational Commission visited the United States. As the Commission reported, "The great industrial and commercial firms are abandoning the traditional methods of waiting for apprentices to 'come through,' and are attempting to manufacture the junior officers, by a rapid process, out of college graduates in technology and commerce."[54] In 1924 the Balfour Committee on Industry and Trade pointed out the tremendous disparity between the United States and Britain in the number of students in management education. The first important governmental initiative to reform British higher education was not undertaken until 1945, however, when the Committee on Education for Management (chaired by the well-known management consultant Lyndall Urwick) was appointed to make policy recommendations.[55]

The British Institute of Management was created in 1947, mainly to foster management education. British interest in the U.S. model of management education was sustained by two reports—one on education for executives and one on university training for engineers—issued by British "productivity teams" that had visited the United States.[56] In the 1950s attempts were made to expand and reorient the British system of higher education to provide managers and technical specialists to industry. But despite these efforts the relationship between education and industry remained under-developed in the 1960s and beyond.[57] Well into the post-World War II period the transformation of the system of higher education to provide the social and technical foundations of management development—a transformation that had occurred in the United States in the first decades of the twentieth century—had simply not taken place in Britain.

Under the National Scheme of Management Studies, most of the post-World War II expansion of higher education took place in technical colleges. T. M. Mosson argues:

> By the late 1950s the National Scheme . . . had fallen into a measure of disrepute. . . . Taken overall the scheme came to be associated by many with a low level of attainment and as a qualification with a lack of social prestige. It is probable that in the eyes of management the better courses run by the better colleges were degraded by association with the worst.[58]

Almost all the courses were taken part time, mainly in the evenings and often over a period of five years. In 1962 only two institutions offered full-time courses. The expansion of management education, therefore, was not designed to develop a new breed of management personnel but was, rather, an attempt to upgrade those already at work.[59]

Even then, middle managers who aspired to upward mobility did not make use of the colleges, viewing them as providing a form of working-class education that might provide satisfactory training for supervisors and foremen. Teachers at the technical colleges generally lacked university degrees, although many had business experience. Top business managers, however, were unwilling to give guest lectures at the colleges.[60]

As for the traditional universities, which had the social standing to appeal to middle and top managers, even by the mid-1960s management studies had not yet been deemed appropriate. Where management courses were taught, they focused on social skills and a widening of intellectual horizons. These courses were most useful to upper-level managers in their late thirties and early forties in transition from technical specialist to general management responsibilities. According to Mosson, "The objective is to enable the specialist turned generalist to use and control the work of specialists, or to enable him to understand the relationship between his firm and the environment."[61]

In terms of management careers, such training was probably too little too late. In the United States, the transformation of specialists into generalists was an essential purpose of management development *within* the firm that built upon the general *pre-employment* educational base, itself shaped by the evolving managerial structures' demands for bureaucratically integrated personnel. Well into the post-World War II period little if any comparable dynamic between corporate management structures and the system of higher education was evident in Britain.

It was not only the institutions but also the culture of management education that differed. In 1930 James A. Bowie, Director of the Department of Industrial Administration at Manchester, wrote, "To British eyes the most striking feature of the average American university is the highly organized character of daily life. . . . Except in some of the greatest universities, the American undergraduate is dominated by his time-table."[62] In his 1954 report *University Education for Business in the U.S.A.*, Norman Hunt, Professor of Organization of Industry and Commerce at Edinburgh, commented on his visit to the Harvard Business School:

> Students are frequently tested and graded, so that they are constantly subjected to pressure of work, shortage of time, and mental strain. This is quite deliberate and is part of the process of education for the hard competitive world of business. It is difficult for anyone with a background of British academic life to understand how this can be part of the activities of the university.[63]

In the 1950s Standard Telephones and Cables sent one of its managers to the Advanced Management Program at the Harvard Business School, but, according to the company historian, "he came back confused."[64]

By the late 1950s the only full-length postgraduate course in administration in a British university catered mainly to American and Canadian students. The Readership in Industrial Administration at Cambridge was endowed in 1954 with American matching funds. In 1968–69, there were only 300 students in M.B.A.-type courses (mostly of one-year duration) in Britain, compared with 19,000 in the United States.[65]

The lack of foundations of management development in the British educational system reflected the paucity of policies to transform specialists into generalists within British industrial firms. Of the 51 large companies included in the Acton Society Trust survey carried out in the mid-1950s, one-third had absolutely no organized system of management training, and only about 10% used internal job rotation as a mode of management development. Silberston argued that among specialists in the auto industry "job rotation is not . . . anything as widespread as it might be" and that the "practical difficulties are often considerable." As late as 1967, W. G. McClelland, Director and Professor of the Manchester Business School, argued the need for managerial job rotation to transform specialists into generalists and permit prospective leaders to escape dead-end jobs. But he went on to remark that it was "surprising how rarely such job rotation was arranged."[66]

The same study that found that the recruitment and training of top British managers had not changed much from the mid-1960s to the mid-1970s also found that production and site managers were drawn mainly from supervisory positions or craft occupations. Moreover, of those who had been classified as managers in 1965, 17% had been demoted to an operative occupation ten years later. Only 4% of the 2,637 managers in the 1975 sample had begun their careers in a managerial occupation. Across all managerial categories, the first jobs of at least one-fifth and perhaps as many as half of those in the sample were as semiskilled operatives.[67]

Throughout the twentieth century bureaucratic segmentation *has* been present in the United States, but it divides shop-floor and clerical workers from professional, managerial, and technical workers, with educational credentials serving as means of allocating people to segments and legitimizing the segmentation.[68] As a general rule, however, U.S. *managerial* structures have been characterized by bureaucratic integration. Conversely, in terms of training and promotion in British industrial bureaucracies, highly trained technical specialists were more closely integrated with shop-floor workers below than with general managers above. Within what we have come to think of as the corporate managerial structure, bureaucratic segmentation remained widespread in Britain as least through the 1950s, and apparently beyond.

IV. Bureaucratic Integration and the Multidivisional Form

Previous comparative research into twentieth-century industrial development has shown that in the United States the multidivisional organizational form served as a potent means of enterprise expansion from the 1920s on, whereas in Britain this organizational form was rare even at midcentury.[69] The characteristic features of the multidivisional form are (1) centralized control over strategic decision making and long-run planning of enterprise activities, (2) the delegation of operational decision making to divisions that are monitored as profit centers, and (3) the rationalization and centralization of key staff functions. By enhancing the capability of top management to coordinate the specialized division of labor, the multidivisional form enables firms to extend the bounds of enterprise rationality, expanding the scope of their activities to a wider range of product lines and more far-reaching market locations.

In other words, the multidivisional form was very conducive to what I have called bureaucratic integration. Centralized control —a necessary but by no means sufficient condition for the success of the multidivisional capitalist corporation—facilitated management development programs that fostered bureaucratic integration. An important element of long-run planning was management development that was not confined to particular functional activities, product divisions, or geographic regions of the firm. Enterprise-wide management development programs made possible job-rotation schemes that involved the movement of people not only among divisions but also from divisions to centralized staff functions. Such career patterns were basic to a continuous process of transforming promising specialists into generalists. By enhancing the prospects for advancement within the firm, enterprise-wide management development programs provided an incentive to the junior or middle manager to identify more strongly with the enterprise as a whole than with a particular work group, specialist activity, or region.

Given centralized control, the key to the success of the multi-divisional form in the United States was the delegation of authority over operational decision making without loss of control by top management over enterprise strategy. The setting up of divisional profit centers and the monitoring of the performance of the divisions did not in and of itself create effective middle management. If middle managers were to be capable of directing the day-to-day operations of divisions along profitable lines, they themselves would have to be capable of coordinating and monitoring a specialized division of labor within their prescribed domains. The development of such generalist capability required the development of specialists who were more or less continuously in the process of becoming generalists. For such a training program to operate effectively the delegation of decision-making authority had to descend well down the managerial hierarchy, with the scope of coordination increasing as managers climbed the bureaucratic ladder.

Given the dependence of top management on employees to whom it had delegated considerable authority, positive incentives of advancement were much more powerful inducements to appropriate performance than were negative sanctions of dismissal. Just as the delegation of authority extended decision-making responsibility down the hierarchy, so open lines of promotion helped ensure that the loyalty of managerial personnel would extend up the hierarchy. Moreover, the very fact that managers could move up the hierarchy made them willing to pass on information and delegate authority to subordinates who might one day take their places, thus extending appropriate training and positive incentives further down the organizational structure. At the same time, by separating control of key staff functions from the divisions, top management ensured that critical information would not become the property of self-serving entities within the organization.

The importance of bureaucratic integration for the success of the multidivisional enterprise helps explain the relatively slow diffusion of the multidivisional form in British industry. By Derek F. Channon's account, in 1950 only 12 firms in Britain had adopted the multidivisional form, and only four of these were wholly British.[70] A necessary condition for long-run coordination of the firm's activities on the basis of the multidivisional form was the centralization of control within the firm. In cases of amalgamation of a number of family firms, the achievement of centralized coordination was often impeded by the persistence of separate family control over the various businesses within the amalgamated organization. It was only when control over strategic decision making had been centralized that top management had the power to delegate authority so that the firm could become involved in a wider array of products and regions.

But centralization of control over strategic decision making did not necessarily mean that top management would be able or willing to create an organizational structure that would permit the successful diversification and geographic expansion of the firm's activities.[71] Even for those large British firms where control over strategic decision making was centralized rather than fragmented, the aristocratic attitudes of the managerial elite combined with shop-culture control of technology made top management unwilling, and perhaps even unable, to delegate authority within the organization. Shop-culture control of technology, moreover, made it extremely difficult, if not impossible, for top management to rationalize and coordinate the functional activities of the firm.

Bureaucratic segmentation thus impeded the unbounding of rationality on the basis of a corporate hierarchy. It made top managers unwilling to delegate authority over operational decision making for fear of losing control of strategic decision making, and rendered them unable to coordinate the specialized division of labor. The evolution of British social institutions, moreover, did little to foster bureaucratic integration as did social institutions in the United States. If anything, twentieth-century expansion of the British educational system served more to reinforce bureaucratic segmentation than to break it down.

Prior to the 1950s, therefore, bureaucratic integration was very difficult in Britain. But it was not impossible. The case of Unilever, the product of the 1929 merger of British-based Lever Bros. with

Dutch-based Margarine Union, illustrates the conditions under which bureaucratic integration was possible even for a firm in which British management was dominant. The case of Unilever also supports the hypothesis that bureaucratic integration was a necessary condition for the success of the multidivisional form.

When Lever Bros. became part of Unilever in 1929, it brought with it 49 manufacturing concerns in the United Kingdom that maintained 48 separate sales organizations. Under Geoffrey Heyworth, who was to become chairman of Lever Bros. and Unilever in 1941, a process of reorganization was begun that continued throughout the 1930s and 1940s, resulting in one of Britain's first and few multidivisional enterprises in the first half of this century.[72]

Bureaucratic integration played an important role in the successful multidivisionalization of Unilever. Whether the founding Lever had himself been adept at delegating authority and developing managers is open to debate, although it does appear that Crosfield's, a pre-1920 acquisition of Lever Bros., had been in the forefront of management development in Britain. Next to Lever Bros., Crosfield's had become Britain's second largest soapmaker, a position that it had attained not so much by advertising effort as by pioneering scientific research. Early on, Crosfield's had begun to employ and promote British science graduates, while at the same time stressing upward mobility for all promising employees. Herbert Davis, who had joined Crosfield's in 1912, became a director of Unilever in the late 1930s and later a vice-chairman and member of the company's strategy-making committee. In general, Crosfield's management had little difficulty becoming integrated into the Unilever structure and supplied much in the way of managerial resources to the giant company.[73]

As part of its rationalization efforts in the 1930s, Unilever began a systematic management development program, apparently unhampered by either British or Dutch family influence.[74] According to Charles Wilson:

> [The 1930s] saw a steady infusion of recruits, a high proportion from the universities but some selected from inside the business. The recruits had to be tried and tested. All this meant continual experiment and interchange between the headquarters and factory

and between factory and factory. There was no room for a class of
permanent central administrators. Men had to move, and the
records show that they did move.

Within a multinational organization, the moves were often from
country to country, so that "throughout the world . . . technicians
and accountants of three or four different nationalities worked
together."[75] Aside from the potential benefits of such movements
for transforming specialists into generalists, the multinational context must have made difficult the survival of British aristocratic
culture that contributed to bureaucratic segmentation in many
large British-based firms.

In a rather thorough description of the multidivisional organizational structure at Unilever in 1950, Geoffrey Heyworth, the
chairman, stated that "there are about 200 people who take on
themselves the decisions which make or mar the success of the
business as a whole," and he asserted that "the biggest job of top
management is to ensure the quality of this 200." He continued:

> To do so it is necessary to know something of the quality of about
> three times that number in order to be able to make the best selec-
> tion when vacancies arise. We not only have to know something of
> these 600, but we have to see that they get opportunities for gaining
> the necessary breadth of experience to be able to fill one of the 200
> posts. This involves planning moves of promising people progres-
> sively. For example, a young production manager in England
> might be moved to an Advisory and Service Department in London
> or Rotterdam for a year or two before returning to a larger operating
> unit, perhaps abroad. He is observed by his immediate superior and
> by the travelling members of top management.

Heyworth went on to say that the war had interrupted the recruitment process, depleting the pool from which the 200 key managers
could be drawn.

> In this situation our rule is that it is better to leave a vacancy un-
> filled than to lower the standard; and if we have to make a choice
> between filling a vacancy in an advisory department and filling one
> in an operating unit, priority is always given to the operating unit,
> because it is no use providing good advice if the operating units are
> not staffed with men of the ability required to carry it out effec-
> tively.[76]

By midcentury Unilever had apparently risen above the social institutions and cultural attitudes that shaped management-succession policies of most large British-based firms. Unilever's mode of management was clearly the exception rather than the rule in Britain. Even those firms that did try to adopt the multidivisional form in the post-World War II decades may not have been very successful in shedding detrimental institutional and cultural influences. Channon shows that there was considerable adoption of the multidivisional form in Britain in the 1950s and 1960s, typically on the advice of the ubiquitous McKinsey & Co. But he raises doubts about the extent of the concomitant changes in management structure and methods:

> Many of the internal characteristics of the corporations adopting multidivisional structure reflected prior structural forms. In particular there was little evidence of change in the reward system, especially as a mechanism to apply *internal* competition for divisional performance.[77]

Even in the context of an attempt at divisionalization of activities and decentralization of authority, the implementation of a bureaucratically integrated managerial structure in late postwar Britain may have faced severe institutional and cultural obstacles, such as (1) a system of higher education that had been shaped in part by the prevalence of bureaucratically segmented managerial structures, (2) the control of technology by shop-floor and shop-culture interest groups, and (3) the persistence of aristocratic values and social class distinctions in the hierarchical ordering of the managerial structure. In the face of these obstacles, insightful executives and experienced management consultants may not have been sufficient to transform the system of incentives, the lines of communication, and the loci of control within a large bureaucratic enterprise to permit managerial structure to make a success of the new organizational form.

Notes

1. The major sources for the British-U.S. comparison are Alfred D. Chandler, Jr., *The Visible Hand: The Managerial Revolution in American Business*, Cambridge, Harvard University Press, 1977; Alfred D. Chandler, Jr., and Herman Daems, *Managerial Hierarchies: Comparative Perspectives on the Rise of the Modern Industrial Enterprise*, Cambridge, Harvard University Press, 1980; Peter L. Payne, "The Emergence of the Large-Scale Company in Great Britain, 1870–1914," *Economic History Review*, 2d ser., 20, December 1967; Alfred D. Chandler, Jr., "The Growth of the Transnational Firm in the United States and the United Kingdom: A Comparative Analysis," *Economic History Review*, 2d ser., 33, August 1980; Alfred D. Chandler, Jr., "The United Kingdom: The Persistence of Family Capitalism," unpublished manuscript, Graduate School of Business Administration, Harvard University, 1984; Derek F. Channon, *The Strategy and Structure of British Enterprise*, Boston, Graduate School of Business Administration, 1973; Leslie Hannah, *The Rise of the Corporate Economy*, 2d ed., London, Methuen, 1983; Bernard Elbaum and William Lazonick, "The Decline of the British Economy: An Institutional Perspective," *Journal of Economic History*, 44, 2, June 1984; Bernard Elbaum and William Lazonick, eds., *The Decline of the British Economy*, London, Oxford University Press, 1985.
2. Alfred Marshall, *Principles of Economics*, London, Macmillan, 1890. E. A. G. Robinson, *The Structure of Competitive Industry*, Cambridge, Cambridge University Press, 1933.
3. Herbert Simon, *Administrative Behavior*, 3d ed., New York, Free Press, 1976.
4. Chester Barnard, *The Functions of the Executive*, Cambridge, Harvard University Press, 1938.
5. "Should a Businessman Be Educated?" *Fortune*, 47, April 1953. Robert N. McMurry, "Man-Hunt for Top Executives," *Harvard Business Review*, 32, 1, January–February 1954.
6. The following summary draws upon Richard Hofstadter and C. DeWitt Hardy, *The Development and Scope of Higher Education in the United States*, New York, Columbia University Press, 1952; Frederick Rudolph, *The American College and University*, New York, Vintage, 1962; Laurance R. Veysey, *The Emergence of the American University*,

Chicago, University of Chicago Press, 1965; E. J. James, "The Origin of the Land Grant Act of 1862," *University of Illinois Bulletin*, 8, 10, 1910; A. C. True, *A History of Agricultural Education in the United States, 1785–1925*, Washington, Government Printing Office, 1929; William Lazonick, "The Integration of U.S. Higher Education into Agricultural Production," unpublished manuscript, Harvard University, 1977; David Noble, *America by Design*, New York, Oxford University Press, 1977.

7. Anglo-American Council on Productivity, *Education for Management*, London, Anglo-American Council on Productivity, 1951, pp. 48–51. Norman C. Hunt, *University Education for Business in the U.S.A.*, Management Education Series No. 1, European Productivity Agency, 1953, p. 11.

8. United States Bureau of the Census, *Historical Statistics of the United States, Colonial Times to 1970*, Washington, D.C., Government Printing Office, 1976, pp. 383, 385–86.

9. Cited in Suzanne Keller, *The Social Origins and Career Lines of Three Generations of American Business Leaders*, New York, Arno, 1980, pp. 133, 135n.

10. J. B. Taylor, "College Education and Business," *Educational Review*, 19, 1900. See also Charles F. Thwing, "College Training and the Business Man," *North American Review*, 177, October 1903; Irvin G. Wyllie, "The Businessman Looks at the Higher Learning," *Journal of Higher Education*, 23, 1952; Mabel Newcomer, *The Big Business Executive*, New York, Columbia University Press, 1955, p. 66.

11. Spurgeon Bell, *Productivity, Wages, and National Income*, Washington, D.C., Brookings Institution, 1940, p. 10; Seymour Melman, "The Rise of Administrative Overhead in the Manufacturing Industries of the United States, 1899–1947," *Oxford Economic Papers*, n.s. 3, February 1951, p. 66; United States Bureau of the Census, *Historical Statistics*, pp. 140–41.

12. Cited in Alfred Lief, *The Firestone Story*, New York, McGraw-Hill, 1951, p. 158. See also Hugh Allen, *The House of Goodyear*, Cleveland, Corday & Gross, 1943, p. 312; Alfred Lief, *"It Floats": The Story of Procter & Gamble*, New York, Rinehart, 1958, p. 157.

13. Boris Emmet and John E. Jeuck, *Catalogues and Counters*, Chicago, University of Chicago Press, 1950, p. 554. Alfred D. Chandler, Jr., *Strategy and Structure*, Cambridge, M.I.T. Press, 1962, p. 238.

14. Keller, *Social Origins*. Newcomer, *Big Business Executive*. "The Nine

Hundred," *Fortune*, 46, November 1952. W. Lloyd Warner and James C. Abegglen, *Occupational Mobility in American Business and Industry*, Minneapolis, University of Minnesota Press, 1955.

15. Noble, *America by Design*.

16. Cited in Noble, *America by Design*, p. 38.

17. *Ibid.*, p. 243.

18. Hunt, *University Education*. Melvin T. Copeland, *And Mark an Era*, Boston, Little, Brown, 1958, chaps. 2, 6.

19. Newcomer, *Big Business Executive*, p. 147.

20. McKinsey cited in Robert K. Merton, "Bureaucratic Structure and Personality," in Merton et. al., eds., *Reader in Bureaucracy*, New York, Free Press, 1952, p. 322. Barnard, *Functions*, p. 222, Newcomer, *Big Business Executive*, p. 135.

21. M. P. McNair, "The Harvard Experiment," in R. J. Mackay, ed., *Business and Science*, London, Sylvan Press, 1931, pp. 75–6.

22. For recent analyses along these lines, with the historical focus more on blue-collar workers, see Richard Edwards, *Contested Terrain*, New York, Basic Books, 1979; William Lazonick, "Technological Change and the Control of Work: The Development of Capital-Labor Relations in U.S. Manufacturing Industry," in Howard Gospel and Craig Littler, eds., *Managerial Strategies and Industrial Relations*, London, Heinemann, 1983.

23. Howard Lee Davis, *The Young Man in Business*, New York, Wiley, 1931, p. 35.

24. Litchfield cited in Allen, *Goodyear*, p. 312. Teagle cited in National Industrial Conference Board, *Company Programs of Executive Development*, Studies in Personnel Policy, No. 107, New York, National Industrial Conference Board, 1950, p. 19.

25. Newcomer, *Big Business Executive*, pp. 80, 112.

26. Keller, *Social Origins*, p. 98. "The Nine Hundred," *Fortune*. See also Warner and Abegglen, *Occupational Mobility*, p. 126.

27. Cited in National Industrial Conference Board, *Company Programs*, p. 23. See also *ibid.*, pp. 28–29, 34, 45–49, 53; John V. L. Morris, *Employee Training*, New York, McGraw-Hill, 1921; Emmet and Jeuck, *Catalogues*, p. 559; Allen, *Goodyear*, pp. 315, 322; Charles L. Walker, "Education and Training at International Harvester," *Harvard Business Review*, 27, September 1949, p. 554; Newcomer, *Big Business Executive*, p. 136; American Institute of Management, *How They Recruit and Develop Their Managers: A Survey of 168 Excel-*

lently Managed Companies, New York, American Institute of Management, 1965.

28. Marshall E. Dimock, *Administrative Vitality*, New York, Harper, 1959, pp. 212–13. On the potential ambiguity between demotion and promotion in "lateral" transfers, see Fred H. Goldner, "Demotion in Industrial Management," *American Sociological Review*, 30, October 1965.

29. Ralph J. Cordiner, "The Implications of Industrial Decentralization," *American Management Association General Management Series No. 134*, New York, 1945, pp. 26–8.

30. *Ibid.*, pp. 27–9.

31. Payne, "Emergence of the Large-Scale Company." Chandler, "Growth of the Transnational Firm." Chandler, "Persistence of Family Capitalism." Hannah, *Rise of the Corporate Economy*. Elbaum and Lazonick, eds., *Decline of the British Economy*.

32. T. C. Barker, *The Glassmakers*, London, Weidenfeld & Nicolson, 1977. B. W. E. Alford, *W.D. & H.O. Wills and the Development of the UK Tobacco Industry, 1786–1965*, London, Methuen, 1973. D. C. Coleman, *Courtaulds*, Vol. 1, Oxford, Clarendon Press, 1969. William Reader, *Imperial Chemical Industries*, Vol. 1, London, Oxford University Press, 1975. Charles Wilson, *The History of Unilever*, Vol. 1, New York, Praeger, 1968.

33. See references in note 31 as well as Leslie Hannah, "Strategy and Structure in the Manufacturing Sector," in Leslie Hannah, ed., *Management Strategy and Business Development*, London, Macmillan, 1976.

34. L. Urwick, "Promotion in Industry," *Public Administration*, 5, April 1927, p. 185.

35. Frank Plachy, Jr., *Britain's Economic Plight*, Boston, Little, Brown, 1926, p. 67.

36. Federation of British Industries, *Stocktaking on Management Education*, London, Federation of British Industries, 1961, p. 58, my emphasis. On these issues generally, see Julia Wrigley, "Seeds of Decline: Technical Education and Industry in Nineteenth Century Britain," in Elbaum and Lazonick, eds., *Decline of the British Economy*; Martin J. Weiner, *English Culture and the Decline of the Industrial Spirit, 1850–1980*, Cambridge, Cambridge University Press, 1981.

37. David Landes, *The Unbound Prometheus*, Cambridge, Cambridge University Press, 1969. Weiner, *English Culture*. David Ward, "The

Public Schools and Industry in Britain after 1871," in Walter Laqueur and George L. Mosse, eds., *Education and Social Structure in the Twentieth Century*, New York, Harper, 1967. Coleman, *Courtaulds*, Vol. 1, pp. 271–72. D. C. Coleman, "Gentlemen and Players," *Economic History Review*, 26, February 1973.

38. Acton Society Trust, *Management Succession*, Acton Society Trust, 1956, pp. 14, 22, 90.

39. Moseley Educational Commission, *Reports of the Moseley Educational Commission to the United States, October–December, 1903*, New York, Arno Press, 1969, p. 184.

40. Michael Sanderson, *The Universities and British Industry, 1850–1970*, London, Routledge & Kegan Paul, 1972, pp. 58–9. Acton Society Trust, *Management Succession*, pp. 8, 128. R. V. Clements, *Managers: A Study of Their Careers in Industry*, London, Allen & Unwin, 1958, pp. 142–48. I. C. McGivering, D. G. J. Matthews, and W. H. Scott, *Management in Britain*, Liverpool, Liverpool University Press, 1960, pp. 65–71. Political and Economic Planning, *Graduates in Industry*, London, Allen & Unwin, 1967. But see the general evidence in D. G. Clark, *The Industrial Manager*, London, Business Publications, 1966, pp. 37–42, as well as the specific case of Courtaulds in D. C. Coleman, *Courtaulds*, Vol. 3, Oxford, Clarendon Press, 1980, pp. 132–37, and Arthur Knight, *Private Enterprise and Public Intervention*, London, Allen & Unwin, 1974, pp. 20, 72, 83, which indicate that the emphasis had shifted to science degrees by the early 1960s.

41. Reader, *Imperial Chemical Industries*, Vol. 1, pp. 92–3, 219. A. E. Musson, *Enterprise in Soap and Chemicals*, Manchester, Manchester University Press, 1965, p. 147. R. W. Ferrier, *The History of the British Petroleum Company*, Cambridge, Cambridge University Press, 1982, p. 339; Barker, *Glassmakers*, p. 236.

42. Sanderson, *Universities*, p. 248. For an example of the impact of wartime loss on managerial succession, see Peter L. Payne, *Colvilles and the Scottish Steel Industry*, Oxford, Clarendon Press, 1979, p. 132.

43. Clements, *Managers*. McGivering, Matthews, and Scott, *Management*, chap. 2. Guy Hunter, *Studies in Management*, London, University of London Press, 1961, pp. 20–1; British Institute of Management, *New Trends in Management Training and Succession*, London, British Institute of Management, 1961. Geoffrey Crockett and Peter Elias, "British Managers: A Study of Their Education, Training,

Mobility, and Earnings," *British Journal of Industrial Relations*, 22, March 1984.

44. Sanderson, *Universities*, pp. 64–5. See also Alford, *Wills*, pp. 281–82.
45. Sanderson, *Universities*, p. 78. Massachusetts Institute of Technology, *Treasurer's Report*, 1913. Cornell University, *Treasurer's Report*, 1913–1914, p. 45. Percy Dunsheath, *The Graduate in Industry*, London, Hutchinson's, 1947, p. 42.
46. Cited in Sanderson, *Universities*, p. 95.
47. Cambridge University Appointments Board, *University Education and Business*, Cambridge, Cambridge University Press, 1945, pp. 39–40. Acton Society Trust, *Management Succession*, pp. 28–9.
48. David Mowery, "British and American Industrial Research: A Comparison 1900–1950," in Elbaum and Lazonick, eds., *Decline of the British Economy*.
49. Robert R. Locke, *The End of the Practical Man: Entrepreneurship and Higher Education in Germany, France, and Great Britain, 1880–1940*, Greenwood, JAI, 1984, pp. 51, 58, 101. Leslie Hannah, *Electricity before Nationalisation*, London, Macmillan, 1979, pp. 218–84.
50. Moseley Educational Commission, *Reports*, p. 57.
51. Cited in Locke, *End of Practical Man*, p. 101.
52. Charles Wilson and William Reader, *Men and Machines: A History of D. Napier & Son, Engineers, Ltd., 1808–1958*, London, Weidenfeld & Nicolson, 1958, pp. 156–59.
53. Peter Young, *Power of Speech*, London, Allen & Unwin, 1983, pp.125, 129–30.
54. Moseley Educational Commission, *Reports*, pp. 56–7.
55. Committee on Industry and Trade, *Factors in Industrial and Commercial Efficiency*, London, His Majesty's Stationery Office, 1924, p. 261. Ministry of Education, *Education for Management*, London, His Majesty's Stationery Office, 1947.
56. T. M. Mosson, *Management Education in Five European Countries*, London, Business Publications, 1965. Anglo-American Council on Productivity, *Education for Management*. Anglo-American Council on Productivity, *Universities and Industry*, London, Anglo-American Council on Productivity, 1951.
57. Mosson, *Management Education*. Weiner, *English Culture*, pp. 132–37. Channon, *Strategy and Structure*, pp. 212–13, 245–46.
58. Mosson, *Management Education*, pp. 163–64.

59. David G. Clarke, "A Survey of Management Education in the United Kingdom," *Journal of Industrial Economics*, 4, February 1956.
60. Mosson, *Management Education*, p. 167. Aubrey Silberston, *Education and Training for Industrial Management*, London, Management Publications, 1955, p. 33.
61. Mosson, *Management Education*, p. 198.
62. James A. Bowie, *Education for Business Management*, London, Oxford University Press, 1930.
63. Hunt, *University Education*, p. 38.
64. Young, *Power of Speech*, p. 183.
65. Ronald S. Edwards and Harry Townsend, *Business Enterprise*, London, Macmillan, 1958, p. 546. Silberston, *Education and Training*, p. 80. Channon, *Strategy and Structure*, p. 246.
66. Acton Society Trust, *Management Succession*, pp. 95–107. Silberston, *Education and Training*, p. 52. W. G. McClelland, "Career Patterns and Organisational Needs," in R. J. Hacon, ed., *Organisational Necessities and Individual Needs*, Oxford, Blackwell, 1968, p. 30.
67. Crockett and Elias, "British Managers," pp. 36–7.
68. Samuel Bowles and Herbert Gintis, *Schooling in Capitalist America*, New York, Basic Books, 1976. Jerome Karabel, "Community Colleges and Stratification," *Harvard Educational Review*, 42, November 1972.
69. Chandler, *Strategy and Structure*. Channon, *Strategy and Structure*. Hannah, "Strategy and Structure," pp. 184–87.
70. Channon, *Strategy and Structure*.
71. For example, see the case of Courtaulds, as set forth in Coleman, *Courtaulds*, Vols. 2, 3.
72. Wilson, *History of Unilever*, Vol. 2, pp. 345ff, 380ff; Vol. 3, chap. 2. Musson, *Enterprise*, chap. 19. Geoffrey Heyworth, "Lever Brothers and Unilever Limited," in G. E. Milward, ed., *Large-Scale Organisation*, London, MacDonald and Evans, 1950.
73. Wilson, *History of Unilever*, Vol. 1, p. 48. D. K. Fieldhouse, *Unilever Overseas*, London, Croom Helm, 1978, p. 45. Musson, *Enterprise*, pp. 145–49, 343–45; chap. 20.
74. Wilson, *History of Unilever*, Vol. 1, chap. 20; Vol. 2, p. 48. Fieldhouse, *Unilever Overseas*, p. 39.
75. Wilson, *History of Unilever*, Vol. 2, p. 316.
76. Heyworth, "Lever Brothers," pp. 177–78.
77. Channon, *Strategy and Structure*, pp. 213–14, emphasis in original.

Comment

Yoshitaka Suzuki
Tohoku University

Professor Lazonick's paper is extremely interesting in that it brings the basic concepts of modern administrative science, which is abstract by nature and not necessarily familiar with the empirical approach, into institutional and historical studies. The performance of management structures depends greatly on the integration of the hierarchy by means of an incentive system, that is, the opportunity for promotion. However, to make this incentive practicable and profitable for the firm requires appropriate "management development" based on pre-employment education, which supplies able specialists who can also be trained as generalists through corporate job-rotation schemes. In contrast to their British counterparts, many American firms achieved bureaucratic integration by offering their employees careers with potentially unlimited upward mobility. The concept of "management development" is useful in explaining this process.

Management development and bureaucratic integration are originally two different things, however, and each poses particular problems for firms. First, how widely and systematically was management development based upon job rotation put into practice among leading American firms, such as Goodyear, Sears, Roebuck, and AT&T? If management development was open to all employees, was it not costly for the individual departments, which always had many newcomers? Was American job rotation just a means of training predetermined future generalists, or was it a selection process in which young specialists were required to work as hard as the existing members of the departments if they wanted to advance? Furthermore, if the supply of generalists was derived from the management development process, why has it often been asserted

that one of the defects of the functionally departmentalized structure was that its top management comprised specialists?

Second, the equilibrium of bureaucratic integration, which consists of the unification of each member's goal with that of the entire
organization and of incentives in the form of promotion, cannot
apply in all circumstances. Since only a handful of people can
climb up the ladder, the majority of people, who are unsuccessful
in gaining promotion, must still believe in the legitimacy of the
system. But this is not easy to achieve. Finally, it is necessary to
integrate hierarchies from top to bottom to attain bureaucratic
integration. Was the segmentation of shop-floor and clerical workers from professional, managerial, and technical workers mentioned
by Professor Lazonick insignificant to American firms?

Response

William Lazonick

Professor Suzuki has raised a number of important issues. By
the 1920s systematic management development was much more
prevalent in the United States than in Britain. But it will require
much more research to document the proportion of large U.S. corporations that had management development programs in the
1920s as well as the impact of the Great Depression on the adoption
and continuation of these schemes.

Undoubtedly there were short-run costs to job rotation, but over
the long run it would have been even more costly to the firm to
confine personnel to narrow functional activities. Without the
prospect of upward mobility within the firm, specialists would have
had less incentive to perform for the firm, and the most able among
them would have had more incentive to leave the firm in search of
advancement.

There is always a danger that functional specialists will rise to top management positions without adequate generalist training. My argument is that decentralization of operations helped overcome this problem because middle managers had to synthesize purchasing, engineering, financial, organizational, legal, and marketing information in making their decisions. The best of the middle managers then provided a generalist-oriented supply of top managers.

The ascent up the managerial hierarchy is not open to everyone. Historically, women have provided a supply of specialists with limited upward mobility, although in the United States the situation has changed dramatically over the last two decades. Others who are dissatisfied with their progress can leave the firm, although, particularly as they grow older and have been with a particular firm longer, to abandon job security by making use of the exit option can be a risky business.

If those who are not promoted view the promotion process as fair, they will be inclined to attribute their lack of vertical mobility to their own inherent limitations. Nevertheless, all organizations (not the least of which are academic) face the problem of motivating older employees who have apparently reached the peak of their productivity potential.

As indicated in my paper, the segmentation of blue-collar and white-collar (mainly female) workers from the managerial bureaucracy was, and remains, an important organizational characteristic of U.S. bureaucracies. Some results of this segmentation have been widespread worker alienation, adversarial union-management relations, and the need for affirmative action legislation. Although the U.S. organizational model has worked well compared with the British, it certainly does not represent the best of all possible solutions to the transformation of individual into collective rationality.

Recruitment and Training of Middle Managers in Japan, 1900–1930

Eisuke Daitō
University of Tokyo

Introduction

It is safe to say that a society has already entered an advanced stage of industrial development when more than 50% of its working population is engaged in occupations in secondary and tertiary industries. All the early developed nations in the West had passed this halfway mark by the end of the nineteenth century.[1] As one might expect, Japan was far behind these industrial pioneers. While Japan reached this point just before 1930, many self-employed "old middle-class" people as well as unpaid family workers still remained in every sector of the economy.[2]

However, a close look at changes in the occupational structure of Japanese society in the early decades of the twentieth century reveals an interesting fact, that of the growth of the "new middle class," which is relevant to the theme of this conference, the rise of managerial capitalism. According to statistics for 1920, when the first national census of population and employment was carried out, about 1,515,000 salaried employees and 16,153,000 manual workers were at work in the Japanese economy.[3] That is, the administrative intensity of the Japanese economy measured by the ratio of salaried employees to manual workers was 9.3%. Regrettably, comparable figures for 1930 are not available because of major changes in census definitions. However, judging from the fact that during the decade the number of white-collar workers grew more rapidly than that of blue-collar workers, we may conclude that the ratio for 1930 was roughly on a par with that of industrialized nations in Western Europe.[4] The purpose of this paper is to examine the cause and effect of this growth of the administrative overhead of the Japanese

business system. In accordance with the project leader's suggestion,
I will focus my attention on the recruitment and training of managerial personnel at the middle and lower levels of managerial
hierarchies.

Theoretically speaking, the growth of middle and lower management can be attributed to the combined effect of the following three
factors. One factor is on the supply side: an increased supply of
well-educated people to firms. In the early stage of industrialization,
since Japan was an industrial latecomer, one of the most crucial
tasks was to develop a high level of human resources and draw
them into productive jobs. During the nineteenth century such
resources had been the scarcest factor of production in the Japanese
economy. The shortage of technical and managerial skills made
it possible for men with these skills to exert a strong influence on the
management of the firms that employed them. This tendency was
strengthened by the traditional practice of Japanese merchant
houses, which gave full authority to their trusted head clerks.[5] In
the first section I will examine briefly how these crucial human
resources were developed in the early stage of industrialization in
Japan.

The second reason for the change in the occupational structure
was the rise of big business, which required extensive administrative
organization. The rise of big business and its elaborate division of
labor among specialized functional units created a sharp increase in
demand for well-trained administrators to plan, coordinate, and
control the activities of various units and personnel. In these firms,
therefore, a substantial proportion of employees was drawn into
administrative and clerical jobs. As is well known, in the early years
of the twentieth century zaibatsu combines, such as Mitsui and
Mitsubishi, set up a central office as a holding company and systematized relationships between it and affiliated companies.[6] In the
second section I will take the case of Mitsubishi as an example and
examine the process of the growth of administrative overhead.
Mitsubishi's policies for the recruitment and training of managerial
staff will also be explored.

The third factor is on the demand side: the shift in industrial
structure. In the early decades of the twentieth century, through the

expansion of such industries as the engineering, chemical, and service industries, which employed large numbers of clerical workers, engineers, sales workers, and administrators, these white-collar groups formed a growing proportion of the labor force. I will discuss several cases in capital-intensive industries and examine their organizational structure at the factory level. It seems likely that as production processes became more capital intensive these industries tended to become more management intensive. Although the factories discussed in the third section were not necessarily big, their activities were so complex and diverse that they had to be placed under an elaborate managerial system.

I

When the political upheaval of the Meiji Restoration of 1868 came to an end, the new state found itself with an urgent need for all kinds of modern skills and knowledge. As is well known, the polity of the Meiji constitutional monarchy was designed after that of Prussia. At first the Japanese army depended heavily on the guidance of French advisers, and the navy drew its model from the Royal Navy of Britain. The idea of compulsory elementary education was introduced from the United States. The field of business and the economy was no exception to this rule.

At first Meiji entrepreneurs tried to depend on the small number of people who somehow had acquired Western business practices and technologies for themselves. Masuda Takashi of Mitsui was the most successful man of this kind. After the Restoration this former cavalry officer of the Tokugawa Shogunate was employed by an American merchant in Yokohama as a clerk and interpreter.[7] Through this practical experience he acquired the skills and knowledge of international trade and became acquainted with many foreign merchants. In 1876, when Mitsui set up a trading firm, he was asked to take office as president of the firm. Under his leadership this firm became the famous general trading firm of Mitsui & Co. Needless to say, however, the supply of self-educated men like Masuda was so limited that it could not fill the increasing demand.

Second, many promising young men were sent abroad or went on their own, in the early years of the Meiji era (1868–1912), to learn how commercial and manufacturing businesses were conducted in advanced countries. Since most of these young men were strongly motivated by a sense of public duty, almost all of them returned to Japan with something that could be put to use for their young nation-state. In this sense, overseas study was a very effective method of education, but the financial burden was sometimes unbearable. One-eighth of the Ministry of Education's budget for fiscal 1872 went for this purpose.[8] To train Yamanobe Takeo, who was to be the chief engineer of the Osaka Cotton Spinning Company, his employer had to pay £150, or about ¥1,500, to an English manufacturer. In 1880, when Yamanobe returned to Japan, he drew a salary of ¥45 a month and two years later was earning ¥60.[9] By comparison, starting wages for male and female workers of the firm were ¥0.12 and ¥0.07 a day, respectively. These figures clearly tell us how highly valued foreign skills and knowledge were for their scarcity and how expensive studying abroad was in those days.

The third method was to bring in foreign experts and advisers. More than 500 foreigners were employed by the Japanese government during the period from 1870 to 1885, when the Ministry of Industry actively promoted government model factories of various kinds.[10] The Ministry of Education also employed many foreign teachers. In addition, private enterprise employed many foreigners during the early years of industrialization. Since many of these foreign experts were enthusiastic, they were very helpful in solving difficult problems of technological transfer to Japan. The problem was that to attract competent foreign experts, Japanese employers had to offer extraordinarily remunerative terms of employment. Some of the salaries paid were higher than those of ministerial-level officials. A mining engineer employed by the house of Sumitomo earned six times as much as Sumitomo's chief executive. In its peak years, therefore, more than 50% of the Ministry of Industry's budget went for the payment of foreigners' salaries, and about 10% of the Ministry of Education's budget was devoted to this.[11] Around 1885, therefore, the Japanese government began an earnest attempt to replace these foreign experts with Japanese engineers and administrators who were self-trained or who had returned from study abroad.

To gain independence from foreign experts, ministries and newly formed government enterprises often set up training programs of their own. A training school for the telegraph and telephone system was the most successful of them.[12] The Meiji government began to construct a publicly owned telegraph network just after the Restoration, and by 1874 construction of the major trunk lines linking the main island of Honshu to Hokkaido in the north and Kyushu in the south was completed. The number of telegraph stations increased rapidly from 18 in 1875 to 1,000 in 1895 and to about 5,000 in 1910. In 1871 the Ministry of Industry set up a small training shop for telegraph operators. Two years later this was remolded into a well-equipped training school, from which about 1,200 students had graduated by 1876. As a result, within a decade foreign engineers and advisers were entirely replaced by Japanese who had been trained at the school. In 1877, when the Ministry of Communications was established, it extended and founded the Tokyo Telecommunication School. The purpose of this school was to train the future managerial and engineering staff of the telephone and telegraph network. Its curriculum covered three distinct fields: administration, telecommunications, and engineering. It was generally recognized that the school could offer a technical education close to one at university level. Since the school turned out about 100 graduates every year, they occupied almost all the key administrative and technical positions of this government-owned enterprise (Table 1).

TABLE 1   Number of Graduates of the Tokyo Telecommunication School.

Period	Administration	Engineering	Wireless	Total
1871–1873	113	—	—	113
1873–1886	1,202	—	—	1,202
1886–1887	71	—	—	71
1887–1890	180	—	—	180
1890–1905	575	442	—	1,017
1905–1909	434	183	—	617
1909–1939	2,043	1,465	342	3,850
Total	4,618	2,090	342	7,050

Source: Ministry of Communications, *Teishin jigyō shi* (History of the telecommunications system), Ministry of Communications, Vol. 1, p. 671.

Such an extensive internal training program could be carried out only by a profitable government-owned enterprise. Private employers had to recruit well-trained people in one way or another from outside or attract personnel of such high caliber and determination that little internal instruction seemed necessary.[13] While the newly established national university began to educate talented students in 1877, it was originally conceived as a means of entrance into the government bureaucracy. In addition, the capacity of the university was so small that demand for university graduates far outran supply during the nineteenth century. In those days, to make matters worse, the social status of those engaged in business or industry was much lower than that of government officials. It was very difficult for private employers to make promising students as well as the public at large realize that higher education was a key prerequisite for a successful career in modern business. Because of the prevailing social climate, which put official above private life, private employers could not attract university graduates.

Despite these difficulties some industries and firms could employ many able people with high educational backgrounds. Mitsui & Co. was a typical example. Since foreign trade in the early years of the Meiji era was dominated by foreign merchants, the government urged wealthy Japanese merchants to engage in foreign trade. Therefore, to run a trading firm was considered a contribution to the national cause. As a result the pioneering firm of Mitsui & Co. acquired enough prestige to attract talented people with a high educational background. As early as 1878 Masuda began to recruit many graduates of the Education Institute of Commerce (later Hitotsubashi University), which was the only center of higher learning for business and industry at that time with the exception of Keiō Gijuku (later Keio University). While he trained them mainly on the job, around 1891 he introduced a trainee system. Under this system selected employees were sent abroad to study foreign languages as well as business practices, and spent about five years away from office duties to complete their studies. At first this system was applied to China but was extended gradually to other areas. According to Masuda, the growth of Mitsui & Co. was due not only to the financial power of the house of Mitsui but also to his efforts in developing human resources within the firm.[14]

We find a parallel instance in banking. Since a well-organized banking system was vital to overcome the economic chaos caused by the Restoration, the Meiji government made every effort to introduce the modern banking business into Japan. After much trial and error in the late 1870s, the government succeeded in persuading not only wealthy merchants but also many ex-aristocrats, such as former *daimyō*, to invest their commutation bonds in banks. As a result, many national banks were founded in the late 1870s. These, together with the private banks founded in subsequent years, formed the core of Japan's banking business. Because of the involvement of many socially prestigious people, bankers were no longer identified with the traditional money-lenders. Moreover, as the banks were established earlier than other modern industries, they played a pioneering role in the modernization and industrialization of the Japanese economy. The national banks were among the first to adopt the corporate form of business organization and to introduce the double-entry bookkeeping system and modern accounting methods. They were instrumental in introducing and popularizing these Western business institutions and techniques. Therefore banks could attract the most competent employees, some of whom advanced into other business fields and produced remarkable achievements. As pointed out by Johannes Hirschmeier, many outstanding entrepreneurs in the Meiji era started their business careers as bankers.[15]

In regard to the employment of university graduates, the case of Mitsui Bank is both interesting and important.[16] As is well known, by the end of the 1880s the bank's performance had deteriorated seriously because a huge number of bad loans had accumulated. Most of them were the result of the bank's dependence on personal connections with government officials. Since the bank depended heavily on privileges granted by the government, many private loans to government officials could not be collected by force. Nakamigawa Hikojirō, who was appointed vice-president of Mitsui in 1891, initiated a radical reform of business policies and began to

TABLE 2   Changes in the Capacity of Institutions of Higher Education.

	No. of institutions				No. of students
	I	II	III	Total	
1895	16	3	44	63	12,382 (0.3)
1905	39	4	14	84	37,180 (0.9)
1915	45	7	56	108	50,470 (1.0)
1925	106	50	101	257	126,842 (2.5)
1935	104	61	143	308	149,030 (3.0)

Note: I=national schools, II=municipal schools, III=private schools, ( )=% of
university attendance.
Source: Ministry of Education, *Nippon no seichō to kyōiku* (Economic growth and
education in Japan), Ministry of Education, 1962.

replace old-style clerks with talented university graduates. Most
of these new appointees had graduated from Keiō Gijuku, which
was founded by Fukuzawa Yukichi to promote practical sciences
and to train potential business leaders to have a spirit of self-respect.
Since Fukuzawa believed in Western liberalism and individualism,
he fought vigorously against the excessive dependence of businessmen on political connections and patronage. His students became
prominent businessmen in various industries in later years. Fukuzawa and his Keiō Gijuku thus contributed much to the early
emergence of professional managers in Japan.

While a few firms and industries could attract talented university
graduates from the early years of the Meiji period, government demand for them in the nineteenth century was so great that most of
them could find jobs in the government bureaucracy. After the turn
of the century, however, things began to change rapidly. As shown
in Table 2, the capacity of higher education expanded yearly. Therefore graduates seeking "good" government jobs found themselves
in a much more competitive situation than before. It became
apparent even to graduates from imperial universities that the
government was no longer able to provide them with ample job
opportunities. From around 1900 onward, therefore, the majority
of university graduates directed themselves toward employment in
the private sector. The increased supply of well-educated people
made it possible for private firms to build up their managerial
hierarchies.

II

In the Mitsubishi zaibatsu not only Iwasaki Yatarō, the founder of the combine, but also his successors as president, Iwasaki Yano-suke, Hisaya, and Koyata, devoted themselves enthusiastically to the management of their family firm. Therefore Mitsubishi's managerial structure was highly centralized compared with that of other zaibatsu, such as Mitsui and Sumitomo. Needless to say, as the firm grew in size and diversified its operations, a more systematized managerial organization emerged. In this respect 1908 was an epoch-making year in Mitsubishi's history, because at this time a radical reform was introduced into its managerial structure.[17] By this time Mitsubishi had extended its business to banking, mining, and foreign trade, while maintaining one of its original businesses, shipbuilding. Each of these activities had been placed under the control of a separate department, and the most pressing managerial problem was that of how to assess the performance of each department. Koyata reformed the firm's managerial structure so that the each department's performance might be seen clearly. Under the new system a certain amount of capital was allotted to three divisions, which could operate their businesses on a self-supporting basis. While they had to pay yearly dividends to the central office, they had the authority to make decisions concerning their own personnel and investments.

In concert with the reform at the top of the firm's organization, a series of rationalization measures was introduced into factories. The factory management system of the shipbuilding division's Nagasaki shipyard was reformed from top to bottom in 1908. The following came into effect at a stroke: a procedure for the exchange and filing of letters, a rule for making cost estimates of engineering works, a procedure for the procurement of raw materials and parts, an inventory control system, a work order and production control system, rules for the recruitment of workers and the determination of wage rates, an elaborate cost accounting system, and so on. According to a history of the shipyard, up to that year it had not had any clearly defined organization or rules by which to manage factory operations. Instead it had depended on customary rules of thumb that had grown up almost spontaneously.[18]

For labor management the shipyard had relied heavily on the inside-contractor system, whose use had allowed avoidance of the responsibility of direct supervision of workers as well as of recruitment and wage administration. Since inside contractors took a substantial kickback from subordinate workers, the latter's will to work was severely weakened. An engineer who was confident that this practice was a stumbling block to the progress of the shipyard's management exerted every effort to abolish it.[19] The abolition of the inside-contractor system was an essential part of the rationalization measures mentioned above. It can readily be imagined that this transformation of labor management entailed an increase in administrative and clerical workers to handle the functions taken away from subcontractors. These rationalization measures also made it necessary for the shipyard to increase its administrative staff. Table 3 shows clearly that the number of salaried employees working for the shipyard increased rapidly after the reform. In contrast, because of the severe economic depression of 1909, the shipyard cut down on the number of manual workers. As a result the ratio of salaried employees to manual workers rose from 4.9% in 1902 to 9.7% in 1890 and reached about 15% in the mid-1920s. One may infer from this that supervision at the Nagasaki shipyard became much closer than before.

It is evident that this trend toward the bureaucratization of management made steady progress not only at the shipyard but also

TABLE 3   Number of Employees at Mitsubishi's Nagasaki Shipyard.

	I	II	Total	I/II (%)
1892	148	3,517	3,665	4.2
1902	269	5,245	5,514	5.1
1906	395	8,946	9,341	4.4
1910	619	5,572	6,371	11.1
1914	902	10,445	11,347	8.6
1918	1,294	14,337	15,631	9.0
1922	1,690	9,250	10,940	18.3
1925	1,215	6,850	8,065	17.8

Note: I=White-collar employees, II=Blue-collar workers.
Source: Hazama Hiroshi, *Nihon rōmu kanrishi kenkyū* (History of labor management in Japan), 1964, p. 437.

in other divisions and factories of the firm. To indicate this trend I have prepared Table 4, which shows the growth of the Mitsubishi zaibatsu in terms of the number of employees during the Taishō era (1912–26). At Mitsubishi, employees were classified into three categories: *seiin, jun'in,* and *kōin. Seiin,* or regular employees, had the most education and the opportunity to reach top executive positions. *Jun'in,* or associate employees, had graduated from middle school and occupied lower-ranking white-collar positions. *Kōin,* or manual workers, generally had the least education.

It is evident from a glance at Table 4 that the number of white-collar workers (*seiin* and *jun'in*) increased disproportionately. The employment of *seiin* increased three times and that of *jun'in* 1.7 times during the Taishō era. This trend was accelerated by the boom caused by World War I and somewhat retarded by the depression after the war. However, in sharp contrast to the drastic fluctuations in the employment of manual workers, white-collar workers, especially *seiin,* enjoyed job security even during the depression.

The rise of white-collar workers at Mitsubishi can be attributed to the following factors. First, the table shows clearly that the firm grew through diversification, which made it necessary to increase the employment of white-collar workers. The growth of the banking, warehousing, trading, and marine and fire insurance businesses, which by the nature of their operations employed a large number of white-collar workers, accounts for one-third of the increase. After the war Mitsubishi diversified into manufacturing electric machines and internal combustion engines by introducing foreign technologies and machines. The concerted effort of many "engineer-administrators" was needed to put the imported technologies and machines into operation. The relative number of white-collar workers at Mitsubishi Electric and Mitsubishi Internal Combustion Engine was larger than that at Mitsubishi Shipbuilding.

Second, an organizational reform introduced in and after 1917 accelerated the trend.[20] Iwasaki Koyata decided to restructure Mitsubishi Gōshi's divisions into a series of separate joint-stock companies. In line with this policy, Mitsubishi Shipbuilding and Mitsubishi Iron Manufacturing were founded in 1917, Mitsubishi

TABLE 4   Number of Employees in the Mitsubishi Zaibatsu, 1912–1926.

Year	Mitsubishi Gōshi				Mitsubishi Shipbuilding			
	I	II	III	Total	I	II	III	Total
1912	1,319	1,815	52,188	55,322	(290)	(708)	(11,496)	(12,494)
1913	1,542	1,844	56,898	60,322	(430)	(633)	(12,778)	(13,841)
1914	1,706	1,942	58,816	62,464	(491)	(686)	(13,909)	(15,086)
1915	1,823	2,000	58,549	62,372	(518)	(722)	(13,876)	(15,116)
1916	2,086	2,273	67,123	71,464	(598)	(811)	(18,163)	(19,572)
1917	1,695	1,641	51,249	54,585	709	944	21,979	23,632
1918	425	158	269	852	913	1,119	26,039	28,071
1919	225	106	240	571	1,085	1,571	32,010	34,666
1920	267	126	279	672	1,268	1,673	30,473	33,414
1921	241	124	287	652	1,158	1,540	26,974	29,672
1922	228	110	276	614	1,188	1,255	19,698	22,141
1923	222	108	371	701	1,094	1,127	17,600	19,821
1924	232	122	337	691	1,054	876	16,741	18,673
1925	246	128	316	690	1,108	824	14,058	15,990
1926	233	138	346	735	1,158	755	14,132	16,045

Year	Mitsubishi Iron				Mitsubishi Warehousing			
	I	II	III	Total	I	II	III	Total
1912								
1913								
1914								
1915								
1916								
1917	100	69	2,332	2,501				
1918	171	187	3,164	3,522				
1919	173	109	2,491	2,803	282	211	1,076	1,569
1920	174	131	2,547	2,852	315	196	1,239	1,750
1921	173	122	2,323	2,618	332	151	1,171	1,654
1922	146	68	1,245	2,618	306	131	915	1,352
1923	119	68	1,194	1,381	309	90	974	1,376
1924	120	66	1,142	1,328	296	110	1,018	1,424
1925	126	69	1,093	1,288	308	126	1,051	1,485
1926	125	62	1,111	1,298	320	145	1,097	1,562

TABLE 4 (Continued)

Year	Mitsubishi Trading				Mitsubishi Mining			
	I	II	III	Total	I	II	III	Total
1912	(273)	(183)	(643)	(1,099)	(552)	(855)	(39,366)	(41,373)
1913	(305)	(255)	(1,192)	(1,752)	(590)	(889)	(42,831)	(44,310)
1914	(332)	(288)	(1,279)	(1,899)	(622)	(879)	(43,350)	(44,851)
1915	(371)	(237)	(985)	(1,593)	(638)	(943)	(43,217)	(44,789)
1916	(396)	(255)	(1,412)	(2,063)	(746)	(1,070)	(46,847)	(48,663)
1917	(438)	(270)	(1,722)	(2,430)	(851)	(1,258)	(49,345)	(51,454)
1918	560	417	2,181	3,158	1,024	1,525	(54,813)	(57,362)
1919	685	530	2,339	3,554	1,072	1,550	(53,905)	(56,527)
1920	746	453	2,292	3,491	985	1,450	(48,993)	(51,428)
1921	790	417	2,209	3,416	945	1,248	(35,115)	(37,308)
1922	755	316	2,273	3,344	896	1,274	(36,081)	(38,251)
1923	786	253	1,577	2,616	836	1,151	(34,153)	(36,140)
1924	637	228	744	1,609	1,000	1,183	(36,107)	(38,290)
1925	712	240	763	1,715	1,048	1,217	(37,843)	(40,108)
1926	725	274	833	1,832	1,098	1,152	(34,869)	(37,119)

Year	Mitsubishi Marine & Fire Insurance				Mitsubishi Bank			
	I	II	III	Total	I	II	III	Total
1912					(99)	(38)	(12)	(150)
1913					(100)	(32)	(10)	(142)
1914					(99)	(32)	(12)	(143)
1915					(125)	(27)	(16)	(168)
1916					(138)	(42)	(18)	(198)
1917					(163)	(40)	(33)	(236)
1918					(195)	(67)	(73)	(331)
1919	27	16	0	43	229	83	98	410
1920	44	33	3	80	263	117	119	499
1921	54	39	5	98	295	167	128	590
1922	63	46	8	117	348	196	166	710
1923	69	58	10	137	391	233	181	805
1924	73	62	11	146	453	301	189	943
1925	83	82	13	178	530	311	203	1,044
1926	98	98	14	210	588	296	212	1,096

TABLE 4 (*Continued*)

Year	Mitsubishi Internal Combustion Engine				Mitsubishi Electric			
	I	II	III	Total	I	II	III	Total
1912								
1913								
1914								
1915								
1916								
1917								
1918								
1919								
1920	85	72	1,156	1,313				
1921	104	109	1,646	1,859	119	110	1,129	1,358
1922	120	120	2,238	2,478	110	112	1,130	1,352
1923	126	121	1,930	2,177	151	170	1,646	1,967
1924	130	126	1,914	2,177	185	195	1,826	2,206
1925	152	121	2,021	2,294	230	223	1,942	2,395
1926	157	130	2,117	2,404	257	263	1,996	2,516

Year	Grand Total			
	I	II	III	Total
1912	1,552	1,969	53,252	56,773
1913	1,779	2,001	58,113	61,893
1914	1,826	2,093	59,966	63,985
1915	2,067	2,109	60,104	64,340
1916	2,335	2,460	69,049	73,844
1917	2,816	2,865	67,096	84,777
1918	3,487	3,743	89,486	96,716
1919	3,827	4,206	92,159	100,192
1920	4,262	4,259	87,101	95,622
1021	4,211	4,027	70,987	79,225
1922	4,160	3,628	64,630	71,818
1923	4,103	3,382	59,636	67,121
1924	4,180	3,271	60,029	67,480
1925	4,543	3,341	59,303	67,187
1926	4,543	3,341	59,303	67,187

Note: 1. I =*seiin*; II =*jun'in*; III =*kōin*.
2. Figures in parentheses are included in figures for Mitsubishi Gōshi.
3. Grand Total figures include residual categories.

Source: Mitsubishi Gōshi Co., *Mitsubishi shashi* (History of Mitsubishi), Mitsubishi Gōshi; reprinted, Tokyo, University of Tokyo Press, 1981.

Warehousing, Mitsubishi Trading, and Mitsubishi Mining in 1918, and Mitsubishi Bank in 1919. By this reform Mitsubishi Gōshi became a holding company that owned almost all the shares of the newly founded subsidiaries and functioned as the central office of the Mitsubishi zaibatsu. Judging from the fact that the number of white-collar workers showed the sharpest increase during these years, many additional managerial personnel had to be recruited to carry out the reform plan.

Third, additional middle managers and engineers were required because the firms of the Mitsubishi zaibatsu introduced new functions and technologies in the course of their development. Following are a few examples.

1. In 1917 Mitsubishi Gōshi set up the Intelligence Department, which was to engage in research on overseas operations and the feasibility of new ventures.[21] This was the first full-scale staff organization that reported directly to the top managers of the Mitsubishi group. While it started with about only 40 members, it grew rapidly. After 1925 most of its functions were taken over by the Information and Research Department, which became the Mitsubishi Institute of Economic Research in 1932.

2. During World War I two research and development institutes were established.[22] One was that of the mining company, and the other belonged to the shipbuilding company. At that time about 100 researchers were working for them. The interruption of the import of technologies from the West due to the war gave a strong impetus to R&D activities. However, these war babies did not grow smoothly after the war.

3. The number of *seiin* employed by Mitsubishi Mining increased from 836 in 1923 to 1,000 in 1924. This increase was due mainly to forward integration into marketing.[23] Since markets for the company's main products, coal and copper, were depressed in those years, the company had to intensify its marketing efforts. At the same time, to cope with slumps Mitsubishi Mining invested substantial money in the mechanization of coal mines. The long-wall mining method, with an extensive conveyor system and improved cutters and explosives, increased the efficiency of mining operations. According to the company history, these rationalization

measures greatly changed the makeup of the work force of coal mines.[24]

4. In 1925 a special committee for labor management was set up. The aims of the committee were explained as follows:

> In recent years, in keeping with the changing political and eco-
> nomic situation, the labor problem in Japan has become increasingly
> difficult and complex. In Gōshi, the Information and Research
> Department is studying the state of affairs both at home and abroad.
> In addition, in every subsidiary firm a department in charge of
> labor management has been established. . . . However, it seems
> necessary to formulate a basic policy concerning the problem.
> This is the reason this committee has been set up.[25]

As mentioned, in the latter half of the 1910s most firms in the Mitsubishi zaibatsu established labor relations departments, to which able university graduates were assigned.[26] The duties of the departments swelled greatly with the enforcement of the Factory Law in 1916 and the Health Insurance Law in 1926.

The increase in white-collar workers made it necessary for the Mitsubishi zaibatsu to systematize employment practices. In the 1910s a series of bylaws concerning the employment of *seiin* was put into effect. First, in 1911 a bylaw for the recruitment of *seiin* was introduced.[27] Its main provisions were as follows: (1) To admit a *seiin*, after examination by a conference of Gōshi's department heads, the president's approval should be obtained. (2) If possible, *seiin* should be recruited from university graduates who have excellent scholastic records, good health, and a steady character. (3) By the end of January each year, department heads should file a report on the number of new recruits as well as the types of positions filled. Although minor modifications were added to the bylaw, this system for the regular central recruitment of university graduates lasted a long time.

Second, in 1913 a ranking system for senior-class employees was established. And in 1916 a bylaw for the promotion of *seiin* became effective.[28] The main clauses of the 1916 bylaw were as follows: (1) A salary scale is fixed according to rank and grade. (2) As a general rule, one can be moved up to the next grade by a periodic pay raise. (3) If necessary, one can be promoted two to five grades at a time. (4) Every April and October, each department head should submit to his superior a list of personnel to be promoted. Two years later a regular performance rating system that covered all *seiin* was introduced. Under this system department heads were requested to file the results of the performance review, which classified their subordinates into five grades.

Third, in 1917 a bylaw prescribing that all employees had to resign when they reached 55 years of age was put into effect.[29] Soon afterward a system of paying a retirement allowance was inaugurated. According to this system, an employee who retired after 25 years of service could receive a lump-sum retirement allowance that amounted to 190 times the monthly salary of his last month with the firm. In addition, he was eligible for a lifelong company pension that was equal to a quarter of his annual earnings.

These bylaws, which covered everything from recruitment and promotion to retirement, clearly prescribed the employment practices for higher-class white-collar workers. In sum, on behalf of the firms of the group, Mitsubishi Gōshi hired personnel fresh from universities, based on an evaluation of school performance and personality. Since universities offered minimal vocational training, new recruits were assigned to positions at the bottom of the managerial hierarchies and were trained mainly on the job. Vacancies above the bottom level were filled not by the hiring of qualified men on the open market but by internal recruitment, promotion from within, and transfer. Decision making on promotions depended heavily on seniority as well as competence. Under these circumstances, employment was considered to be permanent and not to be influenced by short-run fluctuations of product markets. The system of rewards took the form of a series of salary increases over a course of years. Since promotions were among the major rewards that could be given for achievement, they also served to motivate personnel to develop their abilities. Because of these employment practices a series of positions tended to become a career that lasted to the age of mandatory retirement. It may be argued that these bylaws introduced a prototype of the Japanese employment system.[30] In the present context, however, it is important to point out that these employment practices generally followed bureaucratic principles of organizations.

As for training and education, the firms in the Mitsubishi group had good reason to emphasize intrafirm training conducted on the job.[31] Since the firms adopted a policy of internal recruitment, training programs were inseparably related to the system of promotion and transfer. It was not unusual for a higher-class white-collar employee (*seiin*) to be transferred from one office to another every three or four years. A natural inference from the extremely high rate of lateral and vertical mobility of *seiin* within a firm is that the firms maintained a kind of multiple chain promotional plan, which permitted several promotional opportunities through loosely defined avenues of approach to and exit from each position in the managerial hierarchies. In other words, higher-class white-collar employees were called upon to perform various kinds of tasks and to assume increasing responsibility and leadership rather than to specialize in a specific function. They were expected to be ready to acquire new skills and knowledge.

Promotion to top management positions was conducted in the same way. Promising candidates for top management were given various duties and were gradually promoted through a series of selections. In the 1920s, the firms of the Mitsubishi zaibatsu had altogether about 100 directors, an overwhelming majority of whom were inside directors. Although the Mitsubishi zaibatsu's stock ownership was not dispersed, most of the top management positions became a career stage in the life of employed officials rather than the exclusive prerogative of family members.

However, there was an obvious cost to the firms in frequent personnel changes, which sometimes involved functional changes at the same time. Since a substantial portion of employees' careers had to be devoted to on-the-job training for new duties, tasks were likely to be performed less efficiently than if there had been greater continuity of personnel. To deal with this problem experienced lower-class white-collar workers (*jun'in*) were attached to every department. In contrast to *seiin*, they were recruited locally and specialized in a narrow functional field throughout their careers. Theoretically speaking, therefore, it would be sufficient for a new manager to trust experienced subordinates with actual and detailed operations, while all he had to do was establish good human relations with his subordinates. In reality, however, human relations between *seiin* and *jun'in* were sometimes touchy indeed, although the distinction between them was justified by differences in educational background. While the barrier between *seiin* and *jun'in* was somewhat less impermeable than that separating white-collar employees and blue-collar workers, a man who started his career as a *jun'in* was not likely to advance very high in the managerial hierarchies.

III

A modern business enterprise is typically a large vertically integrated firm that has an extensive administrative organization. It performs a variety of functions that would otherwise be carried out by small independent firms that are governed by the invisible hand of the market mechanism. Therefore it can be theoretically assumed that a modern business enterprise has grown by taking over functions of previously independent firms and can prosper because it is controlled more effectively by its administrative organization than by the market mechanism.[32] In the course of its development it may integrate forward and embark on direct marketing and may integrate backward and start manufacturing raw materials and intermediate products that have been bought from outside suppliers.

However, this theoretical assumption does not fit the Japanese experience exactly. While we can point to several facts that seem to conflict with this assumption, the following is of special importance for the purpose of this paper. In the early developed countries, a new firm with limited capital could purcahse rather than manuture raw materials and parts at first, and after a period of profitable operation it might expand its business into processing activities as well as assembly work. But Japanese manufacturers sometimes could not find any reliable suppliers of raw materials and intermediate products that met their requirements both in quality and in quantity. They were therefore forced to make rather than buy all products, especially when quality was of great importance. In fact, some firms went so far as to make everything they could, giving no consideration to the possibility of purchasing from domestic suppliers.

In this regard the sharp contrast between American and Japanese automobile manufacturers in the formative era of the industry is exceedingly illuminating. In the United States, as is well known, independent parts suppliers have been an integral part of the industry from the beginning. Since the skills and machines required for automobile production were "not fundamentally different from those which had already developed for such products as bicycles and sewing machines,"[33] many existing firms in the engineering industry could supply automobile parts. Early automobile factories were therefore essentially assembly plants, which could be built with a small initial investment. In addition, their manufacturing operations could be financed to a considerable degree by buying components on credit and selling finished cars to dealers for cash. This is the main reason that so many firms entered this field.

In contrast to this, pioneering firms in the Japanese automobile industry, such as Toyota and Nissan, were strangers to the existing industrial structure. They demanded new raw materials, new parts, and specialized equipment, most of which required precision work that existing firms could not perform. The automobile firms were severely criticized for their ventures, which were likened to constructing a tall building from the roof down.[34] When Toyota embarked on automobile production in the 1930s, it had to overcome a series of difficulties in procurement.[35] First of all, alloy steels, which were indispensable in automobile manufacture, were not being produced by domestic steelmakers. Toyota had to build its own steel plant. Second, at first Toyota tried to purchase as many parts as possible. For example, important parts for the electric system, such as carburetors, ignition plugs, generators, and alternators, were at first imported from the United States. When Toyota tried to replace the imported parts with domestically manufactured ones, Japanese manufacturers could not supply products of satisfactory quality. In the end, therefore, Toyota began to make most of them itself. Third, since Toyota had to make a variety of parts, it had to develop many kinds of special-purpose machine tools that were suitable only for Toyota. Although some of them were ordered from foreign, mainly American, toolmakers, many were manufactured internally. These were the beginnings of Aichi Steel, Toyota Machine Tools, and Nippon Densō.[36] In this way, Toyota's factories in both Kariya and Koromo were highly integrated for their size from the outset.

Although examples of this sort can easily be multiplied, two more examples will suffice to attest to the fact that Toyota's experience was not an exception.

Hattori Seikō Co. had built up a fully integrated production system of clocks and watches by the end of World War I. After that the firm purchased only watch glasses from a domestic supplier and imported jewels from Switzerland. Not only all the other parts but also many machine tools were manufactured internally. According to Hijikata Shōgo, a director of the firm, the reason the firm built up such an extensive production system was as follows:

> [In the 1890s] when we began to manufacture clocks and watches, Japanese industries had not developed. Therefore we had to make almost all the components of watches and clocks ourselves. We installed a furnace for tempering main springs, a carpenter shop for making wooden frames for wall clocks, a kiln and printing machines for manufacturing enameled dial plates. . . . We had to enter every field, to say nothing of making machine tools.[37]

While this last remark is somewhat exaggerated,[38] it is true that the firm made every effort to build up a fully integrated production system. Its products were sometimes exact copies of American or Swiss watches, but the firm succeeded in developing several highly efficient machine tools and a production control system. An automatic pinion-cutting machine developed by Yoshikawa Tsuruhiko, the firm's chief engineer, was a masterpiece of mechanical engineering.[39] He apparently came up with many ideas on a trip to the United States. Monthly production of watches reached nearly 100,000 in the 1930s.

Niigata Engineering Co. built a new factory in Kamata in 1919. This factory specialized in the production of medium-sized marine diesel engines and made the firm a leading manufacturer in the field. According to the company history, however, "since it was impossible for us to procure parts from subcontractors, even nuts, bolts, and screws had to be manufactured internally. As a result factory managers had to make strenuous efforts to improve production efficiency."[40] To cope with the difficulties a mechanical engineer, Katō Shigeo, introduced the Taylor system in its entirety. He had learned about the system at Tabor Manufacturing Co. in Philadelphia, which was sometimes called a showcase for the Taylor system. In accordance with Frederick W. Taylor's principles, a planning room was set up and functional foremanship introduced. Katō tried to apply Taylor's theory that the added burden of supervisory personnel could be offset by increased efficiency.

From these three cases and other well-known examples, we may draw the following tentative conclusions concerning the structure of factory organization and the function of managers within it. In the early decades of the twentieth century, some big businesses began to manufacture technologically sophisticated products that had previously been imported from Western industrialized countries. These firms' main concern was not to develop new products but to manufacture known products cheaply enough to compete with foreign products, at least in the Japanese market. They sometimes manufactured exact copies of foreign products. At the same time, however, they had to build up a highly integrated production system from the outset. Their factories made use of kinds of processes and equipment that were technologically of the highest grade, by the standards of the time, and that had to be superintended by technical experts. The complexity of the production system also created problems of coordination, which in turn required many managers who had technical knowledge to perform coordinating functions. The firms employed many young engineers, whose supply was increasing rapidly.

From the late 1920s onward, therefore, with the advent of many young engineers, factory organization in the capital-intensive industries underwent a significant change and sometimes developed a unique structure that could be compared to the functional foremanship of the Taylor system.[41] Employers expected young engineers to plunge into the shop to deal with technical difficulties and problems of factory management. Generally speaking, these young men met their employers' expectations. The engineers took over several functions from the foreman and tried to control such factors as manufacturing costs, product quality, inventory levels, intensity of work, and so on in greater detail than before. The basic organizational structure that resulted is shown in Figure 1.[42]

The young engineers were commonly *kakariin*. As is shown in the figure, their offices were near the shop floor because their main duty was to maintain a high operating ratio of expensive equipment, some of which had been imported from advanced countries, and their technical knowledge had to be supplemented by practical experience on the shop floor. It was not unusual, however, for their position in the line of authority of the factory organization to be only vaguely defined. According to the figure, they were staff assitants to the subsection head. In fact, as mentioned above, they took over several of the foreman's managerial functions. At that time there was a marked status discrimination between *kōin* and *shokuin*; *shokuin* tended to give instructions directly to *kōin*, the rank-and-file workers, regardless of the foreman's will. The author-

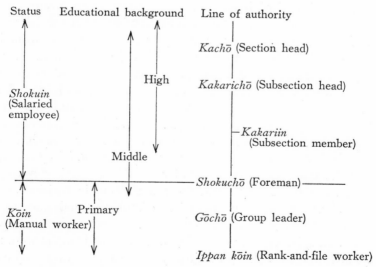

FIG. 1   Model of Shop Organization.

ity of the *shokuin* stemmed partly from the very fact that they were *shokuin*, with a higher educational background than *koin*, and partly from their technical expertise. In any case, their functions were executory in nature, and there was some division of labor among them according to their technical specialties. As a result the shop organization bore a close resemblance to the functional foremanship of the Taylor system.

The position of the foreman was also vague. Although he was engaged in supervisory tasks, he might not consider himself a full-fledged *shokuin* because he had been promoted from *kōin* in recognition of his long service. The position of foreman was commonly regarded as the highest job to which a rank-and-file worker without much educational background could be promoted. Although his influence was waning, he might maintain closer social relations with the manual workers than with the young engineers and could still exert a strong influence on the labor management of subordinate workers.

It was quite natural, therefore, that young, energetic engineers sometimes could not get along with older, experienced foremen. The lack of cooperation between theory-oriented young engineers without practical experience and older, experienced foremen with no theoretical knowledge caused many serious managerial problems. Needless to say, however, many firms benefited from having engineer-administrators in their factories. In cases where much imported technology and equipment had been introduced, some engineers were sent abroad to learn the operational know-how. This was an effective method of developing their technical abilities as well as of improving production efficiency. Most engineers with a middle-level educational background devoted most of their career to a particular factory or a specific functional area. They assumed most of the managerial responsibility for the factory's day-to-day operation. Although they could not make strategic decisions, they introduced many minor changes in technologies and managerial practices that had a significant cumulative effect on cost and productivity. In spite of their efforts, however, these benefits were not always advantageous enough to justify the increased overhead costs that were required to employ many engineer-administrators.

As has been mentioned several times, Japanese firms in technology-intensive sectors were forced to integrate backward from the beginning. To coordinate the activities of the integrated production processes they had to employ many engineer-administrators, considering their size. On the other hand, we may assume that other factors being equal, such as the number of men employed, the more integrated a firm was, the smaller the scale of each integrated production process within the organization had to be. In other words, integration meant small-scale operation, which sometimes hindered engineer-administrators from rationalizing production and managerial practices. It seems reasonable to conclude that few firms could overcome these difficulties.

Concluding Remarks

There is some reason to believe that owner-managers are unwilling to dilute their power and control over their personal or family firms by employing professional nonfamily managers in the managerial organization. It is often argued, therefore, that the rise of the big corporate enterprise brings about a greater dispersion of stock ownership, which in turn results in a decline of the shareholders' power and a steady enhancement of managerial authority. In the history of Japanese business, however, we find a few important exceptions to this rule.

First, many entrepreneurs in the Meiji era had to depend heavily on hired managers who had acquired Western technologies and business practices. Because of the shortage of managerial talent, these managers could exert a strong influence on the management of the firm that employed them. Many important decisions could be initiated only by them. They paved the way for the early development of managerial hierarchies in the Japanese business system.

Second, although a zaibatsu remained a family enterprise, it developed an extensive managerial organization. As is well known, every zaibatsu was dominated by a tightly owned holding company in which the bulk of the family fortune was invested. The zaibatsu family potentially retained absolute power over the holding company as well as a series of operating subsidiaries. However, as was mentioned above, managerial responsibility was vested in hired managers from the early Meiji era onward. With the growing size and complexity of the firm's operations, this tendency grew ever stronger. After the turn of the century the increased supply of university graduates made it possible for big firms to build up extensive managerial structures.

At that time it was common practice for a big firm to classify its white-collar workers into two categories, such as *seiin* and *jun'in* in Mitsubishi. This distinction was quite rigorously geared to educational qualifications. Middle-school graduates went into lower-ranking white-collar positions and university graduates into higher managerial positions. In the case of the Mitsubishi zaibatsu, a series of bylaws that clearly prescribed employment practices for higher-class white-collar workers was introduced. Their employment was considered permanent. They were called upon to perform various kinds of tasks and to assume increasing responsibility rather than to specialize in a specific function. Promotion to top management was conducted in the same way. As a result, most of the top managerial positions became a career stage in the life of successful salaried managers.

Lower-class white-collar workers specialized in a specific functional field throughout their careers. Since pioneering firms in new industries, such as automobile manufacturing, were forced to integrate backward extensively from the beginning, they had to employ many engineer-administrators of this category, considering their size. Factory organization underwent a significant change with the emergence of these engineer-administrators. They took over many managerial functions from the foreman and made important contributions to the rationalization of factory operations. Generally speaking, however, few firms could overcome the disadvantage that stemmed from the complex and small-scale production system.

NOTES

1. Reinhard Bendix, *Work and Authority in Industry*, Berkeley, University of California Press, 1974, pp. 254–55.
2. The proportion of people employed in the service industries was

abnormally high in prewar Japan in comparison with the proportion in other industrialized countries. There were many under-
employed people in these industries. This shift of employment,
therefore, cannot be taken entirely as a sign of industrial maturity.

3. Prime Minister's Office, *Taishō 9 nen kokusei chōsa hōkoku: Kijutsu hen*
(Report of the first national census of 1920: Descriptive volume),
Prime Minister's Office, 1932, p. 144.

4. Bendix, *Work and Authority*, pp. 211–26.

5. For the internal organization of the merchant houses in the Edo
period see Johannes Hirschmeier & Yui Tsunehiko, *The Development
of Japanese Business, 1600–1980*, 2nd ed., London, George Allen &
Unwin, 1981, pp. 38–40.

6. Yasuoka Shigeaki, ed., *Nippon no zaibatsu* (The zaibatsu of Japan),
Tokyo, Nihon Keizai Shimbunsha, 1976.

7. Masuda worked for Walsh Hall & Co. For his experiences in Yokohama see Chō Yukio, *Zaikai hyaku nen* (One hundred years of the
business community), Tokyo, Chikuma Shobō, 1969, pp. 29–41.
This book includes the main part of his autobiography.

8. Herbert Passin, *Society and Education in Japan*, Tokyo, Kōdansha
International, 1982, p. 94.

9. Toyo Cotton Spinning Co., *Tōyō Bōseki 70 nen shi* (70 years of Toyo
Cotton Spinning Company), Toyo Cotton Spinning Co., 1953,
pp. 22–3.

10. Although most of these model factories did not make a profit, they
made a notable contribution to the introduction of Western technologies to Japan.

11. Emi Kōichi, "Meiji no keizai hatten to kyōiku tōshi" (Economic
development and investment in human capital in the Meiji era),
Hitotsubashi ronshū (Hitotsubashi Economic Review), Vol. 48, No. 6,
1962, pp. 97–8.

12. This section is based mainly on Ministry of Communications, *Teishin
jigyō shi* (History of the post and telegraphic service), Ministry of
Communications, 1940, Vol. 1, pp. 610–88.

13. The main source of supply was the government agencies, which
attracted officials by offering remunerative terms of employment.

14. Chō, ed., *Zaikai*, p. 51.

15. Johannes Hirschmeier, *The Origins of Entrepreneurship in Meiji Japan*,
Cambridge, Mass., Harvard University Press, 1964, pp. 248–49.

16. Fujiwara Ginjirō, *Watashi no keiken to kangaekata* (My experiences and
way of thinking), Tokyo, Kōdansha, 1984, pp. 223–31, 285–90.

17. Mishima Yasuo, *Mitsubishi zaibatsu* (The Mitsubishi zaibatsu), To-kyo, Nihon Keizai Shimbunsha, 1981, pp. 81–4.

18. Nagasaki Shipyard Department of Labor, "Nagasaki Zōsensho rōmushi" (History of labor management at Nagasaki Shipyard), Nagasaki Shipyard Department of Labor, mimeographed, 1930, Vol. 2, p. 9.

19. *Ibid.*, pp. 138–40.

20. Mishima, *Mitsubishi zaibatsu*, pp. 85–100.

21. The first head of this department was Okumura Masao. See Nihon Keizai Shimbunsha, ed., *Watashi no rirekisho* (My personal history), Tokyo, Nihon Keizai Shimbunsha, Vol. 17, pp. 9–72.

22. Mishima, *Mitsubishi zaibatsu*, pp. 170–75.

23. Mitsubishi Mining & Cement Co., *Mitsubishi Kōgyō shashi* (History of Mitsubishi Mining & Cement Company), Mitsubishi Mining & Cement Co., 1976, pp. 278–82.

24. *Ibid.*, p. 285.

25. Mitsubishi Gōshi Co., *Mitsubishi shashi* (History of Mitsubishi), Mitsubishi Gōshi Co.; reprinted, Tokyo, University of Tokyo Press, 1982, Vol. 34, pp. 6,881–82.

26. Hirasawa Kan and Nagaoka Tokuji were instrumental in bringing about many reforms in labor management.

27. Mitsubishi Gōshi Co., *Mitsubishi shashi*, Vol. 21, pp. 1,347–49.

28. *Ibid.*, Vol. 22, pp. 1,624–25; Vol. 24, pp. 3,188–90.

29. *Ibid.*, Vol. 26, pp. 3,812–13, 3,911–14.

30. The so-called Japanese employment system at first covered only higher-class white-collar employees.

31. As was mentioned above, universities offered minimal vocational training.

32. Alfred D. Chandler, Jr., and Herman Daems, eds., *Managerial Hierarchies: Comparative Perspectives on the Rise of the Modern Industrial Enterprise*, Cambridge, Mass., Harvard University Press, 1980, pp. 9–14.

33. N. Rosenberg, "Technological Change in the Machine Tool In-dustry, 1840–1910," *Journal of Economic History*, Vol. 22, No. 4, 1963, p. 437.

34. Toyota Motor Corp., *Toyota Jidōsha 30 nen shi* (Thirty years of Toyota Motor Corporation), Toyota Motor Co., 1967, p. 195.

35. Ozaki Masashi, *Toyoda Kiichirō shi* (Toyoda Kiichirō), Jikensha, 1955, pp. 152–75.

36. Toyota Motor Corp., pp. 196–202.

37. Hijikata Shōgo, "Yoshikawa Tsuruhiko ō no koto" (On Yoshikawa Tsuruhiko), *Daini seikō*, No. 5, 1956, p. 2.
38. At first Seikō imported several important parts from Switzerland.
39. Daitō Eisuke, "Pinion jidōki no kaihatsu" (Development of the automatic pinion-cutting machine), mimeographed, 1981.
40. Niigata Engineering Co., *Niigata Tekkō 70 nen shi* (70 years of Niigata Engineering), Niigata Engineering Co., pp. 53–4.
41. This section depends heavily on Okamoto Hideaki, *Kōgyōka to genba kantokusha* (Industrialization and first-line supervisors), Nippon Rōdō Kyōkai, 1966.
42. This is a modified version of a figure in Tsuda Masumi, *Nippon no rōmu kanri* (Labor management in Japan), Tokyo, University of Tokyo Press, 1970, p. 101.

Comment

Takayuki Miura
Fukuoka University

Professor Daitō's study on the formation of middle managers in Japan is a pioneering work. It is both interesting and excellent. I wish to pose three questions, concerning (1) the positioning of engineer-administrators which Professor Daitō stresses, (2) the functions of labor mobility within a firm, and (3) the connection with Professor Lazonick's main theme, that is, a comparative study on the basis of bureaucratic integration and bureaucratic segmentation.

1. According to Professor Daitō, it seems likely that as production processes become more capital intensive, they also tend to become more management intensive. He discusses capital-intensive industries in the third section of his paper. For example, from the outset Japanese automobile manufacturers had to set up a new field of procurement in order to build up a highly integrated production system, and in so doing benefited from having engineer-administrators in their factories. As it happens, the term "engineer" is a key term in Professor Lazonick's paper, as well.

Undoubtedly, since the high marketability of such products as automobiles had been fully demonstrated in the United States, such products were not entirely new in Japan, having been imported from the United States. Therefore, the importance of engineer-administrators may have been evaluated much more highly than that of sales administrators in these industries. However, I wish to ask about the trend in the proportion of engineer-administrators, sales administrators, and commercial administrators (that is, administrators in departments of accounting, personnel, and so on) who, in compliance with the conventional Japanese triad of white-collar workers, later became members of top management in capital-intensive industries. Generally speaking, in Japan university graduates with law degrees were treated with special consideration in the public and private sectors alike during the early decades of the twentieth century. According to Table 2 in Professor Morikawa's response to Professor Yamasaki's comment, the number of top salaried managers with technology degrees increased about 4.5 times during the years 1913–30. However, the percentage of top salaried managers with technology degrees was still only 32.2% in 1930.

   2.   Analyzing the case of the Mitsubishi zaibatsu, Professor Daitō pays attention to the roles of lateral and vertical mobility of employees within a firm. I think that his explanation of vertical mobility is very persuasive. In regard to lateral mobility, however, Professor Daitō's explanation would be well supplemented by Professor Lazonick's explanation. Professor Lazonick notes that promising specialists were periodically rotated from region to region, department to department, and function to function in order to give them a broader understanding of operations necessary for the generalist.

   This reminds me of a recent newspaper article by Makita Hisao. Makita is now the chairman of Nippon Kōkan, one of the biggest steelmakers in Japan. Fifty years have passed since he joined the company in 1934 (23 years as an employee and another 27 years as a director). He writes, "I experienced almost all functions: cost accounting, shop management, purchasing, inventory, sales, personnel, general affairs, labor relations, factory chief, president of a subsidiary, and so on. This experience gladdened and enlightened me. Although I often had a hard time, this valuable experience has been truly helpful, especially after becoming president" (*Nihon Keizai Shimbun*, 3 January, 1985).

   I would like to evaluate the role of lateral mobility as an important function of managerial capitalism. In principle, lower-class white-collar workers were recruited locally, were attached to every department, and specialized in a narrow functional field throughout their career. As Professor Daitō states, "Employment was considered to be permanent and not to be influenced by short-run fluctuations of product markets." Under these conditions, however, what happened in multidivisional enterprises in Japan when one of their divisions became depressed?

Which is the more plausible answer, operation reduction accompanied by layoffs or operation reduction accompanied by the lateral shifting of employees from an unprofitable division to a profitable one? Nagasaki Shipbuilding of Mitsubishi Heavy Industries has implemented a long-term lateral-mobility project since 1979 to cope with the recent shipbuilding depression. The divisions to which employees can be transferred include a wide range inside the Mitsubishi group but outside the company, such as Mitsubishi Motors, as well as inside the company but outside the division, such as Nagoya Aircraft. Even without market coordination, a speedy reallocation of human resources can be achieved through administrative coordination.

Of course there were occasional dismissals in prewar Japan. However, I would like to ask Professor Daitō to what degree lateral mobility in reaction to business trends occurred during the prewar period. In addition, I wonder if Professor Daitō's statistics concerning prewar lateral mobility at Mitsubishi include two types of cases: employees transferred because of business trends and employees transferred to enable them to acquire greater experience.

3. I would like to ask Professor Daitō how we should locate the Japanese characteristics of management development in terms of the classification of bureaucratic integration and bureaucratic segmentation adopted by Professor Lazonick. The very existence of three layers of workers with different educational backgrounds, such as *seiin, jun'in,* and *kōin,* and the more or less segmented system of higher education in Japan seem to have been similar to the British experience. However, almost every higher-level white-collar worker had to start his career as a specialist at the bottom of the organization even though he might be a prospective candidate for top management.

On the other hand, the stress on higher technological education and job rotation for career formation seems to have been similar to the American situation. In the United States a university education was important for rapid promotion "not because of the prestige but rather because of the knowledge that it provided" (Professor Lazonick's paper). However, in Japan "it would be sufficient for a new manager (*seiin*) to trust experienced subordinates (*jun'in*) with actual and detailed operations, while all he had to do was establish good human relations" (Professor Daitō's paper). If that was the case, the situation was fairly complex.

Response

Eisuke Daitō

To offer a precise answer to Professor Miura's first question, we must gather a vast amount of biographical data on top executives in the capital-intensive industries in the early decades of the twentieth century. Although such data are not available, I am sure that most of the Japanese participants in the conference can agree with me on the following: (1) As Professor Miura points out, university graduates with law degrees had an advantage over those with other degrees in the early stage of industrialization of the Japanese economy. This tradition lasted well into the twentieth century, especially at big and bureaucratized firms, such as Mitsui and Mitsubishi. (2) Top managers who had begun their careers as engineers began to play an important role in the decision-making processes of firms in the 1960s and 1970s, when the heavy and chemical industries grew rapidly. (3) Marketing has been the least developed managerial function of manufacturing firms except in a few industries that manufacture consumer durables, such as automobiles and electric appliances. Most manufacturers have relied heavily on the traditional distribution network, which consists of middlemen of various kinds. It seems probable, therefore, that sales managers' power in firms has not been strong.

I am a bit confused by Professor Miura's second question. I contend in my paper that locally recruited white-collar workers (*jun'in*)

were not covered by the lifetime employment system. I prepared
Table 4 to show that their employment was influenced by short-
run fluctuations of product markets. A series of bylaws to which
I refer in the paper defined the rules and procedures governing
vertical movement of centrally recruited white-collar workers (*seiin*)
within the firm. However, Professor Miura seems to ask his question
assuming that *jun'in* enjoyed job security because of lateral mobility
among divisions within the firm.

The third question is very important but difficult to answer. At
Mitsubishi the employees were classified into three categories: *seiin*,
jun'in, and *kōin*. Each had many subcategories. Starting salaries for
seiin differed according to the social prestige of the universities from
which they had graduated, the foremen occupied an ambiguous
position between management and workers, and so on. In short,
Mitsubishi developed a highly segmented hierarchical organization.
To unify this segmented system, the *seiin* had to be generalists and to
establish good relations with their subordinates. In recent years it
has sometimes been stressed that Japanese firms are blessed with
close and harmonious human relations among employees, which
result in high productivity and good business performance. In prewar times, however, the social and economic distance between
managers and workers of various kinds was much greater than
today. It is very likely that Japan was located somewhere between
the two extremes of the United States and the United Kingdom.
At the moment, however, we should refrain from drawing a general
conclusion from a single case study on the Mitsubishi combine.

The Railways and the Development of Managerial Enterprise in Britain, 1850–1939

T. R. Gourvish
University of East Anglia

I

Britain's emergence as the "first industrial nation" in the eighteenth century was based, in entrepreneurial terms, on the owner as manager and on the family-financed firm. Salaried managers, holding positions of responsibility, were not unknown, of course. They emerged, for example, in the chartered trading companies, such as the East India Company, and in the upper ranks of the military. Indeed, in Britain the army quartermaster and the naval captain were perhaps the best examples of managers in the classic period of the Industrial Revolution, that is, between 1760 and 1830.

This is not to say that nonowning, salaried officials were absent from key industries, such as mining, textiles, and metals. But they were not managerial capitalists, and the businesses that employed them were not managerial enterprises. The typical manufacturing enterprise was small, with relatively modest fixed capital requirements, with a labor force that was numbered in tens and hundreds rather than in thousands, and with operations concentrated on one location. Consequently, in the partnership form of organization one of the partners might act as a "managing partner," or a manager might be recruited from among the junior members of the participating families. In many enterprises, entrepreneurs and managers were difficult to distinguish. And where the separation was made, salaried officials rarely took part in strategic decision making. They were often little more than foremen fulfilling supervisory functions at the shop-floor level.[1]

Of the leading industrial countries, Britain was comparatively late in developing managerial capitalism and the large-scale com-

pany on a significant scale. As Leslie Hannah tells us, modern corporations were essentially creations of the twentieth century or,
more exactly, of the 1920s.[2] This lag is usually contrasted with
conditions in the United States and in Germany before 1914, and is
frequently cited when historians seek explanations for Britain's lower
growth rate and loss of world market dominance after 1870. The
prevalence of the family firm and the absence of salaried managers
of high status have been associated not only with constraints upon
investment and technological advance but also with a lower level of
entrepreneurial drive as the dynamism generated by first- and
second-generation owners was dissipated by those who followed.

Recently, Bernard Elbaum and William Lazonick have sought to
connect Britain's relative decline with institutional rigidities in education, finance, labor relations, and state policy. These rigidities are
held to have inhibited the development of the large-scale corporation and market dominance necessary to the successful introduction
of mass-production methods.[3] Controversial and inadequately supported as this thesis is—although we expect more proof to emerge
when the authors' book *The Decline of the British Economy*[4] is
published—it is certainly true that Britain's industrial leaders
experienced, from the mid-nineteenth century onward, a far from
enthusiastic reception from the land-based ruling elite. There was
a general distaste for things industrial, and the socioeconomic advance of an individual or family was expected to involve a move
from industry to finance and land ownership, not vice versa. There
was, then, a growing "sociocultural drag" upon entrepreneurship,
which Martin Wiener has recently termed a "decline of the industrial spirit."[5]

While the importance of social encouragement in industrial success must not be exaggerated—it is not certain that German industrialists fared any better, for example[6]—it does appear that British
industrialists, in their desire to join the established elite, were
induced to divide their time between their businesses and the life
of a landed gentleman, politician, or patron of the arts. This did
not lead immediately to the rise of managerial capitalism, however.
In Britain the "gentleman," or educated amateur owner, to borrow
Donald Coleman's cricketing metaphor, continued to dominate the

"player," or professional salaried manager, until the Second World War and beyond.[7]

II

Whatever may be said for this stereotype of entrepreneurial failure and managerial backwardness, the British railway industry cannot be fitted into it. Recently, historians have done much to rescue the railways from the charge of poor management and disappointing performance during the more mature stage of their operations, that is, after 1870.[8] Furthermore, this new industry, the pride of the Victorian economy, was distinguished by quite novel elements. First, it was a large industry in every way. Its fixed capital needs were exceptionally great. By 1875 the capital raised by U.K. railway companies had reached £630 million, considerably more than the capital raised by such industries as cotton or iron and steel. By 1913 the figure had increased to £1,330 million. Second, the railways' labor force was both large and dispersed. In 1873 it amounted to 275,000 workers, about 3% of the occupied male labor force, and in 1913 there were 643,000 railwaymen, 4.5% of all occupied males. Third, company turnover was high. Gross revenue was running at £52 million a year in the first half of the 1870s, double that of the coal industry, and in 1913 it amounted to £140 million.[9]

Of equal significance for the development of managerial capitalism in the industry, the railways experienced a high level of concentration from an early stage. In 1850, only 20 years after the opening of the Liverpool & Manchester Railway, growth and merger stimulated by an investment mania and intensifying government control left the top 15 companies in control of 61% of U.K. paid-up railway capital and 75% of the industry's gross revenue. By 1870 the same companies controlled 80% of the capital and 83% of the revenue. It is also possible to identify a "big four"—the London & North Western, Midland, Great Western, and North Eastern—which in 1870 accounted for 38% of capital and 44% of revenue. The level of concentration was broadly similar until the Railways Act of 1921 provided for the merger of existing companies into four quasi-monopolistic giants in 1923.[10]

Each of the large companies was in essence a multiunit concern not only providing and selling transport but also manufacturing rolling stock and gas, and sometimes, like the London & North Western Railway, making its own steel rails. Indeed, the railway workshops taken alone rank as large companies in comparison with the rest of British manufacturing.[11] Railway companies were all public joint-stock concerns with limited liability and a dispersed ownership. Each of the major companies must have had at least 20,000 individual investors in an authorized and paid-up capital ranging, in 1914, from £30 million to £204 million. In these circumstances, only the 15–20 directors of the company were in a position to influence directly the policies that it pursued.

This contrasts with the position in most of the manufacturing firms. Even when they were converted from private into public companies, the founding families usually retained controlling blocks of shares. A common strategy was to offer to the public only preference shares or debenture stock, leaving the ordinary capital, and hence voting power, in the hands of the founders.[12] The railway industry also contrasted with manufacturing in the degree of government control to which it was subject. Although the promotion and building of railways in Britain represent a prime example of free-enterprise capitalism on a large scale, the government took an increasing interest in most aspects of railway management. By the turn of the century there was little that the government did not supervise, from merger proposals and financial management to pricing, safety measures, and labor relations.[13] These elements, large, complex companies with a dispersed ownership operating under oligopolistic conditions subject to government control, stimulated a higher level of management organization, making the railways, in Alfred Chandler's phrase, "pioneers in modern corporate management."[14]

Given these conditions, it is scarcely surprising that the railways, Britain's first examples of large-scale industrial enterprise, should have encouraged the separation of ownership and control and managerial capitalism, which may be defined as a situation where "salaried managers occupy positions of top management and make strategic decisions independently of owners."[15] After an initial period of uncertainty from about 1830 to 1850, when railway companies were forced to look outside the industry for managerial recruits, a chief executive emerged in nearly all the major concerns in the person of the "general manager." At the same time, organization of the companies on a departmental, that is, "functional" basis stimulated the emergence of specialist departmental managers —engineers both civil and mechanical, accountants, lawyers, surveyors, and architects. Some of these reached the top as general managers.

Increasingly, however, the railways trained and developed their own managerial talent, with management development concentrated in the traffic or operating department. Although movement of personnel among railway companies and to and from other sectors of the economy did occur, there was a preference for nurturing promising educated recruits by means of special executive apprenticeship schemes. Here would-be general managers were given a thorough grounding in railway management. The first of these schemes appears to have been organized by the Manchester Sheffield & Lincolnshire Railway in the early 1850s and was developed in the 1890s by the North Eastern, which placed particular emphasis on the recruitment of university graduates. This form of management development reached its apogee with the London & North Eastern Railway's traffic apprenticeship scheme in the interwar years. It produced many of the leading managers of the first two decades of nationalized railway administration after 1947.[16]

Before 1923 organization was overwhelmingly centralized in nature, based on the general manager as chief executive at the top. Although there were geographical divisions or districts at a subordinate level, railway headquarters were departmentally structured. Civil engineering (track), mechanical engineering (motive power and rolling stock), operating (carrying traffic), and commercial (selling) functions were separated in varying degrees, and were then coordinated in the strategic decision-making processes of the general manager and the board of directors to which he was responsible. The extent to which general managers made major decisions independently of the board or led the board in making strategic decisions affecting investment, marketing, pricing, and operating naturally varied from company to company. But some examples must be given to demonstrate that managerial capitalism *was* established, in part at least, from the time the major companies first appeared.

Skill in developing cartels to fix prices and traffic volumes, whether formal or informal, enabled Captain Mark Huish to lead the largest joint-stock concern of the day as general manager of the London & North Western from 1846, the date of the company's inception, until his fall from grace in 1858.[17] James Allport frequently dominated the policies of the Midland Railway, both as general manager (1853–57, 1860–80) and as a director (1857–60, 1880–92). The company's decision to establish independent access to London in the 1860s was very much his.[18] Two notable buccaneers, Edward Watkin and James Staats Forbes, proved to be managerial capitalists par excellence for a whole host of railway companies, large and small, in the 1860–1900 period. Beginning their careers as middle managers, then acting as general managers, they usually acted as "chairman and managing director," and at the height of their influence controlled about 14% of the industry's total capital. In addition, they held numerous directorships, often with a managerial function, in other industries, such as insurance, telecommunications, electricity, finance, and manufacturing. While there is no question at all that Watkin and Forbes dominated the overall strategies pursued by their railway companies, it must be conceded that they were themselves dependent in turn on the work of competent executives below them, men such as John Bell and Myles Fenton.[19] By 1914, then, the general manager had become a figure of enormous prestige and power in the railway industry in Britain. Furthermore, the function of managing director, which resembled the president of an American railroad, had been firmly established and could be seen in the role of such executives as James Thompson of the Caledonian Railway and Guy Granet of the Midland.[20]

III

Controversy arises when we examine the relevance of the railways' example to the development of more sophisticated management systems and top-level executive status in the British economy as a whole. The persistence of relatively small family-dominated firms into the twentieth century has led Leslie Hannah to conclude, in *The Rise of the Corporate Economy* (1976), that while it was "possible to discern many of the characteristics of modern corporations in the large railway enterprises"—growth by merger, the separation of ownership and control, professional managers—"the railways presented unique problems different in kind from those encountered in large manufacturing corporations." Because railways were the prime example of social overhead capital in nineteenth-century Britain—above all, a public utility—there was a marked tendency to monopoly and government control "in the public interest" despite the fact that railways had been promoted and financed privately.[21] By implication, then, Hannah sees the railways as an exceptional and not very instructive example for an economy characterized by small productive units and the retention of control by family-based, nonmanagerial capitalists. The transformation in the twentieth century "from a disaggregated structure of predominantly small, competing firms to a concentrated structure dominated by large, and often monopolistic, corporations" owed little to the experience of the railways.[22]

Moreover, Hannah suggests that "there appears to have been little managerial spin-off from . . . the railways to the manufacturing sector. Indeed in the twentieth century such spin-off as occurred appears to have been in the reverse direction."[23] Elsewhere, Hannah has followed Gary Hawke in arguing that railway management resources were rarely if ever transferred to other sectors of the economy,[24] and in his introduction to *Management Strategy and Business Development* (1976) has asserted that "new management methods tended to come from engineers and accountants rather than from men with railway experience."[25] To press this point home, Hannah refers specifically to the example of Sir Josiah (later Lord) Stamp, who was appointed president of the executive of the London Midland & Scottish Railway (L.M.S.) in 1926. The following year he absorbed the position of chairman of the board, thus becoming in effect chairman and managing director of this giant enterprise, with capital in 1923 of £385 million and an annual turnover of £85.5 million, until his death in an air raid on London in 1941. Stamp, a versatile man who had been a civil servant, academic economist, and director of Nobel Industries (from 1926 part of I.C.I.), was recruited for his knowledge of management and administrative systems outside the railway industry. Here, then, was a prime case of spin-off operating *to* rather than *from* the railways.

Hannah's argument that there was little managerial spin-off from the railways to other sectors is rather weak for the period before 1923, at least as far as movements of senior managers are concerned. Such spin-off as occurred was mostly *from* the railway industry *to* other sectors, including insurance, utilities, and manufacturing. James Allport, for example, left the Midland Railway in 1857 to become managing director of Palmer's, the Jarrow shipbuilding firm. Sam Fay, the general manager of the Great Central Railway in the early twentieth century, left to become chairman of Beyer Peacock, the engineering and locomotive building firm. Frank Tatlow of the Midland was chairman of Carpet Trades Ltd. and a director of British Soda, Staveley Coal & Iron Co., and Yorkshire Main Colliery Co.[26] This does not mean that the railways encouraged any significant moves toward managerial capitalism in the British economy, either by presenting nonrailway companies with organizational models or by providing the means to create new, multiunit enterprises. Here the contrast with the United States is striking, of course. In America the emergence of the large railroads and the new corporations was virtually synonymous. However, in Britain the railways made their appearance in the 1820s, when the pattern of economic activity based on textiles, coal, iron, and metals in the midlands, northwest, and Yorkshire was already established. Railways were regarded as merely a superior mode of transport rather than a necessary accompaniment to the establishment of new enterprises exploiting a mass market. Although railways did have an impact in extending the market in such industries as brewing, they also helped to reinforce existing local specialization by family firms. It was not until the end of the nineteenth century that the first managerial enterprises appeared outside the railway industry.[27] Nevertheless, the large railway companies did remain for several decades the only places where managers could operate in a bureaucratic environment divorced from the persistent intervention of owners, and there is no doubt at all that the railways did much to establish the status of the business executive, as seen in the prestigious figure of the general manager.

Returning to Hannah's argument, it is surely misleading to imply, as he does, that railways looked outside for managerial guidance in the interwar years. Stamp of the L.M.S. was very much the exception to the rule of internal succession for senior managers. He was, in fact, the *only* man to come directly from outside the industry to head the executive of a major British railway company between 1850 and the nationalization of the railways in 1947. In any case, what the L.M.S. was attempting to do with Stamp— create a new management structure based on a functional executive committee of the president and four vice-presidents—served as a model for other industrial companies seeking to alter their organizational systems or import managerial expertise. Indeed, many manufacturing enterprises aped an old railway practice in the interwar years, that of recruiting senior military personnel who had taken early retirement.[28]

If Stamp was an example of the railway industry's importation of managerial expertise, then there was a move in the opposite direction in 1929, when Sir Felix Pole, general manager of the Great Western Railway since 1921, resigned to become chairman of the newly formed electrical company Associated Electrical Industries (A.E.I.), a merger of British Thompson-Houston and Metropolitan-Vickers.[29] Hannah appears to have conceded the point in his second edition of *The Corporate Economy*. He cites Michael Bonavia's *Railway Policy Between the Wars* in justification of the argument that manufacturing companies poached young trainee managers from such railway companies as the London & North Eastern because they had no training schemes of their own.[30]

IV

References to the interwar years lead us to the conclusion that the linkages between the railways and the development of corporations in Britain from the 1920s onward have not been fully explored. There is certainly scope for such a study, and as Roy

Church has reminded us, "there is . . . more than an element of truth in the accusation that too many British business historians pay too little attention to the exploration of general business processes and structures, and the connections between business enterprises, industrial and commercial organizations and change."[31] In fact, the problem runs much deeper than this, since there is no modern business history of any of the four railway companies that made up the greater part of the industry after 1923: the L.M.S., L.N.E.R., Great Western, and Southern.

The Railways Act of 1921, operational from 1 January 1923, created an industrial amalgamation in the grand manner. One hundred and twenty-three of the existing two hundred and fourteen railway companies were compulsorily merged into four giant regional enterprises after the failure of plans to nationalize the industry in the wake of the First World War. Although competition was certainly not eliminated, due to the retention of several duplicate routes between the leading industrial centers, the Act established vast areas of railway monopoly until the appearance of an effective challenge from road transport in the 1930s. The four new railway companies were much larger than anything known in the United Kingdom before the Second World War, as Table 1 attempts to demonstrate. While there may be some doubt about the extent to which managerial capitalism took root in the new conglomerates of British industry from the 1920s on—note, for example, the dominance of owner-entrepreneurs in brewing companies, such as Whitbread, and the control of Lever Brothers/Unilever by William Lever to 1925—the railway industry remains the exemplar of interwar corporatism. Stamp dominated the L.M.S. in a highly centralized organization in which the board of directors, which included such businessmen as Alan Anderson, E. B. Fielden, and Sir Guy Granet (the latter an ex-railway general manager), relied upon its executive committee to formulate business strategy. Each of the vice-presidents was responsible for a defined function of management: finance, traffic, engineering, and research. Elsewhere, the more traditional form of railway organization persisted, based upon departments and a nonexecutive board. On the Great Western, this did not prevent Pole and his successor, Sir James Milne, general manager

TABLE 1   Leading U.K. Companies by Issued Capital and Turnover, 1938.

Company	Issued Capital (£ million)	Turnover (£ million)
L.M.S.	413.8	72.5
L.N.E.R.	376.9	53.6
Southern	161.8	25.6
G.W.R.	149.8	31.0
Other companies		
I.C.I.	83.3*	52.8
Lever Bros. & Unilever	72.5**	n.a.
Imperial Tobacco	51.1***	n.a.

    *   Includes external shares in subsidiary companies. W. J. Reader's estimate of capital employed is approximately £96.6 million.
  **   English company only. English and Dutch=£119.4 million.
***   Includes deposits in regard to subsidiary and associated companies.
Sources: *Universal Directory of Railway Officials and Railway Year Book 1939–40*, 1939; Company Records, 1938, Guildhall Library, London; W. J. Reader, *Imperial Chemical Industries: A History*, London, 1975, Vol. 2, p. 497.

from 1929 to 1947, from dominating much of the strategic decision making. Similarly, on the Southern, the successes of that company in the areas of investment, passenger traffic, and diversification are usually attributed to the skill and energy of Sir Herbert Walker, general manager from 1923 to 1937.[32]

How decisions were actually taken is another matter, of course. There is a difference between theoretical dominance of an organization and actual dominance, and it is difficult to find anything for the interwar years' railways to match Geoffrey Channon's impressive analysis of the Midland Railway's decision-making processes in the 1850s and 1860s.[33] Here M.R. Bonavia's work on the L.N.E.R. is at least a starting point. That company certainly possessed an exceptional general manager, Sir Ralph Wedgwood (1923–39), Cambridge-educated and one of the most gifted of a long line of managerial recruits trained by the company and its predecessor, the North Eastern. On the other hand, the L.N.E.R.'s decentralized organization, based on three divisions as geographically based units corresponding to the areas served by the parent companies, the Great Northern, the Great Eastern, and the North Eastern, worked against central control. Furthermore, the board of directors, which like the others had more than its fair share of landed aristocrats and included prominent local industrialists, such as Geoffrey Kitson and Sir Charles Barrie, was not merely a collection of passive spectators. With money extremely tight in a company that was suffering badly from the recession in British heavy industry, the board kept a firm hand on investment and maintenance expenditure, and its committee structure apparently enabled individual directors to play a part in deciding matters of detail. Bonavia's comments may be based on the unsupported recollections of one or two former railway managers—although he himself worked for the company in the 1940s—and they do require substantiation. But they back up the contention that the nature of decision making by salaried railway managers differed from company to company.[34]

It should also be noted that the railway industry was showing signs of being rather ossified by the 1930s. Conservatism and an emphasis on tradition could be vices as well as virtues. With the exception of Stamp, all the general managers of the "big four" companies were internal appointees, as Table 2 indicates. Eleven of the 15 managers had joined the railways straight from school or university. The emphasis on railway training, and on the promotion of managers from within the company structure, had been observable before 1922 but was now intensified following the amalgamations. Channon is particularly critical of the traditional nature of the Great Western's bureaucracy, which was maintained after the 1921 Act, with its "emphasis on single-company men whose careers developed in particular functional departments." The absence of a general management tier supplied with appropriate statistical and financial information was particularly unfortunate, since it encouraged the separation of revenue-producing and cost-producing departments. The government's strategy of imposed amalgamation in 1921 did very little to alter the railways' organizational structures, with the exception of the L.M.S. And it is rather ironic that the Great Western, which was in many ways the most managerially backward of the four companies, should have actually exported a manager to another industry when Sir Felix Pole joined A.E.I.[35]

The L.N.E.R.'s much-vaunted system of management training, the traffic apprentice scheme, also requires critical evaluation. It is certainly true that many gifted managers passed through the company's hands. They included a number of men who rose to prominent positions within nationalized railway management after 1947: Henry Johnson, chairman of the British Railways Board, 1968–71; W. G. Thorpe, deputy chairman, 1969–72; Fred Margetts, board member, 1963–68; A. R. Dunbar, board member, 1963–68; David Bowick, chief executive (railways), 1971–80, and a board member, 1976–80; Robert Lawrence, board member, 1971–83; and several of the general managers, including Gerard Fiennes (Western, Eastern), Lancelot Ibbotson (Western, Southern), and John Bonham-Carter (London Midland). The quality of these managers is not in question, but there is a strong suspicion that the training that helped to take them to the top was ill suited to the changed environment facing the railways after 1930, and particularly after the Second World War. The L.N.E.R. selected about a dozen promising young men each year, half from the universities, half from its own staff. Entry was by competitive examination. This was followed by an intensive three-year period of training in every aspect of railway management outside engineering. Successful apprentices were then deployed in junior posts, such as assistant yard-master or assistant dock agent, where they were carefully nurtured by a senior manager. The system had merits in rewarding junior managers with power at an early stage of their careers. There was a price, however. Successful apprentices had to be prepared to move several times in order to move up the ladder. There was also a decided emphasis on the traffic (that is, operating) side of the railway business. Many of the successful L.N.E.R. apprentices could be criticized for nursing an undue regard for traffic retention without reference to operating costs and profit margins, and for the preservation of a network of maximum size. They were also liable to concentrate on the technical aspects of railway operation to the exclusion of financial considerations.

Stewart Joy, an Australian economist who made his way to the British Railways Board as chief economist via the Ministry of Transport in the late 1960s, was very much an outsider in an organization of insiders. He has been a vocal critic not only of the traffic apprentice scheme but of the career patterns that normally followed the

TABLE 2   Chief Executives of the "Big Four" Railway Companies, 1923–47.

Executive	Education	Prior experience	Age on appointment	Period in office
Sir Felix Pole (GWR)	to age 14	railways only	44	1921–29
Sir James Milne (GWR)	Campbell College, Belfast; Manchester University	railways only	46	1929–47
Sir Ralph Wedgwood (LNER)	Clifton School; Trinity College, Cambridge	railways only	49	1923–39
Sir Charles Newton (LNER)	to age 15	railways, accountancy	57	1939–47
Miles Beevor (LNER)	Winchester School; New College, Oxford	law, R.A.F., railways	47	1947
Sir Arthur Watson (LMS)	Manchester Grammar School; Manchester University	railways only	50	1923–24
H. G. Burgess (LMS)	n.a.	railways only	65	1924–26
Lord Stamp (LMS)	London University	civil service, university chemical industry	46	1926–41
Sir William Wood (LMS)	Methodist College, Belfast	railways only	58	1941–47
Sir Herbert Walker* (SR)			} joint general managers	1923–24
Sir Percy Tempest (SR)	Leeds Grammar; Leeds University	railways only		
Sir William Forbes (SR)	Dulwich School	railways only		1923–24
Sir Herbert Walker* (SR)	North London College School; Bruges	railways only	55	1924–37
Gilbert Szlumper (SR)	King's College School; King's College, London	railways only	53	1937–39

| Sir Eustace Missenden (SR) | to age 14 | railways only | 53 | 1939–47 |
| Sir John Elliot (SR) | Marlborough School; Sandhurst | army, journalism, railways | 49 | 1947 |

* Sir Herbert Walker was first a joint manager, then became manager in his own right in 1924; biographical details are given for the second appearance in the table.

completion of training. Frequent changes of job—often more than
ten times in a decade—may have given young managers a firm
grasp of operating problems in their company but, according to
Joy, inhibited the development of executives with an appreciation of
broader, strategic issues affecting the railway industry. Brought up
in a world where labor was plentiful but capital was scarce, as in
the interwar years, they found it hard to adjust to an environment
in the 1950s when capital was released but there was an urgent
need to improve labor productivity.[36]

Managerial capitalism in the British railway industry must, then,
be associated in the end with conservatism and a failure to adjust
adequately to a changing environment. This is not, of course, a
surprising statement. It was only to be expected that railways
would exhibit such features. In essence the company structure and
a considerable degree of government control had been established
by the early 1850s, and the main elements of the industry's steam-
based technology had been perfected by the 1870s. There were
comparatively high salaries and a high social status for successful
managers, and job security was greater than that existing in many
British industries hit by postwar recession and, from 1929, the Great
Depression. Appointing boards had no need to take risks in appointing general managers with no prior experience of rail transport.

This does not mean that promising managerial talent was excluded at executive levels below the very top. John Elliot, who
became general manager of the Southern Railway in the last few
months before nationalization in 1947, had been recruited from
Fleet Street in 1925 at assistant general manager level to improve
the flagging public relations image of the company. The L.M.S.
did not stop recruiting from outside with the appointment of Stamp.
Arthur Pearson was another journalist who went on to pursue a
successful railway career, first as personal assistant to the vice-
president, Sir William Wood, in 1934. Sir Harold Hartley had a
distinguished military record and had acquired considerable experience in a variety of fields before his appointment as vice-president
(research) in 1932.[37] Nevertheless, the majority of railway managers were home-grown products, brought up in an environment
steeped in notions of loyalty, discipline, and traditional practices.

The nature of managerial capitalism in this industry can only be understood by a closer examination of executive actions. But it is clear that the essential ingredients of this divorce of ownership and control—large capital inputs, oligopoly, multiplant operations, and a dispersed labor force—were established features of the railways long before they surfaced elsewhere in British industry. In the interwar years the position of the "big four," the four giant corporations that unlike most of British manufacturing were not forced to compete in shrinking world markets, was quite distinct. Yet the organizational solutions that each offered after 1923 belied the similarity of their market position and had much to do with the relative strengths and weaknesses of the major constituent companies. This fact served to set limits to the opportunities for strategic decision making by the general manager as chief executive.

Finally, a word about the transition from salaried manager to owner-director. An earlier study has shown that 48% of the leading general managers appointed in the 1850–1922 period were eventually given a seat on the board of directors.[38] Most of them also enjoyed access to stocks and shares on favorable terms, particularly when new issues were floated. In any case, a salary of £6,000–£10,000 a year before 1914—enjoyed by the top executives—was sufficient to turn a salaried manager into a part-time *rentier* capitalist. Although the scope for incorporation into the ranks of the owners naturally declined with the restructuring of the industry after 1923, it still occurred. Sir Guy Granet, for example, was chairman of the L.M.S. before Stamp succeeded him in 1927. Only the coming of war prevented men like Milne and Wedgwood from joining the boards of their companies (railways were managed by a Railway Executive Committee of general managers on behalf of the government from 1939 onward, and this body had to be kept distinct from representatives of the private owners). Of course the real opportunities for managerial capitalism came with the nationalization of the industry in 1947. Very few salaried managers were investors in British Transport stock, the guaranteed, fixed-return stock that was offered to the railway shareholders in compensation. The task of the managers was management pure and simple. Obligations to the new "owners," the nation, were more remote than ever: to provide "adequate railway services" and to "break even taking one year with another."

As the privately owned railway industry reached its mature stage, the evidence of its *direct* influence upon the development of managerial capitalism in other sectors receded. There is little evidence of a transfer of particular skills. Multidivisional enterprises may have been interested in what Stamp was attempting at Euston, headquarters of the L.M.S., with a comparatively small central staff of fewer than 120 people. But they were also interested in the developments at I.C.I. and elsewhere, and in the best American practice. The influences promoting corporate growth, mergers, and professional management hierarchies in manufacturing tended to be different from those that had encouraged these elements in the railway industry in the nineteenth century. They called for different solutions. In the world of the 1930s bankers and accountants made more promising consultants and executive recruits than did railway managers.

NOTES

1. S. Pollard, *The Genesis of Modern Management*, London, 1965, pp. 136–59, 250–72.
2. L. Hannah, *The Rise of the Corporate Economy*, London, 1976; 2nd ed., 1983, chap. 7.
3. B. Elbaum and W. Lazonick, "The Decline of the British Economy: An Institutional Perspective," *Journal of Economic History*, Vol. 44, 1984, pp. 567–83.
4. Oxford, 1985, in press.
5. M. J. Wiener, *English Culture and the Decline of the Industrial Spirit 1850–1980*, Cambridge, 1981, pp. 127–66. For a critical review see K. Burgess, "English Culture and the Decline of British Economic Power: An Historical Perspective," Roehampton Institute of Higher Education Inaugural Lecture, 1982.
6. I am grateful to Hartmut Kaelble for this point.
7. D. C. Coleman, "Gentlemen and Players," *Economic History Review*, 2nd ser., Vol. 26, 1973, pp. 96–116. An annual cricket match was played between gentlemen (amateurs) and players (paid profes-

sionals) until 1962, and county cricket teams were customarily captained by Oxbridge-educated amateurs until the 1960s.

8. R. J. Irving, "The Profitability and Performance of British Railways, 1870–1914," *Economic History Review*, 2nd ser., Vol. 31, 1978, pp. 44–66. T. R. Gourvish, "The Performance of British Railway Management After 1860: The Railways of Watkin and Forbes," *Business History*, Vol. 20, 1978, pp. 186–200. R. J. Irving, "The Capitalization of Britain's Railways, 1830–1914," *The Journal of Transport History*, 3rd ser., Vol. 5, 1984, pp. 1–24.

9. T. R. Gourvish, *Railways and the British Economy 1830–1914*, London, 1980, pp. 9–10.

10. *Ibid.*, p. 10.

11. C. Shaw, "The large manufacturing employers of 1907," *Business History*, Vol. 25, 1983, pp. 52–3. On an employment basis, the Great Western Railway ranks sixth, the London & North Western tenth, and the North Eastern seventeenth.

12. This can be observed in the conversion of brewing companies after 1886, for example.

13. Gourvish, *Railways and the British Economy*, pp. 49–56.

14. A. D. Chandler, Jr., "The Railroads: Pioneers in Modern Corporate Management," *Business History Review*, Vol. 31, 1965.

15. H. Morikawa, conference brief for Fuji Conference, 1985.

16. T. R. Gourvish, "A British Business Elite: the Chief Executive Managers of the Railway Industry, 1850–1922," *Business History Review*, Vol. 47, 1973, pp. 289–316, reproduced with revisions and additional data as "Les dirigeants salariés de l'industrie des chemins de fer britanniques, 1850–1922," in M. Lévy-Leboyer, ed., *Le patronat de la seconde industrialisation*, Paris, 1979, pp. 53–83.

17. T. R. Gourvish, *Mark Huish and the London and North Western Railway: A Study of Management*, Leicester, 1972.

18. G. Channon, "A Nineteenth-Century Investment Decision: The Midland's London Extension," *Economic History Review*, 2nd ser., Vol. 25, 1972, pp. 448–70. T. R. Gourvish, "Sir James Joseph Allport," in D. J. Jeremy, ed., *Dictionary of Business Biography*, Vol. 1, London, 1984, pp. 42–5.

19. Gourvish, "The Performance of British Railway Management," pp. 190ff. T. R. Gourvish, "Sir Myles Fenton" and "James Staats Forbes," in Jeremy, ed., *Dictionary of Business Biography*, Vol. 2, pp. 338–39, 392–95.

20. Gourvish, "A British Business Elite," p. 313.

21. Hannah, *Corporate Economy*, p. 12.

22. *Ibid.*, 2nd ed., 1983, p. 1.

23. *Ibid.*, 1st ed., 1976, p. 88. This emphasis has been dropped in the second edition, p. 79.

24. G. R. Hawke, *Railways and Economic Growth in England and Wales 1840–1870*, Oxford, 1970, pp. 384–88. L. Hannah, "Mergers in British Manufacturing Industry 1880–1918," *Oxford Economic Papers*, Vol. 26, 1974, p. 13. L. Hannah, "Managerial Innovation and the Rise of the Large-Scale Company in Inter-War Britain," *Economic History Review*, 2nd ser., Vol. 27, 1974, p. 258.

25. L. Hannah, ed., *Management Strategy and Business Development*, London, 1976, p. 3.

26. Gourvish, "A British Business Elite," pp. 297, 314.

27. These remarks are a response to criticisms offered by Alfred Chandler and William Lazonick.

28. Hannah, *Corporate Economy*, 1st ed., p. 89.

29. Here it should be noted that Pole had developed a training scheme for managers in the early 1920s and had fully realized the weaknesses of the G.W.R.'s departmental system. Having made little impact in his attempts to change it, he appears to have become a convert to the multidivisional form of organization. I am grateful to Geoffrey Channon for this point.

30. Hannah, *Corporate Economy*, 2nd ed., p. 79, citing M. R. Bonavia, *Railway Policy Between the Wars*, Manchester, 1981, p. 35.

31. R. A. Church, "Business History in Britain," *Journal of European Economic History*, Vol. 5, 1976, p. 218.

32. F. Pole, *His Book*, Calcot Place, 1954. G. Channon, "The Great Western Railway Under the Railways Act of 1921," *Business History Review*, Vol. 55, 1981, p. 203ff. C. Klapper, *Sir Herbert Walker's Southern Railway*, London, 1973.

33. Channon, "A Nineteenth-Century Investment Decision."

34. M. R. Bonavia, *Railway Policy*, pp. 6–7, citing A. A. Harrison and G. R. Hayes. See also M. R. Bonavia, *The Organisation of British Railways*, London, 1971, pp. 26–31.

35. Channon, "The Great Western Railway," p. 207.

36. S. Joy, *The Train That Ran Away*, London, 1973, pp. 32–3.

37. J. Elliot, *On and Off the Rails*, London, 1982. A. J. Pearson, *Man of the Rail*, London, 1967.

38. Gourvish, "A British Business Elite."

Comment

Kishichi Watanabe
Kyoto Sangyo University

Since my knowledge of British railways and their management is very limited, it is hard for me to criticize Professor Gourvish's paper. After explaining my understanding of his paper briefly, I would like to pose some comments and questions from the viewpoint of the entire discussion of managerial capitalism at this conference.

Dealing with the development of managerial enterprise in British railways, Professor Gourvish distinguishes two periods of development divided by the Railways Act of 1921: the early stage of managerial enterprise from 1850 to the early 1920s and the later stage from 1923 onward.

It is well known that Britain emerged as the "first industrial nation" in the eighteenth century and established the modern factory system in key industries, such as textiles, steel, mining, and metal works, based on owner-manager and partnership-family enterprises. As Professor Gourvish says, "the typical manufacturing enterprise was small, with relatively modest fixed capital requirements, with a labor force that was numbered in tens and hundreds rather than in thousands, and with operations concentrated on one location." He adds that "of the leading industrial countries, Britain was comparatively late in developing managerial capitalism and the large-scale company" owing to its managerial backwardness and "sociocultural drag." The delay of British industries in developing big business, with its mass-production system, salaried managers, managerial hierarchies, and separation of ownership and control, is pointed out by Professor Chandler and contrasted with the cases of the United States and Germany.

Although British key industries continued to be managerially backward, Professor Gourvish emphasizes, the railway industry produced the only case of managerial enterprise and was the pioneer of modern business enterprise from an early stage. That is, the railway industry was a large industry with a high level of concentration from an early stage, mergers took place partly at the instigation of the government, the labor force was both large and dispersed, and separation of ownership and control appeared.

As a result of the concentration of railway enterprises, the "big four" companies—the London & North Western, Midland, Great Western, and North Eastern—dominated the industry until the Railways Act of 1921. Each of these companies was a "multiunit concern not only providing and selling transport but manufacturing rolling stock and gas, and sometimes . . . steel rails." These public joint-stock companies with limited liability and a dispersed owner- ship had at least 20,000 individual investors and an authorized capital ranging from £30 million to £204 million in 1914.

In regard to business organization and decision making in these leading companies, the various units and the centralized structure were organized in such a way that salaried managers occupied the top- and middle-management positions and the "general manager" as chief executive made strategic decisions. But the position of the general manager was not clear; that is, whether the general man- ager had a seat on the board of directors and whether his function was generally like that of a modern corporate president varied from company to company. According to Professor Gourvish "48% of the leading general managers appointed in the 1850–1922 period were eventually given a seat on the board of directors." Middle managers directly responsible to the general manager, such as managers of civil engineering, mechanical engineering, operations, accounting, and other divisions and departments, made tactical decisions that dealt with the day-to-day activities of their divisions and departments. A unique educational system to recruit railway managers was set up in "special executive apprenticeship schemes" under which many general managers were trained. Therefore, the leading salaried managers in railways were produced by an intra- company education system and were not recruited from outside the company. It is remarkable that managerial enterprise, characterized by managerial hierarchies and the separation of ownership and control, were created in British railways at an early stage of development.

"The Railways Act of 1921 . . . created an industrial amalgamation in the grand manner," writes Professor Gourvish. "One hundred and twenty-three of the existing two hundred fourteen railway companies were compulsorily merged into four giant regional enterprises," the London Midland & Scottish, London & North Eastern, Great Western, and Southern. In the 1930s these companies were much larger than any other manufacturing enterprises in England, as Professor Gourvish shows in his paper. The business structure was a highly centralized organization, where the general manager still played a very important role in decision making but with the executive committee making the final strategic decisions. Each vice-president, as a middle manager, was given the responsibility for "a defined function of management": traffic, engineering, finance, and research. It requires further study to ascertain whether the L.M.S. and the L.N.E.R. established decentralized organizations, but in the case of L.N.E.R. the three divisions of the Great Northern, the Great Eastern, and the North Eastern worked against central control. The traffic apprentice scheme still worked remarkably well and produced many able salaried managers.

However, Professor Gourvish points out that the ossification of the managerial capitalism of the British railways was connected with conservatism; this included the managerial bureaucracy and the training system of the apprentice scheme, under which managers tended to be ill suited to a changing business environment and to find it hard to make strategic decisions from a broad viewpoint; they tended to neglect costs and financial problems and place too much emphasis on the technical aspects of operations. Another feature of British managerial capitalism in the railways is that the "transition from salaried manager to owner-director" occurred in the 1850–1923 period. Most general managers received high salaries and had "access to stocks and shares on favorable terms." Professor Gourvish says that "a salary of £6,000–£10,000 a year before 1914—enjoyed by the top executives—was sufficient to turn a salaried manager into a part-time *rentier* capitalist." But it is not clear whether most top decision makers were such capital-holding owner-managers.

In his concluding remarks Professor Gourvish observes that "the real opportunities for managerial capitalism came with the nationalization of the industry in 1947. Very few salaried managers were investors in British Transport stock. . . . The task of the managers was management pure and simple." It is a very interesting view that the maturity of managerial capitalism in British railways, which were based on private enterprise, was reached with the first stage of nationalization, struggling with the ossification of the managerial bureaucracy.

I would like to ask Professor Gourvish some questions:

1. How many miles of track and how many workers did each big company have? These facts are important for an understanding of the scale of each enterprise in connection with business structure. For example, the Pennsylvania Railroad Company in the United States had 6,000 miles of track in 1874 and more than 11,000 miles in 1906, and employed 50,000 workers in 1890 and more than 103,000 in 1906.

2. Can you show me an organizational chart of a big company in the nineteenth and twentieth centuries that indicates the positions of general manager, president, managing director, chairman, and board of directors?

3. Can you give details on the institution of the traffic apprentice scheme? What were the conditions of enrollment?

4. From the viewpoint of the comparative study of managerial capitalism, it is interesting that both British and American railroads produced managerial enterprise, although some features of each railway differed in scale and performance. And it is important that managerial enterprise emerged in the same industries and at the same time, after the mid-nineteenth century, in both countries. The common causes of the rise of modern enterprise in that industry may have been large size, requiring large capital and labor forces; the complexity of business functions; the necessity of safety and publicity; economies of speed; and the same technological background. However, the most important factor may have been the

entrepreneurship of salaried managers who pursued the rationalization of management in their business.

Key industries in the industrial revolution, such as textiles and steel, and newer ones, such as mass-produced light machinery and specialized heavy industries, failed to develop managerial hierarchies of salaried managers. My question is why those industries did not learn modern management techniques from the railway experience in the nineteenth century. In other words, why did managerial capitalism, produced by British railways in the nineteenth century, not spread to other industries? Professor Gourvish shows one example of exporting managerial experience, the "spinoff" of managers from the railways to other industries, in the case of Sir Felix Pole, who became general manager of the Great Western Railway in 1921 but resigned in 1929 and became chairman of a new electrical company. But Pole seems to have been very much the exception in Britain.

In the case of the United States the modern managerial enterprise that American railroads created contributed to the development of other industries, such as steel, electricity, and chemicals. For instance, Andrew Carnegie, who innovated the early mass-production system of steel and its management, had worked for the Pennsylvania Railroad Company for 12 years and introduced its management methods into his steel-manufacturing concern.

Why did the British industrial entrepreneurs and business elite in the late nineteenth century prefer traditional management to modern business enterprise using managerial hierarchies and fail to harvest much fruit from the latter despite the existence of the managerial enterprise in British railways? The fundamental cause may have been their social and cultural values and their freedom of choice. If so, the managerial enterprise as a business institution is neither historically determined nor an inevitable phenomenon.

My question, however, is what social and cultural values discouraged British entrepreneurs from innovating new business institutions.

A Comparative Study of the Managerial Structure of Two Japanese Shipbuilding Firms: Mitsubishi Shipbuilding and Engineering Co. and Kawasaki Dockyard Co., 1896-1927

Takao Shiba
Kyoto Sangyo University

Introduction

In this paper I would like to discuss the relationship between the structure of a company's top management and the characteristics of its management policy. Two examples were selected for this purpose: Mitsubishi Shipbuilding and Engineering Co. and Kawasaki Dockyard Co. These two companies, pioneers in the Japanese shipbuilding industry, were founded in the 1880s, when Japan started to modernize. They actively introduced Western technology and made efforts to build bigger and better ships, while other shipbuilders, except for naval dockyards, continued to use less advanced technology. As a result, these two companies became pre-eminent in the Japanese shipbuilding industry.

The two companies developed in very different ways. Mitsubishi's development was steady, but Kawasaki followed an unstable course. While the former expanded step by step, the latter grew rapidly through the use of aggressive strategies. At one point Kawasaki earned big profits and became the largest Japanese manufacturing firm through the success of its aggressive strategies, but soon after, its business came to a standstill because of overextension. This was followed by a protracted reconstruction. Mitsubishi, however, was not damaged badly even in severe depressions because of its cautious business practices.

Why did the two firms develop so differently? The difference lies in the structure of their top management. From early in its history Mitsubishi had several managers with many years' experience in the shipyards. On the other hand, one man controlled Kawasaki for a long time. This fact caused the difference in their managerial policies.

I. The Founding of the Mitsubishi and Kawasaki Shipbuilding Business

Both Iwasaki Yatarō, founder of Mitsubishi Co., and Kawasaki Shōzō, founder of Kawasaki Dockyard Co., started their ship-building businesses on a full scale by purchasing government-owned shipyards.[1] But there were two great differences. First the facilities of the shipyards they bought were not the same. The Nagasaki shipyard, which Iwasaki Yatarō bought, had facilities and equipment superior to those of the Hyōgo shipyard, which Shōzō purchased. For example, the former had a big dock, but the latter had no dock at all.[2] Second, there were great differences in financing. Yatarō had accumulated huge profits from his shipping activities and mines,[3] whereas Shōzō's profits from dealing in sugar were much smaller.[4]

Whether a shipbuilding firm had a dock was of great importance in this period, since more profit could be made from ship repairs than from shipbuilding, for which there was little demand in Japan. A shipyard with no dock could not repair big ships, and Kawasaki could not build a dock because of lack of funds. On the other hand, Mitsubishi Co., which was established after Iwasaki Yatarō's death in 1885 by his successor, began to invest substantial funds to improve the facilities and equipment of the Nagasaki shipyard in the late 1890s, even though it was already the largest yard in the Japanese private shipbuilding industry. Since it did not have sufficient facilities or equipment to build big ships, Mitsubishi had to update them to develop its shipbuilding business at a time when larger and larger ships were in demand.[5]

Shōzō was aware of the disadvantages of his shipyard but could not alleviate the situation for three reasons. The biggest reason was lack of funds. In addition, it was very difficult for him to personally direct the expansion of the business because his health was poor. More-over, he lost two children in an accident,[6] and although he adopted his nephew Yoshitarō, this adopted son was too gentle to run the business.[7] The situation became serious after the Sino-Japanese War of 1894–95. Although there was a great demand for repairs of big ships after the war, his shipyard could not repair big ships because, as mentioned above, it did not have a dock.[8] Shōzō decided to raise capital to build a dock converting his business to a joint-stock company and introducing new management.

The new company was started in 1896, and Shōzō selected Matsukata Kōjirō as its president. Matsukata was the third son of Matsukata Masayoshi, a former prime minister and a powerful politician at that time, and had experience as a company director.[9] As Matsukata's father came from the same district and was a close associate, Shōzō knew Matsukata's character and ability. Matsukata was only 31 years old, but Shōzō set up the top management of the new company in a way that gave the new president unrestricted control. First he retired from top management and became an adviser though he was the biggest shareholder with 50% of the shares. The other 18 shareholders were all family members or acquaintances, including Matsukata, who held 2.5%.[10] Although five directors and two auditors were selected from among these shareholders, there were only two executive directors, Matsukata and Kawasaki Yoshitarō, who became vice-president. All the others were dummy directors.[11] Shōzō created this top-management structure to allow the young president to exercise his talent freely. As a result the new firm, named Kawasaki Dockyard Co., Ltd., was run by young executives (Yoshitarō was only 28 years old). Perhaps Shōzō made his nephew vice-president to prevent Matsukata from gaining complete control, but Yoshitarō was too gentle to control the aggressive Matsukata and preferred the role of assistant. As a result, Matsukata soon had full control, contrary to Shōzō's expectations.

The adoption of this management system spelled success for Kawasaki Dockyard. The company underwent a complete transformation by investing aggressively to improve facilities and equipment under the direction of Matsukata, who liked expansionist policies. After building a dock in 1902, the company raised funds for expansion by increasing capital and issuing debentures from 1904 to 1906. As a result the company doubled in size and was able to build ships of more than 3,000 gross tons by 1906.[12]

There were few changes in its top management structure during this period. Indeed Matsukata and Yoshitarō, especially the former, increased their control when their main opponent, Watanabe Hisashi, retired from his directorship. Watanabe was Shōzō's oldest employee and the president of the newspaper company that Kawasaki controlled. He had expected to be appointed to an important position when Shōzō re-formed his shipbuilding business, but Shōzō preferred Matsukata and appointed Watanabe a mere dummy director. Watanabe complained about this treatment and confronted Matsukata about management policies. Finally he retired.[13] As a result there was now no one on the board of directors who could stand up to Matsukata.

Mitsubishi Co. adopted a different management system for its shipbuilding department. As mentioned above, the head of Mitsubishi Co. decided to enlarge its shipbuilding business in the late 1890s, but this intention could not be realized immediately because of a disagreement among the managers of the Nagasaki shipyard.[14] In 1897 the president of Mitsubishi Co. therefore appointed Shōda Heigorō, a general manager of the company, chief manager of the shipyard and had him direct the improvement of facilities and equipment. Aggressive investment in facilities and equipment followed, and Mitsubishi Co. continued to invest huge amounts in the shipyard until around 1910.[15] Although Shōda remained chief manager of the shipyard until 1906, he returned to the head office in Tokyo in 1901 and also worked as a general manager. So a senior assistant manager actually directed the shipyard after 1901. He was an engineer who had been employed in the shipyard ever since it was government owned. Thus the actual power to run the shipyard was, to some extent, delegated to an engineer with shipbuilding experience.

This transfer of power was completed in 1906, when Shōda retired as chief manager of the shipyard and Maruta Hidemi, who had been an assistant manager and engineer, replaced him.[16] Meanwhile, Mitsubishi Co. had established a new shipyard in Kobe, the biggest trade port in Japan. The company also appointed an engineer chief manager of the Kobe shipyard, so that management of the shipbuilding business was in the hands of managers with shipbuilding experience from this time on.[17] This situation did not change when a shipbuilding department was established to control the two shipyards in 1907, nor when the department was made a division in 1908.[18]

II. Mitsubishi and Kawasaki During World War I

World War I had a great effect on the development of Japanese shipbuilding. Although the Japanese shipbuilding industry had been expanding its capacity and accumulating technology, its market was so small that development was slow. Only five private firms could build ships of more than 1,000 gross tons before World War I.[19] The war created a big market for the Japanese shipbuilding industry as submarine action destroyed many ships and military transport increased in Europe. As a result Japanese shipbuilders received many orders.

In the face of this huge demand, Japanese shipbuilders wanted to build as many ships and earn as much profit as they could. They expanded their facilities and improved shipbuilding methods so that they could build many ships quickly. Most of them adopted the practice of building identical ready-made ships for this purpose. If they waited for orders before starting to build ships, the time spent planning to suit the needs of each customer and gathering the necessary materials reduced the number of ships they could produce in a given time. In addition, the price of materials was rising rapidly, and shipbuilders lost money when the price of materials exceeded contract estimates. Furthermore, they could make more profit by selling ships after completion because the price of ships was also going up.[20]

Kawasaki Dockyard enthusiastically adopted the ready-made method. Although it built ships to order at the beginning of the war, it later specialized in mass production of identical ready-made ships, which it called "stock boats," and refused all special orders after the end of 1915. As a result Kawasaki Dockyard was able to build 36 merchant vessels, about 210,000 gross tons, in only four years.[21]

These huge ships brought a great deal of profit to the company, which sold not only to Japanese shipping agents but also to foreign shipping firms and the U.S. government.[22] The company's profit during the war was over ¥90 million,[23] most of it acquired by selling these ships (of course the company also built warships and manufactured other products, such as locomotives and iron pipe).

The wartime boom also prompted Kawasaki Dockyard to go into steelmaking. The reason for this was that Belgium and Germany could not export steel because of the war and Britain prohibited the export of steel in 1915. Thus the United States became the only source of steel for Japan, which had a low steel-production level, and prices rose rapidly.[24] Given this situation, Kawasaki Dockyard decided to produce its own steel in 1915, when it adopted the stock-boat policy. In 1917 the company started to build a big steel plant.[25]

It may safely be said that Matsukata chose these two aggressive strategies because the top-management structure of the company had not changed much. In fact Matsukata was now stronger than ever because Shōzō, the only person who had been able to control him, had died in 1911. Although two directors were added in 1915, they were both engineers who had worked under Matsukata for a long period. Moreover, they remained managers in the shipbuilding and machinery-manufacturing departments after becoming directors.[26] Therefore they had little power to restrict Matsukata's actions.

Compared with Kawasaki Dockyard, which made huge profits under Matsukata's direction, Mitsubishi made fewer profits from its shipbuilding activities. Mitsubishi Co. converted its shipbuilding division to Mitsubishi Shipbuilding and Engineering Co., Ltd., in 1917. The combined profit of the shipbuilding division from 1914 to 1917 and of Mitsubishi Shipbuilding and Engineering in 1918 was about ¥39 million,[27] only one-third that of Kawasaki Dockyard. The reason for this was that Mitsubishi did not change its shipbuilding policy as thoroughly as did Kawasaki Dockyard. Although Mitsubishi built some ready-made ships, these numbered only 17, about 53,000 gross tons altogether, or 24% of its total production of about 220,000 gross tons.[28] Instead Mitsubishi emphasized the building of ships ordered by Japanese shipping agents and the Japanese Navy. As mentioned above, however, these ships were not profitable because the prices of materials and ships were rising rapidly. Warships were especially unprofitable because they took a long time to build. Indeed, Matsukata of Kawasaki Dockyard tried to avoid receiving orders for warships because of their unprofitability.[29]

Although it is not clear why Mitsubishi decided to emphasize the building of special-order ships and warships, the following points may be instructive. First, the managers of the shipbuilding division of Mitsubishi Co. thought carefully about the wartime boom. The head office of the shipbuilding division, for example, issued a warning to its shipyards in 1916, when the price of ships was already three times as high as before the war, "not to act radically, because a reaction to the boom was inevitable."[30] Such warnings were later repeated. The chief manager of the shipbuilding division at that time was Maruta, who had been the chief manager of the Nagasaki shipyard after Shōda.

Second, Iwasaki Koyata, who was already the de facto head of Mitsubishi Co. before the war though only a vice-president, was strongly convinced that management must avoid speculation. In 1920 he said that he intended to prevent speculation "to acquire undue profit in the hope of making a fortune at a stroke."[31] Since the top management held such opinions, the shipbuilding division could not behave in an openly speculative way even if given the power to use its own judgment. The building of identical ready-made ships was speculative because it anticipated rising ship prices.

On the other hand, it is likely that Matsukata did not see speculation as a sin and wanted to profit as much as possible from rising ship prices. For example, he refused to sell stock boats around the end of war because he judged that the price of ships would continue to rise.[32] He did not have complete confidence in the development of a boom when he decided to start building stock boats, but his judgment was vindicated in 1916 when he went to the United States and Europe to secure steel and study the situation in Europe.[33] After trying to secure steel in the United States, he traveled to London and Paris and stayed in Europe until the end of the war, observing conditions. During his absence there was little change in the top management of Kawasaki Dockyard because Matsukata managed the company by telegraph.[34]

In the short run, Matsukata's visit to Europe had a beneficial effect on the company because he closed a deal with a British shipping agent in London to sell 12 stock boats.[35] The important decision to increase production of stock boats in 1917 was probably based on Matsukata's judgment of the development of the war.[36] As a result the company had many ships in 1918,[37] when Japan exchanged ships for U.S. steel, making a huge profit.[38] In the long run, however, Matsukata's stay in Europe had a bad effect on the company, because he stayed in the countries concerned so long and observed their conditions so closely that he misjudged the development of the postwar economy. He judged that there would be a huge demand for large-scale transportation for a long time because the European countries were too heavily damaged to reconstruct quickly.[39] He thus made the very important decision to enter the shipping business full-scale by building more ships. After Matsukata returned from Europe in November 1918, Kawasaki Dockyard established Kawasaki Steam Ship Co., Ltd., in April 1919 and took part in the establishment of Kokusai Steam Ship Co., Ltd., which was set up by Japanese tramp agents and shipbuilders who had some unsold ready-made ships, in July of the same year. He gained control of the latter company by investing the most ships.[40] Kawasaki Dockyard continued to build many ships, holding some of them in the shipping department it established during the war but investing most of them in the two steamship companies. As a result Kawasaki Dockyard controlled the second biggest shipping group in Japan.[41]

This venture failed, however, since world shipping was greatly depressed after the war, contrary to Matsukata's expectations. Although demand for goods for European reconstruction stimulated shipping for a short time, shipping charges dropped rapidly after 1920. As a result the two shipping companies, Kawasaki S.S. and Kokusai S.S., were badly hurt and could not pay a stock dividend.[42] Kawasaki Dockyard's shipping department also made scant profit. In short, Kawasaki Dockyard was not able to recover the funds that it had invested in the many ships it had built.

In the same period, the management system of the newly created Mitsubishi Shipbuilding and Engineering Co. changed. The shipbuilding division's head office was the smallest in Mitsubishi Co. For example, it had only one-third the staff of the coal-mining division even in 1916.[43] After the formation of the new company, however, the head office was strengthened and the size of its staff doubled.[44] Moreover, the head office's organization was improved and top management was strengthened. Originally Mitsubishi Shipbuilding had nine directors and three auditors, with Iwasaki Koyata, president of Mitsubishi Co., as president. But it is likely that Iwasaki was just a figurehead and that the three executive directors actually managed the company. After only six months Iwasaki retired as president and was succeeded by Takeda Hideo in May 1918. Takeda, who had been an engineer and a vice-admiral,[45] and three executive directors managed the company from this time on. Two of these executive directors were engineers, and the third had been an assistant manager of the shipbuilding division of Mitsubishi Co. from 1913 to 1915, though he was not an engineer.[46] Although the chief managers of the Nagasaki and Kobe shipyards were also directors, the rest of the directors and the auditors were managers of other subsidiaries and divisions of Mitsubishi Co. or were members of the Iwasaki family.[47] They did not participate in the daily operation of the company.

If we compare the top management of Mitsubishi Shipbuilding with that of Kawasaki Dockyard, we can see that whereas Kawasaki was completely controlled by one man, Mitsubishi was managed by a group of directors, most of whom had an engineering background. These differences had an important effect on the development of the two companies in the long depression that followed World War I. Kawasaki collapsed because of the aggressive policies of Matsukata, whom no one in the company could control. Mitsubishi, on the other hand, was cautious and succeeded in minimizing the damage of the depression.

III. Aggression and Caution During the Depression

Although Matsukata had been brought to Kawasaki Dockyard as a hired manager by Shōzō, his position changed substantially after World War I. When he became president of the company he held only 1,000 shares, and though he and his family bought more, their total holding was only 9,363 shares (4.6% of total issued stock) just before the war. As the Kawasaki family held about 70,000 shares (35.4%) at that time, Matsukata was clearly inferior in terms of ownership.[48] Nevertheless, he was able to exercise strong leadership for two reasons. First Shōzō supported him, and secondly, Yoshitarō, who became vice-president on behalf of the Kawasaki family, remained Matsukata's faithful helper. The attitudes of these two members of the Kawasaki family made it possible for Matsukata to exercise autocratic power. However, the relationship between Matsukata and the Kawasaki family changed greatly after the war, Matsukata having bought large blocks of shares in 1916 and 1919. By May 1919 he and his family held 133,252 shares (14.8% of total issued stock), while the Kawasaki family held only 127,376 shares (14.2%).[49] But this situation did not last long. By November 1919 Matsukata's holding had dropped to 87,227 shares (9.7%), while the Kawasaki family now held 160,476 shares (17.3%).[50]

The rapid changes in Matsukata's stockholding were probably related to the increase in company capital that occurred in February 1919, when the first payment was transferred from reserves in order to pass on to shareholders some of the profits made during the war.[51] Matsukata probably used this opportunity to increase his holding. Certainly he did so when the company doubled its capital in August 1921. At this time, too, the first payment was transferred from reserves,[52] and Matsukata bought about 12,000 shares before the increase in capital. After this operation he and his family held 322,934 shares, or 17.9% of the total stock.[53] On the other hand, the Kawasaki family's holding was reduced to 7.4%, because it had sold half its holding just before the increase in capital. Thus the relationship between Matsukata and the Kawasaki family was completely reversed.

As shares in Kawasaki Dockyard were already dispersed,[54] Matsukata's holding was large enough to enable him to control the company. In addition Yoshitarō, the only man able to restrain Matsukata, died in July 1920. Although Yoshitarō had remained Matsukata's helper, Matsukata could not ignore him completely because he was the son-in-law of the founder and an original partner. Therefore his death removed the final restraint on Matsu-kata. Although one of Yoshitarō's sons became a director after Yoshitarō's death, he never became an executive director, and it was only after Matsukata's retirement that the Kawasaki family was able to install a representative as an executive director.[55]

As mentioned earlier, Kawasaki Dockyard's shipping ventures failed and the company lost most of the profit it had made during the war.[56] In addition, its shipbuilding business, except for the building of warships, declined for two reasons. First, demand for ships fell substantially and competition among shipbuilding companies became very keen. The second, crucial, reason was that the relationship between Japanese shipping agents and Kawasaki Dock-yard was now very bad because during the war Kawasaki had refused orders from shipping agents and had specialized in building stock boats. As a result the company received no orders from Japanese shipping agents,[57] and its financial position gradually worsened. The conclusion of the Naval Armament Limitation Treaty in 1922 added to Kawasaki Dockyard's difficulties, since it resulted in a reduction in the building of warships.[58]

Kawasaki Dockyard had previously invested heavily to improve facilities and equipment because the Japanese Navy had suggested that it would order many warships, including some big battleships. The navy planned to increase armaments during World War I. The expansion plan was enlarged more and more as time went on. In 1920 the final plan was established. According to this plan the navy would have a huge fleet, with eight battleships and the same number of battle cruisers. To complete this fleet the navy drew up a grand scheme to build 120 naval vessels, including four battleships and four battle cruisers. This, however, necessitated many shipbuilding facilities. Therefore the navy requested shipbuilding companies to enlarge their facilities.[59] Kawasaki Dockyard invested huge funds in facilities and equipment. But the navy's expansion plan was curtailed by the Naval Armament Limitation Treaty, and many orders for warships, especially battleships and battle cruisers, were canceled. It was difficult to recover the funds invested, and the financial state of Kawasaki Dockyard worsened.

Given this state of affairs, the top management of Kawasaki

Dockyard chose to enter new fields of production rather than reduce the size of the company. The company thus began to invest again in new facilities and equipment although there was overcapacity in the shipbuilding division. Because of its poor financial situation the company had to raise the necessary funds by borrowing from financial agencies and issuing debentures. Interest on these debts soon put further pressure on company finances.[60]

The choice of this course of action can probably be ascribed to Matsukata's personality, as he is said to have hated to retreat. Indeed, he said that he made the decision because he feared decline.[61] It was, however, very risky, given the company's financial position, and some journalists began to point this out around 1923.[62] Nevertheless, Kawasaki Dockyard did not modify its course. Matsukata, as president and largest shareholder, was beyond the control of the directors even when their number was increased to 13 in 1920. Most of the new directors were in fact employees who had long worked under Matsukata and were appointed by him as a reward for their long years of service.[63] It was only natural that such directors would not oppose him. Therefore the company could not modify its course unless Matsukata himself modified his way of thinking.

Compared with Kawasaki Dockyard, Mitsubishi Shipbuilding acted very carefully. By 1918 it had established management by directors with engineering backgrounds. They then proceeded to reduce investment in some divisions on the one hand and invest in the facilities and equipment needed to build warships on the other, based on the assumption that the Japanese Navy would order many ships, including some large battleships.[64] Mitsubishi Shipbuilding, however, began to reduce its size as soon as the navy's plans were altered by the Naval Armament Limitation Treaty. Mitsubishi Shipbuilding began to discharge workers from the Nagasaki shipyard in February 1922, just after the treaty was signed. In all, the company discharged more than 6,000 workers from the Nagasaki and Kobe shipyards in only two years. By 1925 the number of workers was half that in 1921, just before the conclusion of the treaty.[65] In addition, the company streamlined its structure by closing down unprofitable sections, although it aggressively promoted those from which stable profits were expected. As a result of this streamlining, Mitsubishi Shipbuilding's fixed assets in 1926 were 90% of those in 1921.[66]

Mitsubishi Shipbuilding's management at this time seemed to place the most stress on the accumulation of technology and internal funds. The above-mentioned streamlining can be regarded as an indication of this intention. In addition, the company accumulated profits by controlling dividends, and thus had substantial internal funds in the second half of the 1920s despite the deepening depression.[67] These funds were used to beef up technology and thus fostered the company's further development.[68]

The basic top-management structure of Mitsubishi Shipbuilding remained unchanged throughout the depression in the 1920s. Although Takeda retired as president in 1925, the next president was an engineer who had worked at the Nagasaki shipyard for many years and had been an executive director of the company since 1920.[69] These two, with the other executive directors, managed the company from the head office. Important decisions were, of course, made by the board of directors, but the executive directors took a leading role, too. For example, according to the minutes of the board meetings, the executive directors and the chief managers of the two main shipyards, who were also directors, proposed subjects for the other directors to discuss.[70] In sum, the six directors, including the chief managers of the main shipyards, led the company's management.

We must not forget, of course, that Mitsubishi Co. had the power to appoint directors and auditors in its subsidiaries and to make final decisions on budgets and settlement of accounts. Moreover, decisions of the board of directors had to be reported to the president of Mitsubishi Co. and obtain his approval before action could be taken.[71] This meant that Mitsubishi Shipbuilding's management could not run the company as it pleased.

IV. Conclusion

In 1927 Kawasaki Dockyard came to a standstill. The direct cause of its paralysis was a shortage of working funds caused by the collapse of its main bank in the financial crisis that year. An underlying cause, however, can be found within the management of the company itself. Its aggressive plans during the depression only enlarged its losses, since interest on borrowing undertaken to set up new departments rapidly absorbed falling profits. As a result, the company lacked working funds and had to borrow more money in the second half of the 1920s. Mounting debts finally caused the company to collapse.

These debts were a function of Matsukata's aggressive strategies, and his one-man rule was in turn attributable to the company's founder, who hoped to develop Kawasaki Dockyard by allowing Matsukata free rein to exercise his management ability. Matsukata, with the founder's support, wielded his power as if he were the owner rather than a hired manager. This system was effective as long as the shipbuilding market was expanding. Kawasaki Dockyard became a major shipbuilder, and Matsukata's power within the company grew accordingly. In addition, he bought so many shares that his holding surpassed that of the founder's family, and he was able to control the company in both name and fact. However, the situation changed greatly once he had established complete control. The long and severe depression that plagued the Japanese shipbuilding industry after World War I required a cautious attitude in the management of shipbuilding companies, but Matsukata did not modify his aggressive attitude. The result was the collapse of his company.

In contrast, the top-management structure of Mitsubishi Shipbuilding was such that it was impossible for one man to run the company alone. The system of hiring managers who had worked in the shipyards for many years was established early, and as most of these managers were engineers, the departments they managed tended to follow a steady course. The managers' policies during World War I are the best example of this. The system did not change when the shipbuilding division was changed to a joint-stock company but instead was strengthened by an increase in the number of managers. Moreover, Mitsubishi Co. checked management decisions. Therefore there was no way for extreme strategies to emerge. Although this system tended to restrict profits in prosperous periods, as during World War I, it also worked to reduce losses in the postwar depression.

Notes

1. These two were managers in the shipbuilding business. Iwasaki Yatarō had owned a small ironworks in Yokohama since 1875. Since the ironworks was too small for building large ships, only a few small steamboats could be built there. Kawasaki Shōzō managed a small shipyard in Tokyo. His shipyard made only a few small boats, too. See *Mitsubishi Jūkōgyō Kabushiki Kaishashi* (The history of Mitsubishi Heavy Industries), 1956, pp. 31–3; Mishima Yasuo, *Hanshin zaibatsu*, Tokyo, Nihon Keizai Shimbunsha, 1984, pp. 350– 55.

2. For the difference in the capacity of these two shipyards see Kobayashi Masaaki, *Nihon no kōgyōka to kangyō haraisage: Seifu to kigyō* (The industrialization of Japan and the disposal of government-owned plants), Tokyo, Tōyō Keizai Shinpōsha, 1977, pp. 277–79.

3. Iwasaki Yatarō's business generated accumulated profits of about ¥6,400,000 from 1875 to 1885. See Hatade Isao, *Nihon no zaibatsu to Mitsubishi* (Japan's zaibatsu and Mitsubishi), Tokyo, Rakuyū Shobō, 1978, p. 25.

4. Kawasaki Shōzō's accumulated profits are difficult to ascertain, but judging from the records, his yearly income in the sugar-dealing business was about ¥35,000. Thus his accumulated profits were very small compared with Iwasaki's. See Mishima, *Hanshin zaibatsu*, pp. 355–61.

5. Mishima Yasuo, ed., *Mitsubishi zaibatsu*, Tokyo, Nihon Keizai Shimbunsha, 1981, pp. 189–96.

6. Mishima, *Hanshin zaibatsu*, pp. 368–70.

7. *Ibid.*, p. 370.

8. During the war Japan imported many big ships because many of the ships held by Japanese shipping agents were used for military transport. As most of the imported ships were old, they had to be repaired after the war. However, only Mitsubishi's Nagasaki shipyard could repair such big ships. See Teratani Takeaki, *Nihon kindai zōsen shi josetsu* (An introduction to the history of modern shipbuilding in Japan), Tokyo, Gannandō Shoten, 1979, pp. 83–4.

9. Matsukata Kōjirō had an excellent education for his time. After
    graduation from Daigaku Yobimon (later Tokyo Imperial Uni-
    versity), he went to the United States and took a doctorate in civil
    law at Yale University. He also studied at the Sorbonne in Paris.
    See Yamauchi Seikei, *Hyōgo ken jinbutsu retsuden* (Biographies of fa-
    mous people from Hyogo Prefecture), 1914, p. 345.
10. First business report of Kawasaki Dockyard Co., Ltd.
11. *Kawasaki Jūkōgyō Kabushiki Kaisha shashi* (The history of Kawasaki
    Dockyard Co., Ltd.), 1959, p. 659.
12. Shiba Takao, "Kawasaki Zōsensho ni okeru Meiji 30 nendai no
    kakudai undō" (The movement to expand Kawasaki Dockyard in
    the third decade of the Meiji era), *Kōnan ronshū*, Vol. 6, 1978, p. 48.
13. Tazumi Toyoshirō, *Gendai Hyōgo ken jinbutsu shi* (A history of famous
    people from Hyōgo Prefecture in recent years), Tokyo, Ken'yūsha,
    1911, pp. 268–69; *Kōbe Shinbun 70 nen shi* (Seventy years of the
    Kobe Shinbun), 1968, pp. 17–23.
14. This dispute is said to have been caused by a difference in the
    way of thinking about the shipbuilding business between a chief
    manager who was not an engineer and the engineers of the Nagasaki
    shipyard. See Biographical Committee of Iwasaki Hisaya, ed.,
    Iwasaki Hisaya den (A biography of Iwasaki Hisaya), 1961, pp. 385–
    86. But Morikawa Hidemasa has recently presented a different view
    of the dispute; see Morikawa Hidemasa, "Iwasaki Yanosuke
    jidai no Mitsubishi no top management" (The top management
    of Mitsubishi in the time of Iwasaki Yanosuke), in Tsuchiya Moriaki
    and Morikawa Hidemasa, eds., *Kigyōsha katsudō no shi teki kenkyū*
    (Historical research on entrepreneurial activities), 1981, pp. 56–61.
15. Mishima, ed., *Mitsubishi zaibatsu*, pp. 194–97.
16. Nagasaki Shipyard Shokkō-ka, *Mitsubishi Nagasaki Zōsensho shi* (A
    history of the Mitsubishi Nagasaki shipyard), Vol. 1, 1928, pp. 34, 36.
17. The man who was appointed chief manager of the new shipyard
    was the senior assistant manager of the Nagasaki shipyard. *Ibid.*,
    p. 74.
18. The chief manager of the Kobe shipyard became the first chief
    officer of the shipbuilding department. The second chief officer
    was Maruta Hidemi, and the third was an engineer who had
    graduated from Kōka Daigaku (Industrial University). Mitsubishi
    Co., *Mitsubishi Gōshi Kaisha shashi* (History of Mitsubishi Gōshi),
    Vol. 21, reprinted, Tokyo, University of Tokyo Press, 1980, p. 1,033;
    Vol. 22, p. 1,572; Vol. 27, p. 3,639.

19. Kaneko Eiichi, ed., *Gendai Nihon sangyō hattatsu shi, IX Zōsen* (History of the development of modern Japanese industry, Vol. 9 Shipbuilding), Study Group on the Development of Modern Japanese Industry, 1964, p. 156.

20. Teratani, *Kindai zōsen shi*, pp. 222–37.

21. *Kawasaki Jūkōgyō shashi*, p. 708.

22. *Ibid.*, pp. 257–58.

23. Thirty-sixth to forty-seventh business report of Kawasaki Dockyard.

24. Teratani, *Kindai zōsen shi*, pp. 228–31.

25. Shiba Takao, "Taishō ki kigyō keiei no takaku teki kakudai shikō to sono zasetsu" (The aspiration for diversified expansion of business management in the Taishō era and its frustration), *Osaka Daigaku keizaigaku* (Osaka University ecomomic studies), Vol. 28, No. 2–3, 1978, pp. 108–11.

26. *Kawasaki Jūkōgyō shashi*, p. 659.

27. Mishima, ed., *Mitsubishi zaibatsu*, p. 209.

28. *Ibid.*, p. 208.

29. Okada Keisuke, *Okada Keisuke kaikoroku* (Memoirs of Okada Keisuke), Mainichi Shimbunsha, 1950, pp. 30–1.

30. *Mitsubishi shashi*, Vol. 26, p. 3,499.

31. Biographical Committee of Iwasaki Koyata, ed., *Iwasaki Koyata den* (A biography of Iwasaki Koyata), 1957, pp. 196–97.

32. Uchida Shin'ya, *Fūsetsu 50 nen* (Fifty years of trial and tribulation), Tokyo, Jitsugyō no Tomo Sha, 1953, p. 29.

33. Fortieth business report of Kawasaki Dockyard, p. 2.

34. Matsukata kept in contact with the head office by using the London office of Suzuki Trading Co., one of the largest trading companies in Japan at that time. See *Kawasaki Jūkōgyō shashi*, p. 978.

35. Matsukata closed this deal himself. See Shimizu Ken'ichi, "1920 nendai ni okeru zōsen daikigyō no chikuseki kōzō" (Shipbuilding enterprises in the 1920s), *Ritsumeikan keizaigaku* (Ritsumeikan economic studies), Vol. 25, No. 5–6, 1977, p. 191.

36. Fortieth business report of Kawasaki Dockyard, p. 3.

37. At that time the company had eight ships. See Shiba, "Taishō ki kigyō keiei," pp. 105–6.

38. For this exchange program see Teratani, *Kindai zōsen shi*, pp. 213–54, 390–411.

39. Society to Honor Kaneko and Yanagida, ed., *Kaneko Naokichi den* (A biography of Kaneko Naokichi), 1950, p. 194.

40. Shiba, "Taishō ki kigyō keiei," p. 115.

41. *Kawasaki Kisen 50 nen shi* (50 Years of Kawasaki Steam Ship Co., Ltd.), 1969, p. 47.
42. Shiba, "Taishō ki kigyō keiei," p. 117.
43. *Mitsubishi shashi*, Vol. 26, pp. 3,568–71.
44. List of members of Mitsubishi Co., and its subsidiaries, 1918.
45. Biographical Committee of Takeda Hideo, ed., *Takeda Hideo den* (A biography of Takeda Hideo), 1944, p. 164.
46. *Mitsubishi shashi*, Vol. 22, p. 1,960; Vol. 23, p. 2,382; Vol. 24, p. 2,791.
47. *Ibid.*, Vol. 28, p. 4,234.
48. Thirty-fifth business report of Kawasaki Dockyard.
49. Forty-fourth business report of Kawasaki Dockyard.
50. Forty-fifth business report of Kawasaki Dockyard.
51. *Kawasaki Jūkōgyō shashi*, p. 690.
52. *Ibid.*
53. Fifty-first business report of Kawasaki Dockyard.
54. The number of shareholders increased from 18 in 1896 to 1,333 in 1914, when World War I broke out. The number increased steadily during the war, reaching 4,950 by November 1919. The number increased further to 9,745 by November 1921. At that time the combined holdings of the ten largest shareholders were 36.6%, including Matsukata's holding of 16.6%. *Kawasaki Jūkōgyō Kabushiki Kaisha shashi: Nenpyō shohyō* (The history of Kawasaki Dockyard Co., Ltd.: Chronological tables and statistics), 1959, pp. 334–39.
55. *Kawasaki Jūkōgyō shashi*, p. 664.
56. Shiba Takao, "Fukyō ki no ni dai zōsen kigyō" (A comparative study of two big shipbuilding firms during the post-World War I depression), *Keiei shigaku* (Japanese business history review), Vol. 18, No. 3, 1983, p. 15.
57. *Ibid.*, p. 6.
58. Shiba, "Taishō ki kigyō keiei," p. 126.
59. Kaneko, ed., *Sangyō hattatsu shi*, Vol. 9, pp. 205–7.
60. Shiba Takao, "Kin'yū kyōkō ji ni okeru keiei senryaku no hatan to sono seiri: Kawasaki Zōsensho no baai" (The collapse of business strategy and its settlement during the monetary crisis: The case of Kawasaki Dockyard), *Keiei shigaku* (Japanese business history review), Vol. 15, No. 1, 1980, pp. 39–41.
61. Matsukata's statements at the sixty-second and sixty-third general meetings of Kawasaki Dockyard stockholders, 1928.
62. Shiba, "Taishō ki kigyō keiei," p. 127.

63. *Kawasaki Jūkōgyō shashi*, p. 659.
64. Shiba, "Fukyō ki no ni dai zōsen kigyō," pp. 12–3.
65. *Ibid.*, p. 18.
66. *Ibid.*, pp. 18–9.
67. *Ibid.*, pp. 22–3.
68. *Ibid.*, pp. 23–4.
69. *Mitsubishi Jūkōgyō shashi*, p. 151.
70. Mitsubishi Heavy Industries, Ltd., "Materials for Compilation of a History of the Company."
71. Mishima, ed., *Mitsubishi zaibatsu*, pp. 91–3.

Comment

Kesaji Kobayashi
Ryukoku University

Professor Shiba's paper discusses the relationship between managerial hierarchies and business performance. Both Mitsubishi Shipbuilding and Kawasaki Dockyard had nearly the same managerial structure to coordinate the various business activities of their enterprises, but by 1930 the former company had established itself as a zaibatsu-type enterprise, while the latter went bankrupt during the economic crisis in 1927 after showing "the progressive aspects of managerial enterprises," as Professor Morikawa says in his paper. Despite its failure, the Kawasaki Dockyard case provides very interesting evidence concerning the effectiveness of a managerial hierarchy led by a mighty entrepreneur. According to Professor Morikawa's classification, Kawasaki Dockyard was a firm that shifted from Y to Z_2, that is, from an enterprise with a larger number of joint stockholders than of salaried managers on the board of directors, to one in which salaried managers accounted for more than two-thirds of the directors. But this transformation was the result of a business failure in the latter half of the 1920s, so Kawasaki Dockyard would have been either Y or Z_1 in the period that Professor Shiba's paper treats.

The leading figure in Kawasaki Dockyard's managerial hierarchy was Matsukata Kōjirō, a dictatorial entrepreneur who joined Kawasaki as a salaried manager but soon became owner-manager by acquiring a large share of the company's stock. During World War I his aggressive business strategy was rewarded with marvelous performance, bringing the company handsome profits. But immediately after the war, with the coming of a depression in the shipbuilding industry as well as the shipping industry, his expansionary strategy brought about the reverse effect, and with the Japanese

Navy's change of plan because of the Naval Armament Limitation Treaty, Kawasaki Dockyard completely lost its market base, resulting in the total failure of 1927.

Mitsubishi Shipbuilding's strategy was far sounder. Measures to rationalize the company, including the discharge of employees, were forcefully pursued. And in this survival strategy Mitsubishi Shipbuilding showed its superiority to Kawasaki Dockyard. In fact, the top management of Mitsubishi Shipbuilding included many executives who could check the company's strategy from various points of view. As Professor Shiba points out, this was one of the most conspicuous characteristics of Mitsubishi Shipbuilding's managerial hierarchy. Kawasaki Dockyard's structure lacked such a checking system, leaving the important decision making to one man, Matsukata.

Having summarized the paper, I would like to comment on the following three points. First, was Matsukata's dictatorial leadership due to his managerial ability or to his position as the largest stockholder? Second, Professor Shiba writes that "as most of these [Mitsubishi Shipbuilding's] managers were engineers, the departments they managed tended to follow a steady course." But this statement seems to be based on an a priori judgment that engineers could make sounder decisions. Historically, engineer-type entrepreneurs were apt to put too much emphasis on technological aspects, neglecting other aspects of business. In Mitsubishi Shipbuilding, was the check by Mitsubishi Co. (the parent company) more important than that by engineer-managers? And third, I would like to know more about the motives behind Kawasaki Dockyard's diversification strategy during the depression era, because I have heard that Matsukata hated to discharge employees.

This paper seems to emphasize not only the importance of the formation of managerial hierarchies but also the importance of the personnel in such a hierarchy.

Response

Takao Shiba

1. I think that the source of Matsukata's dictatorial leadership was his managerial ability rather than his position as the largest stockholder, because his dictatorial leadership was established before he became the largest stockholder. As mentioned in my paper, under his direction Kawasaki Dockyard expanded in size and ship-building capacity. As a result, the company ensured its position as second only to the shipbuilding division of Mitsubishi Co., which could use the vast funds of the Mitsubishi zaibatsu. Moreover, Matsukata's aggressive policies brought huge profits to his company during World War I. This performance strengthened his leadership.

2. Indeed, engineers could not always make sounder decisions. In many cases engineers put too much emphasis on technological aspects and neglected business aspects. I think, however, that there are two types of engineers. One type is an engineer who tends to pursue technology for its own sake; the other is an engineer who becomes a manager using the knowledge and judgment acquired in his training as an engineer. Mitsubishi Co. appears to have segmented engineers into these two types during a certain term of employment and promoted the latter type to top management. Therefore we do not see the former type as engineer-directors in Mitsubishi Shipbuilding and Engineering Co. before World War II.

Professor Kobayashi's second question includes another point: How did the parent company affect the decision-making process of the top management of Mitsubishi Shipbuilding and Engineering Co.? This is a very difficult question, since we have no detailed records of decision making in the Mitsubishi zaibatsu. But again I think it is clear that Mitsubishi Shipbuilding's decision making was very steady and cautious.

3. Kawasaki Dockyard's diversification strategy during the de-pression was based on two motives. One was Matsukata's paternal-istic feeling, as Professor Kobayashi points out. But there was

another motive. This was Matsukata's intention to forge a new way for his company, whose shipbuilding business had been reduced and whose shipping business was at a standstill.

The Development of Managerial Enterprises in India

P. N. Agarwala
Educational Consultants (India) Ltd.

I. Historical Background

Prior to the presence of Portuguese, Dutch, British, and French trading companies from the closing years of the fifteenth century to the early nineteenth century, when the monopoly of the East India Company to trade with India was ended by the British Parliament, Indian and Arab merchants had dominated India's manufacture of textiles, including cotton and silk; its trade in precious stones, spices, and other luxury items; and its foreign commerce. Many of India's manufactured goods were carried by sea and overland through the Arab countries of the Middle East and Lebanon to Egypt and Europe. After Saladin's success during the Crusades and the fall of Constantinople in 1453, the European powers sought an alternate route to India by circumnavigating Africa. Indian textiles were prized in Southeast Asia—present-day Burma, Sri Lanka, Thailand, Malaysia, Indonesia, Indochina, and the Philippines, East Africa, and even the distant South American and Caribbean regions. Commerce and industry were dominated by certain castes and communities, such as the Gujarati Banias, Bhatias, Parsis, Khoja, and Bohra Ismaili Muslim traders in western India; the Marwari Banias in central and eastern India; the Chettiars in South India; and the Banias and Khatris in North India.

The managing agency system, which began with the founding and operation of a life insurance corporation, was later extended to the management of coal, jute, tea, and engineering companies pioneered by the British houses. This system was adopted in Bombay and later extended to the rest of India. One of the main reasons for the rise and growth of the managing agency system was the need

235

to provide continuity in management, since many of the expatriate British personnel used to return or retire to Britain. The other compelling reason was the scarcity of risk capital, as there were no stock exchanges or money markets through which to raise capital. The nobility and the other land-owning classes that had surplus savings preferred to invest them in real estate and jewelry and to indulge in conspicuous consumption.

It is against this background that industrialization in India in the modern sense took root around the middle of the nineteenth century, when the first textile mill was pioneered in Bombay by a Parsi entrepreneur, Cawasji Davar. Simultaneously the jute industry was pioneered by Scottish entrepreneurs around Calcutta; Auckland set up the first jute mill; and tea plantations, coal mines, and engineering establishments were started by British houses in Assam, Bengal, and Bihar. The development of the railroad system began in 1853, when the Bombay–Thana railway line was opened. Later the Calcultta–Ranigunj line was commissioned by various British interests, who set up railway companies to span the subcontinent. Much of the railway system operating in India was complete by World War II. The American Civil War provided the impetus for the start of industrial enterprises, particularly textile mills in western and later central India. The combined paid-up capital of joint-stock companies amounted to over £30 million by 1865.

II. The Rise and Growth of Joint-Stock Companies in the Nineteenth Century

Modern business corporations in India were greatly subject to foreign influence and traditions. The ancient indigenous institutions of the guild type and territorial or community groups of businessmen and skilled artisans had almost withered away by the end of the eighteenth century in the fluid political situation following the collapse of the Mogul Empire and the struggle for supremacy among the Marathas, Jats, Sikhs, and Rajputs in which the British emerged triumphant.

India exported very substantial quantities of cotton textiles to Europe almost to the end of the eighteenth century, and large quantities of yarn to China and Japan in the second half of the nineteenth century, enjoying a substantial comparative cost advantage. Parsi merchants like Jamshedji Jeejibhai, Khurshedjee Rostomjee Cama, Nusserwanji Tata, and his son Jamshedji Tata all started their enterprises by trading with and going to China. The pioneering Bengali merchants traded mostly in jute, rice, seed, and other products, and they were important middlemen for British private trade in the eighteenth century and the first half of the nineteenth century. The leading spirit among them was Dwarakanath Tagore. He had been a promoter and large shareholder of the Union Bank, Steam Tug Association, Bengal Tea Association, India General Steam Navigation Company, and Bengal Coal Company. His firm collapsed in 1851. He was the grandfather of the poet Rabindranath Tagore. Later the Bengalis showed a marked aversion to risk taking, investing mostly in real estate and engaging in government service, teaching, law, and medicine. In the nineteenth century there were few suitable managers and accountants to man the banks and the financial houses. There was also a dearth of trained and experienced personnel in merchant houses; people holding obscure positions in old established banks were eagerly sought by the new class of promoters.

The Wadias were the master shipbuilders from the eighteenth century onward. They built many ships for the China trade and for the East India Company. In the mid-nineteenth century, when the Crown took over the company, the Wadias branched out into textiles. The Petits set up a number of textile mills in Bombay, as did the Jewish house of Sassoons and also Ibrahim Currimbhoy, who had 13 textile mills before the 1933 collapse. Among Gujaratis, Thackersey and Khatau set up cotton mills in Bombay.

The Crimean War in the 1860s deprived the world markets of hemp. Jute became a big business and was eagerly sought not only for packing but also for defense purposes. What the American Civil War had done to foster fortunes in cotton, the Crimean War did for the jute industry. By 1865 tea had also become a big business, and 62 tea companies had been registered in India in addition to 30 sterling companies. Highly paid managers with large staffs were immediately sent to superintend the tea-owning properties in

Assam and North Bengal. Had it not been for the subordination of the national interests of India to those of Britain in industrialization and transport development, India might well have reached the stage of managerial capitalism much earlier.

Most of the European managing agency houses, such as Andrew Yule and Bird, were controlled by the Yule and Benthall families and were run as partnerships. Expatriate British personnel were hired by these houses on the basis of family background, the school tie, and the old boy network. Those who made their mark rose to become directors or junior partners. The emphasis was largely on on-the-job training rather than professional competence or functional specialization.

In the Indian managing agency houses, the dominant business castes and community provided the nucleus for managerial decision making pertaining to investments, expansion, diversification, product planning, pricing, and hiring of key personnel. Most of those hired were close relatives, members of the community, people drawn from the place of origin of the merchant entrepreneur, and trusted friends. Promotion was largely determined by loyalty and trust gained through long years of work, not by professional background or merit alone. Very few technical institutions had been set up to teach engineering, medicine, and science; enterprising students went abroad to the United Kingdom, Germany, and the United States for higher education and professional training.

The government's vacillatory policy regarding the development of the iron and steel industry and shipping was vividly illustrated in the setting up of the basic and key industries and shipping even when raw materials like iron ore and coal were found in abundance alongside the bulk cargo freight.

III. The First Managerial Entrepreneurs

The rate of growth of total agricultural production and the rate of growth of industrial production were both low until the eve of World War I, and the share of industrial workers in the total work force underwent hardly any significant change. Although India was the first oriental country to feel the impact of industrialization, Japan, which started later and with fewer natural resources, forged ahead far more rapdily. Modern industry in India, barring ordnance factories, was largely in the private sector. Up to 1914 there was virtually complete free trade. Among the modern industries the most important were cotton and jute manufacturing, coal, tea, and engineering. Steel rose after 1907, when Tata Steel was established in Jamshedpur and the Steel Corporation of Bengal began to produce steel at a plant at Kulti that had earlier produced pig iron.

The cotton industry was dominated by Indians, while the jute industry remained almost the exclusive preserve of Europeans, mainly Scots. The major portion of the cotton yarn output was exported to China, and some was even sent to Japan until 1893. Both industries were almost entirely dependent on imports of capital, machinery, and spares from the United Kingdom. These two manufacturing industries alone accounted for more than half the total imports of machinery and millwork.

Tariff protection would have made all the difference in fostering faster growth of finer counts of cotton textiles and yarns. Indian mills perforce had to concentrate on the production of goods that could be woven with yarn of up to 40 counts. The twin policies of free trade and financial orthodoxy continued to strangle government initiative in the industrial field. Most of India's trade and industry was geared toward the foreign market. The railway network was focused primarily on servicing the ports. There was no domestic production of railway cars, locomotives, or rails, all of which were imported from the United Kingdom. Had there been a sustained growth of investment fostered by the kinds of deliberate government policies that had already become familiar through the experience of Prussia and Japan, resources for further investment would also have expanded at a more positive rate. A high rate of growth of investment would have resulted in a high rate of growth of capital and intermediate goods and would have helped managerial capitalism if only appropriate policies had been pursued. From 1880 to 1914 India was practically the only sizable economy that was forced to pursue a policy of free trade and nonintervention in the industrial field. The tax system was quite regressive from the mid-1880s onward, and only minuscule amounts were spent on education.

In the face of this challenging environment entrepreneurs like Jamshedji Tata, Sir Rajadranath Mookerjee, and later Hirachand Walchand, Sir Purshottamdas Thakurdas, Shriram, and Kirloskar pioneered industries like iron and steel, power generation, textiles, shipping, construction, sugar, engineering, automobiles, aircraft, chemicals, and agricultural implements. Jamshedji Tata introduced ring spinning in the 1880s at around the same time that the process was introduced in Manchester, and with great perseverance was able to lay the foundations of the steel industry at Jamshedpur. Tata pioneered scientific and industrial research and the power grid for electricity generation in Bombay and introduced the elements of modern management in the running of the Tata enterprises. This tradition was carried on by Jamshedji Tata's sons Sir Dorab and Sir Ratan, who hired experienced professional personnel for the running of their industrial enterprises, such as Sir Jehangir Ghandy, who became the first Indian general manager of the Tata Iron and Steel Works at Jamshedpur. Tata also hired Sir Homi Mody, A. D. Shroff, and senior retired government officials like Gulam Mohammad and Sir Ardeshir Dalal, besides Seth and Hinge in its chemicals and oils plants.

Sir Rajadranath Mookerjee graduated from the position of civil engineer and petty contractor to head the firm of Martin Burn, which set up the Indian Iron and Steel Works at Kulti (Asansol). The firm was also engaged in the building of light railways, large construction projects, and power and water supply schemes in many Indian cities. Indian Iron and Steel was the second largest steel enterprise, next only to Tata. Martin Burn was originally an English house, where Sir Rajadranath became the first Indian partner through sheer merit. The company was largely professionally managed by engineers and technocrats and had established a high reputation for efficiency.

Sir Purshottamdas Thakurdas had made his mark in the cotton business and was a director of more than 65 companies (the largest number of directorhsips held by an individual at the time). He was the chairman of the Oriental Government Life Assurance Company, the largest life insurance firm in the country, and presided over the East India Cotton Exchange for many years. He was one of the authors of the Bombay Plan formulated by eight Indian industrialists in 1944, was associated with many government commissions, and was the first president of the Federation of the Indian Chambers of Commerce and Industry, set up in 1927. He may be said to represent the beginnings of managerial capitalism inasmuch as he did not own any industrial enterprise.

Hirachand Walchand started out as a construction contractor but was fired with the vision of setting up such basic and key industries as automobile and aircraft manufacture, engineering, and shipping. A self-made entrepreneur, he laid the foundations of these industries and engaged in innovative projects. He fostered the professionalization of managment in his enterprises and was not given to any speculation or brokerage, a background that characterized many other industrialists. Sir Visvesvariya, who had been a chief engineer and *dewan* (prime minister) of Mysore State, pioneered the concept of state enterprises by setting up Mysore Silk, Mysore Sandal Wood, and Badravati Iron and Steel Works, and conceived of economic planning for industrialization far ahead of any of his contemporaries.

Shriram began as an assistant secretary in Delhi Cloth and General Mills, where his father, Madan Mohan, had been a paid secretary. The mill had originally been set up by the Gurwala family, who were the treasurers to the Mogul court and had been rated as the Rothschilds of India by contemporary British authorities. Shriram, who may be described as a product of managerial capitalism, succeeded in expanding and diversifying the mill to make it one of the largest industrial groups in the country. Shriram followed the Tata example of harmonizing industrial relations, emphasized scientific and industrial research, and favored professional management.

Kirloskar, who had a technical background, set up a company to manufacture iron plows and other agricultural implements. His firm has expanded and diversified considerably and is professionally managed. Of 14 directors, only one has been drawn from the

Kirloskar family. Professionals like M. B. Jambekar, Gurjar, and A. K. Phalnikar were hired at senior levels.

IV. Impact of World War I and the Interwar Years

During World War I India became a major supply center for defense supplies for the war against the Central Powers, particularly Turkey. This no doubt gave the existing industry a fillip, since imports were curtailed after 1916. Even so, no effort was made to set up any basic or key industries in the fields of capital goods, machinery, rolling stock, or chemicals. Limited efforts were initiated for direct and indirect military supplies and were chiefly concentrated on developing small-scale industries. There was no systematic policy of helping new industries through financial assistance or market guarantees, even for government purchases. At the end of World War I a department of industries was set up to supply commercial intelligence and render technical advice and assistance to minor industries and to organize demonstrations of cottage industries.

The interwar years witnessed a dramatic decline in the terms of trade, and India's position as an exporter of primary commodities made it extremely susceptible to the agricultural depression that set in 1926–27. In the late 1920s and in the 1930s a policy of deflation was pursued vigorously although a massive program of public works was the need of the hour.

In the early years of industrialization prior to World War I, few qualified Indians were available to man and run modern business corporations. Initially entrepreneurs and foreign capital had to be imported, though some managerial talent was no doubt forthcoming from the small Parsi community, which had had exposure to Western technology, was given to overseas travel, and mixed easily in social and business circles abroad. Even on the eve of World War II foreign enterprises still dominated some of the major industries, such as jute mills, tea plantations, coal mines, and engineering. The bulk of investment went into extractive or plantation industries aimed at the export market.

Discriminating protection on a halting and limited scale was introduced after 1923 in the wake of severe competition from

Belgian steel and was extended to sugar, paper, cement, and cotton textiles in the 1930s. This helped lay the foundations of the sugar, cement, and paper industries, but overall the Great Depression severely affected the agro-industrial sector. A brief respite in 1935–36 was followed by the severe recession of 1937–38, which was relieved only by the outbreak of war in 1939–40.

The caste system was one of the factors that retarded the business activity of capitalist enterprises in modern India. The Indian merchant class in Bombay led by the Parsis, Jews, and other outward-looking communities displayed much greater entrepreneurial dynamism than did the merchant class in Calcutta and Madras. Capital raising was perforce confined to India's own resource groups, as financial and capital markets had not been developed. Capital was raised mainly on the basis of the credit standing and business acumen of a small number of successful entrepreneurs.

The transition to salaried managers was therefore extremely slow in coming, as the resource groups wanted to retain financial and managerial control over operations. The factors of production necessary for carrying out business activities were subjected to the restrictions of prevailing social customs. Neither capital nor labor was effectively mobile. The consumption habits of the people were essentially conditioned by the caste to which they belonged as well as by their personal status. The Marwari community has till recently continued to engage in business activities in traditional styles.

The larger Indian industrial houses, which had set up the sugar, paper, and cement industries in the wake of tariff protection, reaped a rich bonanza during World War II and the immediate postwar years. Wartime profits and the phenomenal stock exchange boom of 1943–46 helped them consolidate the hold of their combines and paved the way for their mammoth expansion and diversification in the post-independence years. This was greatly facilitated by easy access to bank credit and the life insurance funds controlled by the groups. The combines purchased many of the European concerns that sold their holdings in the postwar era. Even though the Marwari interests had acquired substantial shareholdings in the jute and coal sector, the management of these units remained largely in European hands until the late 1940s and early 1950s.

The European houses had introduced a system of hiring young executives in their covenanted cadres, but they were hired largely on the basis of their school and family backgrounds rather than on the basis of professional competence and merit. Indian firms with the exception of Tata, Martin Burn, and Indian Iron and Steel, and to a lesser extent Shriram, Kirloskar, Mahindra, and Thapar, continued to fill their top executive positions with loyal and trusted kinsmen or members of their communities and villages and to employ technical personnel only in fields where they could not muster their own kith and kin to fill the positions.

The multinationals in India, such as Imperial Tobacco, Imperial Chemicals, Dunlop, Lever, Union Carbide, Firestone, the oil companies—Shell, Exxon, Caltex—and the pharmaceutical companies, began to hire professionally qualified managers around the mid-1950s, when import subsitution on a massive scale led to expansion and diversification. The entrepreneurial base that was so narrow has shown signs of broadening in the past three decades owing to the large spurt in industrial development in the post-independence era.

The industrial policy resolutions of 1948 and 1956 helped lay the basis for a massive spurt in the expansion and diversification of the industrial sector. Industrial production has increased fivefold in the last 35 years. Thanks to the population upsurge in the past 37 years and the massive investments in successive five-year plans, a sheltered market has grown up; and absence of any real competition has helped the established industrial houses to grow very rapidly. The House of Birla has grown more than 37-fold in the last 37 years. Tax incentives, liberal depreciation allowances, and generous loans from financial institutions have enabled the large houses to grow phenomenally. Houses like Thapar, J. K., D. C. M., Mafatlal, Bangur, and Goenka have grown many times over. Reliance Textiles, founded by Dhirubhai Ambani, who was a mere clerk 20 years ago, has blossomed into a textile and petrochemical complex with a turnover of over 5,000 million rupees and is slated to double its turnover in the next three years.

Much of the spectacular growth has been in the nontraditional sectors of chemicals, pharmaceuticals, fertilizers, synthetic fibers and textiles, consumer durables, engineering, plastics, and electronics, while the older industries, such as textiles, jute, sugar, and paper, have been languishing for want of modernization. Industrial sickness has gripped many of the traditional sectors, largely because of misconceived policies and lack of professional management.

With a view to controlling the concentration of economic power among the large industrial houses, the government has introduced many licensing controls as well as the Monopolies and Restrictive Practices legislation. The managing agency system was formally abolished on 3 April 1970. But despite all these rigorous rules and procedures, the large industrial houses have managed to retain effective control over their enterprises. They still control the key and strategic decision-making areas of investment, expansion and diversification, pricing, product planning, and hiring of key personnel—almost all the areas of top management and corporate planning.

Many professional salaried managers have been hired at the operational level—production and maintenance, inventory and materials management, industrial relations, accounting, and public relations—but with few exceptions the corporate boards are still largely controlled by the industrial houses through their nominees, friends, and relatives. The large industrial houses have thus managed to retain their dominant hold and are now in the process of putting family members who have received a professional education in top executive positions. The separation of corporate ownership and control has become an accepted phenomenon in the West, but in India salaried managers do not yet occupy top management positions and make strategic decisions independent of the owners in any of the large industrial houses with the exception of Tata and, to an extent, Kirloskar, Mahindra and Mahindra, Larsen and Tubro, Escorts, Godrej, Bajaj, and the multinationals. No doubt the expansion and diversification of the operations of these industrial houses have necessitated the introduction of salaried managers at the intermediate and near-top levels, but the large industrial houses have managed to retain effective control over their corporate boards through their nominees, relatives, and friends even when their own family members have not provided enough progeny to fill the key positions.

The Birlas alone, who are ranked as the second largest industrial house, next only to the Tatas, manage more than 150 companies. Of these, 77 are directly controlled by their kith and kin. The salaried executives who have risen to high positions in their corporate structure include D. P. Mandelia and his son S. P. Mandelia. D. P. Mandelia joined the Birlas in his teens and has risen to the position of their principal adviser. His son S. P. Mandelia manages the Century Rayon complex in Bombay. Other top executives from outside the Birla family circle are Saboo, Hada, and Shah, who reached their present positions by gaining the trust and confidence of the Birla group in the course of long years of loyal service. Although the Birlas have introduced a system of daily reporting (the Perta system of accounting) for actual production, profit and loss, and so on against predetermined targets and for capital investment, they continue to rely on their traditional style of management. The complexity of running their diversified industrial interests has been overcome by the proliferation of their own progeny and by the expansion of the group through matrimonial alliances and the bringing of trusted community and village members into the fold. The Kanorias, Mohtas, Kotharis, and Khaitans are subgroups of the Birla conglomerate. D. P. Khaitan was a brilliant solicitor and chief legal adviser of the Birlas who enjoyed a share in the partnership. The other members of the subgroup are interrelated.

The J. K. group originated in Kanpur and has grown phenomenally in the last 45 years. It now has large interests in Bombay, Calcutta, and Kota (Rajasthan). The major units, such as Raymonds, J. K. Synthetics, J. K. Chemicals, and J. K. Paper, Cement, Sugar, Textiles, and Tyres are under the full control of the extended Singhania enterprise. Salaried managers, such as Nowlakha and Pai, hold important positions at the operational level but have not been vested with key decision-making authority.

The Mafatlal group has been split up among three brothers for taxation purposes and to overcome the Monopolies and Restrictive Trade Practices Commission's capitalization ceiling of 200 million rupees for each industrial house. Even though Mafatlal is generally regarded as a relatively progressive house and has expanded and diversified from textiles, sugar, and jute into petro-chemicals and dyestuffs, to be rated as the third largest industrial house in the private sector, the key decisions continue to be made by members of the charmed circle (the extended family). Similarly in the case of the Shriram group, while salaried managers like S. Ratnam, Y. T. Shah (a former secretary of commerce), and Dharmvira (a former cabinet secretary and governor) have been brought in at high operational and advisory levels, the key decisions are still the prerogative of Bharat Ram, Charat Ram, their sons, and the sons of the late Murlidhar-Bansidhar and Sridhar (all descended from Shriram). In the case of the Thapars, who have emerged as the fifth largest industrial group in the last two decades, the real decision-making power rests with Lalit Mohan Thapar and his brothers Madan and Inder even though top executives like N. M. Wagle, formerly of I.C.S., have been brought in to manage one of the largest enterprises, Greaves Cotton.

In the case of the Bangurs, who have earned a reputation of being very solid in finance, real estate, and shares, the only major outsider brought in to enlarge and manage their operations in Bombay and Karnataka has been G. D. Somani, who had been a prominent broker. In the case of the Goenkas, who in recent years have emerged as the largest takeover group, the real decision-making powers rest with R. P. Goenka, who has recently acquired control of the Ceat, Dunlop Tyre, and Bayer operations in India as well as 20 other foreign affiliates, along with his brothers K. P. and J. P., who like the Mafatlals have become independent entities to overcome government regulation. The top decision-making power in the Sarabhai group has been vested in Gautam Sarabhai, son of Ambalal Sarabhai, and top executives like Bhatt have been eased out. In the Lalbhai group the key decisions are made by a triumvirate comprising Arvind Lalbhai and Kasturbhai's sons Shrenik and Siddarth, who manage the textile group and the chemicals and dyes group, respectively.

Even though public financial institutions have their nominees on the boards of many of these enterprises, normally they do not interfere with the key decisions made by the chief executives or the groups' representatives. In the existing milieu these nominees are easily influenced to go along with the decisions of the de facto controllers. Somehow the industrial combines have thus far managed to survive and grow in changing circumstances through recent makeshift arrangements to bring in salaried managers mainly at the operational and advisory levels.

The increasingly felt need for professional talent in top management is being partly met by the hiring of outside consultants and advisers with information, experience, and know-how in their specialized fields. There is no doubt that the number of salaried managers is greater than that of owner-managers, but in the peculiar socioeconomic conditions prevailing in India the owners have somehow managed, through close linkage with the political leadership and top bureaucracy, to retain their stronghold in an environment that is subject to very rigorous government rules and procedures at almost every stage of industrial operations. Only now are licensing controls beginning to be liberalized with the raising of the level for MRTP companies from 200 million to 1,000 million rupees in view of the steep inflation since the original ceiling was fixed a decade and a half ago.

In the Indian context the members of the founding families have rarely lost their incentive for achievement because of the punitive rates of taxation, including heavy estate duty and wealth tax, and the diminution of power, patronage, and prestige through the loss of control of a large industrial group. With the abolition of the feudal vestiges of *rentiers* and of princely privileges, there is little incentive left to maintain the property of the family, particularly as there is no wealth tax on corporate assets. The current rates of estate duty run to 85% on more than 2 million rupees' worth of property, to which are added a succession certificate and valuation charges at 5%, leaving a residue of barely 10% in the present inflationary spiral. Even the cost of a reasonably good house in the metropolitan cities of Bombay, Delhi, and Calcutta is presently more than 2 million rupees. In addition to the very high income tax, there is a 12.5% surcharge and, to compound it all, a compulsory deposit that leaves a fifth or less of total income. On top of this, there is a wealth tax based on the current value of assets and bearing no relation whatever to the historical cost or the current income derived from property. In some cases the total tax incidence reaches the prohibitive level of around 100% and therefore leaves no incentive whatever to the individual owner. There is considerable tax evasion. Some tax relief is now in sight. It has been proposed to abolish estate duty in the 1985–86 budget, and the compulsory deposit and surcharges have been dropped.

Despite their phenomenal growth over the past 43 years, Indian industrial enterprises are still puny by international standards. Not a single private-sector house is listed in *Fortune*'s list of the 500 top companies outside the United States. Therefore, it has been possible thus far to cope with the existing red tape and highly bureaucratic procedures by bringing in professional talent and salaried managers at the intermediate and liaison levels.

In the United States, Western Europe, and even Japan the separation between ownership and management has become almost complete because the controlling stock interest is often held not by individuals but by mutual benefit funds, pension funds, banks, and trusts. The management of a big corporation thus has become a free-floating center of power, subject only to the market, takeover bids, trade union pressure, and government intervention. There has also been an increasing recognition of the concept of the corporate management's social responsibility. Nonpropertied managers, unlike owner-managers in the developed countries, are responsible not only to shareholders but to a host of other groups, such as consumers, workers, the government, and above all society at large. This movement has helped develop the concept of professional nonpropertied managers. However, in India this development is still in the nascent stage. Only the Tatas have accepted the concept of social responsibility. Other industrial groups have tried to draw consolation from their charitable trusts devoted to education, hospitals, the provision of rest houses for pilgrims, the building of temples, and so on, all activities that qualify for tax exemption. Many of the industrial combines, including Tata and Birla, have drawn profusely on the funds of the temple trusts, which are based on the donations and offerings made to these institutions by followers in the community, at low rates of interest.

The developed countries have replaced owner-managers with a new class of nonpropertied managers who owe their position to managerial ability rather than property ownership. Their social

backgrounds, training, and experience make them both think and
act differently from owner-managers. The emergence of managerialism has led to fundamental changes in the ideology of business. The
old picture of a ruthless, self-interested company director has given
way to the picture of the modern, nonpropertied, professional corporate director responsible to society at large and free to subordinate the old-fashioned hunt for profits to a variety of other quanti-
tatively less precise but qualitatively more worthy objectives. In
India, however, in the absence of any real competition in the
domestic market owing to the rigors of licensing and in the absence
of any foreign competition owing to stringent import controls and
continuing constraints on foreign exchange, the transition to managerial capitalism has not yet progressed in any significant measure.

With selective liberalization in very recent years, there is an
emerging prospect of salaried managers moving up to higher levels
of decision making. A modest beginning has been made with the
introduction of professional managers into board rooms, but Indian
corporate management as a whole still has a long way to go before
it can catch up with its counterparts in developed countries. It has
to overcome its own resistance to change in a traditional culture.
So far, adaptation to change has been half-hearted, making the
transition to a new productive order incomplete.

Often the board functions like a shadow king, while real decisions
are made by executive management. The majority of the large
private-sector companies in India continue to be controlled by
powerful families or groups. A good board organized on functional
lines could be of immense help to the executive management of the
corporation. This may become more evident when the public
financial institutions take a more direct interest in the active functioning of the boards of companies in which they have invested large
amounts of capital, and in ensuring that the right kind of competent
and professional men are adequately represented on these boards.

V.   The Growth of the Public Sector

On the eve of the transfer of power in 1947, public ownership
extended to the railways, post and telegraph service, and ordnance
factories. In the post-independence period there has been a phenom-

enal growth in the public sector. In 1951 five public-sector corporations were set up—the biggest being Sindri Fertilizers—at a capital cost of 310 million rupees. Three one-million-ton steel plants were set up in the late 1950s and early 1960s. In the 1960s and 1970s the public sector was greatly expanded, and coal, copper, zinc, and lead mines were nationalized.

In the last 33 years the public sector has grown to include 214 corporations involving a capital outlay of 350,000 million rupees. This sector embraces a very wide spectrum of enterprises: oil and natural gas exploration, production, refining, and marketing; steel production except for Tata Steel, the only private-sector steelmaker; a considerable part of fertilizer production; coal, copper, zinc, manganese, lead, and most iron ore mining; aircraft manufacture; a very substantial part of shipping; a large share of bulk pharmaceuticals manufacture; a fair share of the manufacture of earth-moving and telephone equipment; and a substantial share of the manufacture of machine tools, watches, tractors, and incandescent bulbs. The government has taken over well over 100 ailing textile mills and many large engineering companies; airlines and a host of other service-sector enterprises, including State Trading; some ailing sugar, jute, and cement plants and tea plantations; and a fair share of the hotel industry. All life insurance business was nationalized in 1955. The Imperial Bank of India, which was acting as a government treasury in all of India's 300-odd districts, was also nationalized in 1955; and 14 major joint-stock banks were nationalized in 1969, followed by six other banks in recent years. Today 85% to 90% of the banking sector is nationalized; the only exceptions are foreign banks and small indigenous banks. The general insurance companies, covering fire, marine, accident, and other nonlife insurance, were nationalized in 1971. The total capital of these publicly owned enterprises, together with the central atomic power generation plants and other public utilities, amounts to 1,000,000 million rupees.

Besides the central government undertakings, a large number of state government undertakings have been set up to manage buses and other nonrailway public transport, irrigation, and hydroelectric power projects. The total public-sector investment considerably outweighs the total private-sector investment. There are presently 60,000 joint-stock companies operating in India. Their combined capitalization amounts to 250,000 million rupees, of which the 300 largest companies account for 175,000 million rupees. The small-scale sector has grown rapidly in the last two and a half decades.

Although the public sector was conceived as an instrument of state policy and was designed to run on commercial lines, over the past three decades it has developed a fairly bureaucratic pattern and style of management. The chiefs and functional directors of the 200-odd public-sector corporations are screened and selected by the Public Enterprises Selection Board set up by the government, and these appointments are further subject to the approval of the Appointments Committee of the cabinet, comprising the prime minister, the finance minister, and the minister of the ministry to which the undertaking is administratively subject. The finance ministry and the administrative ministry are normally represented on the board of the enterprise, and all significant matters involving investment, pricing, expansion, diversification, and determination of pay scales are subject to the approval of the administrative and finance ministries.

In 1969 the government set up the Bureau of Public Enterprises to coordinate the operations of public enterprises and to serve as a data bank and monitoring mechanism to oversee their performance. The bureau, however, also functions in a typically bureaucratic fashion and has not been able to play an effective coordinating role to ensure optimal efficiency in the running of public enterprises.

When the public enterprises were being set up in the 1950s, the government deputed a large number of retired and serving civil servants and bureaucrats to fill the senior and top positions in these enterprises. The experiment of creating an industrial management pool was attempted in 1958–59, but the very strong opposition of entrenched civil servants and bureaucrats managed to strangle this venture at birth. There was no further recruitment after the initial 100-odd people who were drafted from professional and management disciplines. The bureaucrats and civil servants, having had no exposure to the management of industrial enterprises and no management training, imposed wholesale the archaic rules and procedures for district administration that had been introduced by the colonial administrators in the second half of the nineteenth and the early part of the twentieth centuries.

These fundamental and supplementary rules, formulated at a time when the government followed a laissez-faire policy, were wholly unsuited to the running of modern commercial and industrial undertakings. The main emphasis in the observance of these rules was a kind of proprietory audit. There was no concept of corporate planning, predetermined target setting, monitoring and performance appraisal, and midterm review, and no exposure to operating in a competitive framework. Therefore the ethos of a management culture has not been cultivated. To cap it all, the administrative ministry very rarely delegates any autonomy to the chief executive and the board for strategic decision making. Furthermore, the tenure of the chief executive and the functional directors is generally set at two years and is further subject to the relationship with the administrative ministry. Thus no real decision-making power is vested in the enterprise on a long-term, continuing basis, nor can any succession planning be attempted in such circumstances.

At the lower and middle levels the public sector has no doubt been able to attract professionals, as it offers comparatively secure tenure at these levels, but the avenues for promotion do not normally extend beyond the senior operating levels; few recruits have managed to reach the higher echelons of management. There have been two notable exceptions. One is S. M. Patil, who rose to become the chairman of Hindustan Machine Tools, which manufactures machine tools, watches, tractors, printing machines, and incandescent bulbs, and put the company in a sound growth pattern. Patil had a private-sector background with a strong technical base. He managed to professionalize the company's operations and diversify its activities in a competitive framework. The other notable professional manager is Krishnamurthy, who revamped Bharat Heavy Electricals, one of the largest public-sector groups in the area of power plants. These two companies were rated as highly progressive and very well managed in a survey of the All India Management Association conducted in 1984.

Three of the top 10 public-sector profit-making companies—the

Oil and Natural Gas Commission, Oil India Limited, and Indian Oil Corporation—are engaged in petroleum exploration, production, refining, and marketing. The others include the giant state trading monopoly organizations—the State Trading Corporation and the Minerals and Metals Trading Corporation—Indian Air Lines Corporation, Neyveli Lignite Corporation, Central Coalfields, Bharat Heavy Electricals, and Hindustan Machine Tools. All enjoy a monopolistic position except for Hindustan Machine Tools, which functions partly in a competitive framework. The bulk of the State Trading Corporation's profits accrues from the canalized sector, which is not exposed to any competition whatever. If the profits of the monopoly organizations were set off against the loss-making enterprises, the public sector collectively would show a very large operating deficit. Even after the windfall profits of the monopoly organizations are added in, the net return from the public sector is nominal and clearly reflects the lack of efficiency and sound management of these undertakings. Most of the prices in the public sector are administered prices, which have little relation to market forces or domestic or international competition.

In the case of multinationals operating in India, the parent companies no doubt play a major role in investment decisions, expansion, diversification, product planning, and corporate planning. However, most of these enterprises are managed by professionally trained salaried managers, and a systems approach is invariably followed. The parent company does not interfere in the day-to-day management of these enterprises, and considerable latitude is afforded in matters of pricing, industrial relations, and research and development.

Under the Foreign Exchange Regulation Act many foreign companies have diluted their shareholdings to conform to the 40% ceiling laid down by the Reserve Bank of India. Only multinational companies engaged in priority, high-technology, 100% export, and basic sectors are permitted to have 51% foreign shareholdings. Despite this dilution many companies have managed to retain effective control by wide dispersal of their shareholdings. There has been substantial investment in the pharmaceuticals sector in the past two and a half decades, but recently, owing to stringent price controls, there has not been much accent on further expansion. There has been considerable dilution in many of the Sterling Tea companies, where British investments predominated. Other sectors dominated by multinationals are in the area of consumer goods, such as soap, detergent, edible oils, cigarettes, packaged tea and coffee, beverages, baby food, chocolate, and cosmetics, as well as in tires, fertilizers and explosives, tin containers, aluminum, dye-stuffs, and engineering—all areas where consumer preferences and brand loyalties have been built up over the years.

Ajit Haksar, who originally worked for Hindustan Thompson, a U.S.-based advertising agency, rose to become the first chairman of India Tobacco, a subsidiary of British-American Tobacco. He was instrumental in diversifying operations into a chain of hotels with Sheraton collaboration, paper and board manufacture, and marine-product exports. Prakash Tandon was made the first chairman of Hindustan Lever in the early 1960s; he was followed by Varadarajan, who now heads the Council of Scientific and Industrial Research. Hindustan Lever has diversified from edible oils, soaps, and detergents to tea, animal feed and fertilizers.

Other notable managerial professionals include Keshub Mahindra. He heads the Mahindra and Mahindra group, which manufactures jeeps, tractors, textile machinery, and so on. His father and uncle held senior executive positions in the private sector and the government, and his shareholding in the enterprise is a bare fraction of 1%. Similarly, Har Parshad Nanda started out in the agency house of Escorts and has been instrumental in making it one of the fastest-growing industrial complexes, accounting for 85% of the motorcycle production and 23% of the tractor production in India. The company also has other engineering products. His own shareholding is minuscule. K. G. Khosla, who began as a trainee and salaried employee of Delhi Cloth and General Mills (part of the Shriram group), now heads the Khosla Compressors unit—the largest company of its kind in India.

Godrej started out in a small way as a manufacturer of iron safes and security equipment, and in the post-independence era has diversified into the manufacture of refrigerators, typewriters, soap and detergent, edible oils, and other products. The Bajaj group, which may also be said to be largely manned by professionals, has made its mark internationally in the export of scooters to Indonesia, Taiwan, and Mauritius, and has built up a high reputation for business ethics, customer quality, and after-sales service. Both Ramakrishna and Rahul Bajaj are qualified professionals, and their products have earned a high reputation for quality and service.

VI. Business Training and Associations

Management institutes: The Indian institutes of management in Calcutta and Ahmedabad were set up on the pattern of M.I.T. and the Harvard Business School in the early 1960s, and the Bangalore Institute was established around 1974. (A fourth institute is expected to be set up in Lucknow in 1985.) These three management institutes produce about 500 M.B.A.s every year. Other well-known management institutes have been established in Bombay, Jamshedpur, and Delhi. Some 45 universities have also introduced management courses, though many of them do not have the specialized and highly trained faculty needed.

Six to seven thousand trained managers are required annually, and the number is expected to reach around 10,000 before the end of the 1980s. Most of the graduates of the three institutes of management are able to obtain positions in large private- and public-sector corporations and have little difficulty in reaching good middle-level operating positions during the first ten years. Positions at the senior and top levels are less plentiful, however, and these managers do considerable job hopping in the later years of their careers.

Management associations: The All India Management Association was formed in 1958–59 and celebrated its silver jubilee in May 1984. It is now starting to provide professional training programs in multidisciplinary areas. It has branches in important metropolitan and industrial centers. The management movement is no doubt gaining momentum, and graduates of the three prestigious management institutes are receiving increasingly wider acceptance by commerce, industry, and government.

Chambers of Commerce and Industry: The membership of the Associated Chambers of Commerce and Industry, which is an offshoot of the Bengal and other European Chambers of Commerce and Industry, is drawn mainly from multinational and professionally managed companies, while the membership of the Federation of the Indian Chambers of Commerce and Industry reflects the traditional large industrial houses (largely family controlled) and some professionally managed enterprises.

Significant movement in the corporate sector toward the full-fledged emergence of salaried managers in top management positions can only be expected in coming years, when the liberalizing policies now being initiated have had time to open up wider avenues for the rise of managerial capitalism in India.

Comment

Shin'ichi Yonekawa
Hitotsubashi University

In Japan there are two separate groups working on comparative economic history. Some scholars are engaged in comparing Japan with the West, and others are interested in the comparison of Japan and developing countries. In my view, however, the two groups should be integrated. Only multifaceted comparative research can facilitate understanding of the historical position of the Japanese economy. Professor Agarwala's paper is most welcome for this reason.

Professor Agarwala is a well-informed scholar with a retentive memory, and his paper on Indian business history is full of invaluable facts based on records to which not only non-Indian scholars but also Indian scholars do not have easy access. His paper contains information on a number of Indian businessmen in addition to an analysis of India's economic and business history. His description is so wide-ranging and detailed that even scholars unfamiliar with the economic history of India can understand the outline of India's capitalistic development. Here I wish to summarize his remarks in reference to the rise of managerial capitalism or, to be exact, its immaturity, in India.

According to Professor Agarwala, "Indian corporate management as a whole still has a long way to go before it can catch up with its counterparts in developed countries." India's economy has been changing, but its salient characteristic is slowness to change. There are several reasons for this: the caste system, colonialism together with free trade, the controlled economy after independence, and British influence on management and education. These are major restraining factors that have retarded the business activities of capitalist enterprises in modern India. However, there have been exceptional cases of well-known individual salaried managers. According to Professor Agarwala's paper, the large industrial houses have managed to retain their dominance by providing their family members with professional education, while filling lower- and middle-management posts with salaried managers. The future emergence of top salaried managers is more feasible in subsidiaries of foreign firms.

The last three decades have witnessed phenomenal growth in the public sector. The top management of public enterprises, however, is often occupied by retired or serving civil servants, with the result that the ethos of a management culture has not been cultivated.

Following are my impressions of Professor Agarwala's paper. First, in discussing India's economic history, we cannot ignore the managing agency system. In India the Companies Act was enacted in 1857, modeling itself on the British Companies Act of 1856. Company management, however, was accompanied by the managing agency system: Companies were actually managed not by directors but by managing agents. Company directors were merely a formality. What matters here is that managing agents were the largest stockholders as well as directors of the companies of which they were nominated as agents. (Since 1970 the agency houses have been reorganized as holding companies and continue to control their business groups.) Thus there was no separation of management control from ownership. Controlling a number of companies, each agency house formed a business group similar to that of the zaibatsu in Japan. Zaibatsu (business groups owned by families) differed from agency houses, however, in that they were in effect managed by salaried managers. In this context, I would like to say that his assertion of a dichotomy between corporate ownership and management control owning the managing agency system tends to cause misunderstandings.

Next I would like to note Professor Agarwala's use of the term "managerial entrepreneur." Were the managerial entrepreneurs discussed in his paper professional owner-managers from the start, or did they become owner-managers later? My guess is that in India the latter has been the rule. On the other hand, as Professor Agarwala mentions, professional owner-managers are now appearing in industrial houses. Institutions of higher education are numerous in developing countries. The second generation of founding families is blessed with the opportunity to study at these institutions. It would be possible, therefore, for these families' progeny to continue to control business groups. In Asian countries, Korea in particular, a number of zaibatsu-like business groups exist. It is true, however, that the predominance of family-controlled business groups is associated with the social value system of the society as a whole. The influence of families tends to wane with the birth of modern society. Professor Agarwala's paper is most useful for consideration of the tendencies of business groups in developing countries.

Large Firms in Small Countries:
Reflections on the Rise of Managerial Capitalism

Herman Daems
Katholieke Universiteit Leuven

The rise of managerial capitalism is closely connected with the development of large hierarchies that own and manage a variety of operating units in order to coordinate activities, allocate resources, and control performance. This close, but not perfect, connection is a consequence of the efficiency gains that can be made in large hierarchies by entrusting the functions of risk bearing, decision ratification, and decision making to separate economic agents. Much is known about the economic, technological, and organizational factors that contribute to the development of large hierarchies. The size of the market has been shown to be an essential factor.[1] This might suggest that in small countries the rise of managerial capitalism will be much slower than in large countries.

This paper focuses on the development of large hierarchies in small countries. Special attention is given to the case of Belgium. The focus on small countries is relevant because it provides a new perspective on the role of the size of the home market for the growth strategies of large industrial hierarchies. It will be shown that the size of the country is not a significant factor for the comparative position of large enterprises in Europe. Belgium offers an interesting case because it illustrates how managerial capitalism spreads and how managerial, financial, and family capitalism coexist.

The following definitions are important for this paper. Managerial capitalism is a system that separates risk bearing, decision ratification, and decision making. When risk bearing and decision ratification are combined in one economic agent, the system is called financial capitalism. Family capitalism combines all three functions in one agent.[2] Hierarchies are institutions that consolidate ownership and organize supervision.[3]

I. The Comparative Position of Large Firms in Small Countries

1. National Characteristics

Table 1 provides information on the national characteristics of large European industrial hierarchies in 1980.[4] An industrial hierarchy is defined as a large firm that on a consolidated basis employs more than 10,000 people worldwide. The cutoff point of 10,000 is somewhat arbitrarily chosen, and some companies barely missed making the limit. However, in most cases this limit guarantees that the firm owns and manages a variety of operating units and thus can be considered a hierarchical system. In this way it was possible to gain a first indication and a minimum estimate of the importance

TABLE 1   National Characteristics of Large European Enterprises.

	1	2	3	4	5	6	7
Austria	2	7	75.7	2.6	40.5	9,120	
Belgium	6	11	116.3	5.1	35.5	11,000	1.3
Denmark	3	6	67.2	4.5	30	12,940	1
Finland	8	5	51.1	15.6	34.4	8,690	1
France	43	60	652.4	6.6	36.3	10,680	1.8
Germany	57	76	822.7	6.9	44.9	12,450	2.1
Ireland	1	2	17.6	5.7	32.3	4,390	0.8
Italy	14	36	388.6	3.6	37.7	5,690	0.8
Luxembourg	1	1	4.5	22.2	38.6	11,640	—
Netherlands	10	15	160.2	6.3	32	10,620	2
Norway	2	5	55.8	3.4	30.1	11,360	1.4
Spain	6	20	209.3	2.8	36.4	5,310	0.3
Sweden	26	12	124.6	20.1	32.5	12,820	1.9
Switzerland	15	9	100.1	14.9	39.3	14,970	2.3
United Kingdom	119	40	513.9	23.2	39	7,170	2.1
United States			2,554.4		31.4	10,650	1.9
Japan			1,045.1		34.9	8,720	2.4

Column 1=Number of firms, Column 2=Hypothetical number of firms, Column 3= GNP in Billions of US $, Column 4= (1)/(3), Column 5=% employment in industry, Column 6=GNP per capita in US $, Column 7=R&D as % of GNP.

of industrial hierarchies for the organization of economic activities in Europe. In constructing the list from a variety of sources care was taken not to include subsidiaries of non-European companies.

Of the 313 large firms that fit the above-mentioned criteria 239, or 76%, originate in one of the following large European nations: France, Germany, Italy, Spain, and the United Kingdom. The United Kingdom tops the list comfortably, with Germany and France at a comparable distance. Italy and Spain are far down the list. Together France, Germany, and the United Kingdom are responsible for 219, or 70%, of Europe's large industrial hierarchies. The remaining 74 firms come from Europe's small countries.

The fact that such large nations as France, Germany, and the United Kingdom provide the home base for most of the enterprises on the list reflects their economic size. With 59.2% of the combined gross national product of the European nations that are covered in the list generated in these three large countries, it is no surprise that a majority of the large firms are of French, German, or British nationality. But these figures also point to important differences among countries. One way to study these differences is to redistribute the 313 large firms over the countries on the basis of each country's GNP. Column 2 of Table 1 shows the results of this hypothetical reallocation. It is clear that more industrial hierarchies operate from Finland, Sweden, Switzerland, and the United Kingdom than from the average European country. To illustrate: If the United Kingdom followed the average European pattern, it would only have had 48 companies in 1980 instead of 119. Germany and France, on the contrary, had fewer large firms than they could have had on the basis of their GNP.

Another way to analyze the national differences is to divide the number of large firms operating from one country by the country's GNP. The results of this simple but revealing calculation are given in column 4 of Table 1. In such countries as Austria, Italy, Spain, and Norway the number of large industrial hierarchies is rather small in relation to economic size. Belgium, Denmark, France, Germany, Ireland, and the Netherlands hold an intermediate position. But Finland, Luxembourg, Sweden, Switzerland, and the United Kingdom have many more large enterprises than economic size alone would suggest. The positions of Luxembourg and Ireland are of course special because of their exceptionally small size.

The conclusion that is suggested by these simple calculations is that remarkable national differences exist in the appearance of large hierarchies and presumably in the position of managerial capitalism. Regardless of size, some countries appear to have provided a more fertile environment for the development of large enterprises than others.

What accounts for the observed national differences? Several explanations can be suggested. First, in all fairness it should be pointed out that the differences may be caused by imperfections in the data. As suggested above, the 10,000-person limit for inclusion in the list of large European hierarchies is somewhat arbitrary. However, other cutoff points lead to similar conclusions. Second, countries differ in their degree of industrialization. Column 5 of Table 1 provides a rough indicator of industrialization. The indicator is the share of the industrial sector in total employment. The data suggest that the relationship between industrialization and the number of large industrial hierarchies is not close. Sweden, with many industrial hierarchies, scores low on industrial employment. Germany, with a smaller relative number of large firms, is Europe's most industrialized country. Third, the countries' historical development differs. Again it is difficult to find an obvious link. Early industrializers, such as Belgium, have fewer large companies than a late industrializer like Sweden. Another way to look at the influence of historical development is to see whether countries with higher prosperity have more large enterprises. Column 6 of Table 1 gives data on GNP per capita. Once more a simple relationship between level of development and large enterprises fails to come through. Fourth, the countries' technological capacity is unequal. Simple measures of technological capacity are not available. One possible but imperfect indicator is the ratio of research and development expenditures to GNP. Column 7 of Table 1 gives the relevant information. The data, with the exception of those for Germany, suggest a positive relationship between R&D intensity and the number of large firms. This relationship is illustrated in Figure 1. The figure is consistent

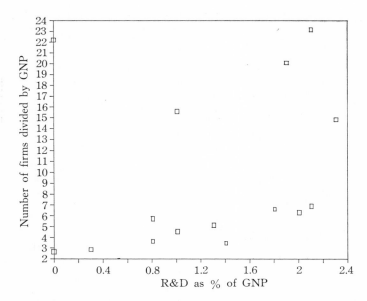

FIG. 1 Relationship of Large Firms to R&D, by Country.

with theoretical insights and empirical findings about the development of large firms and multinational enterprises.[5]

Following are the tentative conclusions. The size of a country's economy does not appear to have a major influence on the number of large enterprises that it brings forth. The observed differences in the comparative position of large hierarchies are not easy to explain. Industrialization and historical development do not appear to provide an easy explanation. Technological capability is the only factor so far that seems to have an effect on the comparative position of large hierarchies. This may point to the crucial importance of technological factors in the development of managerial capitalism. This tentative conclusion can be reinforced by analyzing the industries in which the large hierarchies operate.

2. *Industrial Characteristics*

Table 2 sheds light on the industrial characteristics of large

TABLE 2 Industrial Characteristics of Large Firms in Small Countries.

	Aus-tria	Bel-gium	Den-mark	Fin-land	Ire-land	Luxem-bourg	Nether-lands	Nor-way	Swe-den	Switzer-land
13	0	1	0	0	0	0	1	0	0	0
22	1	2	0	0	0	1	1	0	5	1
24	0	0	0	0	0	0	0	0	1	1
25	0	1	0	1	0	0	3	1	0	4
31	1	2	0	2	0	0	1	1	4	1
32	0	0	0	0	0	0	0	0	3	5
33	0	0	0	0	0	0	1	0	0	0
34	0	0	1	0	0	0	1	0	3	3
35	0	0	0	0	0	0	0	0	2	0
36	0	0	0	2	0	0	1	0	2	0
37	0	0	0	0	0	0	0	0	1	1
41	0	0	1	0	0	0	1	0	0	1
43	0	0	0	0	0	0	0	0	0	0
44	0	0	0	0	0	0	0	0	0	1
46	0	0	0	2	0	0	0	0	2	0
47	0	0	0	1	1	0	0	0	3	0
48	0	0	0	0	0	0	0	0	0	0
49	0	0	1	0	0	0	0	0	0	0
Total	2	6	3	8	1	1	10	2	26	18

13=Coal, oil & gas, 22=Iron & steel, 24=Stone, clay & glass, 25=Chemical industry, 31=Metalworking, 32=Nonelectrical machinery, 33=Office equipment, 34=Electro-technical equipment, 35=Car manufacturing, 36=Other transport equipment (ship-building), 37=Optical & other instruments, 41=Food & beverages, 43=Textiles, 44 =Leather & footwear, 46=Lumber industry, 47=Paper & printing, 48=Rubber & plastics, 49=Miscellaneous.

hierarchies. Only the small countries are covered in the table. In this way it is possible to reduce the effect of the size of the domestic market on the industrial characteristics of large enterprises. The table suggests a number of important conclusions.

Three industries are particularly attractive to large enterprises: metalmaking (six out of ten countries), metalworking (seven out of ten), and chemicals (five out of ten). Metalmaking and chemicals are basic industries with substantial economies of scale in production. Basic industries supply inputs for other industries. The desire, justified or not, to protect these inputs has led many small countries to develop and support large enterprises that produce these inputs. Some care is required here. Many of the large enterprises that operate in the metalmaking industry are not multiunit hierarchies. Very often they are single-plant firms. Consequently, the metal-making enterprises are not a sign of the spread of managerial capitalism in the countries concerned. It is interesting to note the close connection that exists between the metalmaking and the metalworking industries. Countries with many large companies in metalmaking will typically also have large companies in metal-working.

Sometimes the presence of a large company in a specific industry reflects the comparative advantage of the country in that industry. Geography gives Finland and Sweden a comparative advantage in timber exploitation, paper, and shipbuilding. It is in these three industries that the Finnish and Swedish hierarchies operate. Similarly, a Dutch shipbuilding enterprise was among Europe's large enterprises in 1980. Since then this particular enterprise has been dissolved.

What is striking about the remaining industries is that few of them serve mass consumer markets. Most of the large enterprises from small countries that operate outside the basic industries have selected large but specialized markets in which to pursue a strategy of growth. By focusing on the production of highly differentiated products for specialized markets, the companies are able to avoid a direct confrontation with competitors from large countries. These competitors can use their large home market to gain cost advantages that are unavailable to the companies from small countries.

However, there are some notable exceptions: Volvo and Saab-Scania from Sweden in car manufacturing, the Dutch company Philips in a variety of industries, and in food, Nestlé from Switzer-land and Heineken from the Netherlands. These companies oper-ate in mass markets, but very often they have positioned themselves with quality differentiated products in higher-priced segments of the mass markets. Sometimes the companies entered these markets because an early innovation gave the company a first-mover advan-tage in the market on which it could build to compete with the competitors from large countries.

These observations about national and industrial characteristics suggest the following conclusions about the comparative position

TABLE 3   Share Represented by Enterprises or Establishments of Enterprises
variables; years around 1975).

	Cutoff point	Year	Number of employees	Production
Australia (1)	> 25%	1972–73	28.5	36.2
Austria (1)	> 50%	1973	20.1	22.1
Belgium	> 10%	1975	33.0	44.0 (6)
Canada	> 50%	1974	43.1 (1)	51.1 (1)
Denmark (2)	> 50%	1976		8.8 (7)
Finland (1)	> 20%	1976	4.2	4.2
France (3) (4)	> 20%	1975	19.0	27.8
Germany	> 25%	1976	16.9	21.7 (6)
Italy (8)	> 50%	1977	18.3	23.8 (6)
Japan	> 25%	1978	1.8	4.2 (7)
Norway	> 20%	1974	12.3 (1)	18.7 (1)
Portugal	> 50%	1975	7.0	9.6
Spain	> 50%	1971		11.2
Sweden	> 20%	1976	8.6	10.8
United Kingdom (1)	> 50%	1973	10.8	15.3

(1) Establishment-based data, (2) Excluding oil refining and car assembling, (3) Including natural gas, (4) Excluding food industries, (5) Value for fire insurance only,
10.0%, value for fire insurance plus shares on 31 December 1974, 10.8%, (6) Turnover, (7) Sales, (8) Data on the basis of a survey covering 1,079 corporations that on

and development of managerial capitalism in European countries
in general and small countries in particular. Large-scale hierarchies
and, presumably, managerial capitalism have not developed evenly.
The data used here show that among the small countries Sweden,
Switzerland, and, somewhat surprisingly, Finland have evolved
much more than other countries (even the large ones) toward
managerial capitalism. A small domestic market does not seem to
hinder the development of managerialism. In general, two closely
interrelated factors are of crucial importance for this development:
technological capability and the ability to supply differentiated
products for special markets. In the second half of this paper the
validity of these factors will be evaluated for the case of Belgium.

II.   The Organization of Belgian Industry

In Belgian industry four types of companies are clearly discern-
ible. The first type consists of large Belgian-owned and -operated

with Foreign Participation in Manufacturing Industry (Percentages for selected

Value added	Wages and salaries	Invest-ments	Profit	Assets
34.3	31.3	31.3		
22.5	21.9	20.4		
51.0 (6)	46.1 (1)			53.9
5.3				
24.5	21.6	28.7	29.4	
				22.1
			6.9	4.2
18.0 (1)	8.6 (1)	10.6 (1)		10.0 (1) (7) (5)
9.9	9.4	5.7	11.7	8.9
14.7	12.5	15.8		

31 December, 1977, represented 2.4% of existing corporations and 63.9% of the total equity of existing corporations.
Sources: OECD (1981) and Van den Bulcke et al. (1979).

companies. As can be seen from Table 1, only six Belgian industrial enterprises employed more than 10,000 people in 1980. No accurate data exist on the impact of these industrial enterprises on the Belgian economy, but based on some information about value added by company, I estimate that they account for less than 5% of GNP.

The second type consists of companies that belong to one of Belgium's financial and industrial groups. These groups are federations of companies that are held together by holding companies and interlocking directorships. Groups are different from managerial hierarchies because they often have only a partial ownership in their affiliated companies and they have no central office to manage the group. There can be no doubt about the impact of these groups on the Belgian economy. In 1971 they held about 12% of all risk-bearing assets in Belgium.[6]

The third type consists of subsidiaries of foreign multinational enterprises. Table 3 provides some information about the impact

TABLE 4   Size Distribution of Multinational and Belgian Firms in Belgium, 1970.

No. of employees	Multinational		Belgian	
	Firms (%)	Employment (%)	Firms (%)	Employment (%)
1– 19	11.63	0.4	81.39	12.83
20– 49	17.61	1.84	9.75	11.04
50– 99	17.94	3.93	4.11	10.39
100–199	17.44	7.88	2.36	11.8
200–499	19.6	18.55	1.58	17.53
500–999	10.8	21.4	0.53	13.05
>1000	4.98	45.97	0.27	23.36
ABS figures	602	192,107	38,182	1,051,433

Source: Van den Bulcke et al. (1979).

of these foreign subsidiaries on the Belgian economy and compares it with the impact of foreign subsidiaries on other countries. Some 33% of total employment is provided by foreign subsidiaries. Their influence is also clear in the list of the 100 largest companies operating in Belgium. Many of the companies on that list are foreign owned. Table 4 reports data on the size distribution of foreign-owned companies and compares this with the size distribution of Belgian-owned companies.[7]

The fourth type of company is suggested by Table 4. Most of Belgium's companies are small and medium-sized. The data contained in Table 4 reveal that more than 90% of companies employ fewer than 50 people. Together these companies are responsible for 23% of employment.

The nature of Belgian capitalism is linked to the types of companies. Managerial capitalism is most likely to be associated with type 1 and type 3, the large Belgian enterprises and the foreign subsidiaries. Financial capitalism is characteristic of type 2, the financial and industrial groups. Family capitalism is the hallmark of type 4, the small and medium-sized enterprises. These classifications are useful, but they have to be treated with care. Several of the large enterprises that belong to type 1 are also members of financial and industrial groups that hold a considerable share of their equity capital. Consequently, what managerial capitalism exists in Belgium is largely imported. This raises the question of why Belgium and other small countries have experienced this particular development. To deal with this question the four different types of companies will be reviewed in somewhat greater detail.

1. The Large Belgian Companies

Six Belgian enterprises can be considered large hierarchical organizations. Petrofina, founded in 1920, is engaged in the production, refining, shipping, and distribution of oil. Cockerill-Sambre is a state-owned steel company. The company is the result of innumerable mergers and reorganizations throughout its history. One of its constituent companies was founded in 1842. Solvay, founded in 1863, is one of the world's largest chemical companies. Bekaert, founded in 1880, is a metalworking company with a strong market position in steel wire. Fabrique Nationale (FN) is best known for its firearms but also has other products in the metalworking and machinery industries. The company was established in 1884. Metallurgie Hoboken-Overpelt, founded in 1908, is a nonferrous-metals producer with strong market positions in special markets.

The founding dates illustrate that these companies go back a long way in history. Unlike large companies from large countries, their growth was rather slow. Their industrial activities fit the general pattern that was outlined in the first half of the paper. The basic industries are represented by Petrofina, Solvay, Hoboken-Overpelt, and Cockerill-Sambre. The first three have reached a position among the large European enterprises because of their technological capabilities in their own fields. Cockerill-Sambre survived because the government supported it. The two other large companies are examples of growth by product differentiation in specialty markets.

None of Belgium's large companies operates in mass consumer markets. Some of them have tried but failed. In the interwar years Fabrique Nationale attempted to diversify into car manufacturing. Despite FN's efforts to differentiate its cars on the basis of durability, design, and performance, it could not compete successfully in an industry where cost cutting through volume production was the key to strategic success. Other Belgian companies tried to enter the car-manufacturing industry around the same time, but they all failed.[8] Today Belgium has a sizable capacity for car production, but all the production is done by foreign enterprises. Recently Bekaert tried to use its technological expertise in steel wire to enter the kitchen-utensils market but had to give up quickly.

Another way to illustrate this point is to refer to the companies that started as Belgian companies but were later taken over by foreign multinationals. Gevaert et Cie, founded in 1894, became a major producer of photographic paper[9] in the interwar years. The company is now owned by the German company Agfa, itself a subsidiary of Bayer.

Management of the large companies that are discussed here remains largely in the hands of engineers. Engineers have led these companies through their long history. Given the businesses in which the companies operate, it is likely that this will remain so. As suggested above, many of the companies are partially owned by financial groups. This is the case for Petrofina, FN, and Hoboken-Overpelt. The exceptions are Solvay and Bekaert, where family ownership is still very important. In terms of management and organizational structure, however, Bekaert closely resembles the standard model of a managerial enterprise.

2. Financial and Industrial Groups

Financial and industrial groups are the most typical institution of Belgian capitalism. The groups use holding companies and interlocking directorships to knit companies together. The holding companies issue securities to finance their controlling interests in industrial corporations and banks. In this way the financial groups act as financial intermediaries that organize securities substitution.[10]

The groups emanate from the oldest financial institution in the Belgian economy, the mixed bank. The first mixed bank was founded in 1822. In the middle of the nineteenth century the mixed banks were forced to take equity participations to cover the loans they had made to companies. After World War I the mixed banks showed dramatic growth. But the economic and financial conditions of the early 1930s proved disastrous for some mixed banks' strategy of financing long-term commitments with short-term funds. The banking legislation of 1935 forced the banks to separate banking activities from business activities. The groups created holding companies to maintain control over their affiliated companies.

Groups supply risk capital to members of the group and ratify decisions of the boards on which they are represented. Consequently, groups are typical institutions of financial capitalism. Until recently each group was involved in a wide range of activities. Very often there was no common denominator in the group's portfolio. This has made it nearly impossible to set up a central office that can decide on strategy and coordinate activities. Even performance monitoring has not been carried out in a systematic way. Most groups do not have a formal organization structure, and few services are offered centrally.[11] The total absence of modern management methods reflects the role that the groups traditionally have seen for themselves. They consider themselves suppliers of risk capital. In the 1980s this strategy has changed. The leading group, Société Générale de Belgique, is reorienting its portfolio of participations around a few industries. This enables the group to play a more meaningful role in the management of its affiliated companies. The Société Générale is beginning to develop central office functions, such as strategic planning and personnel management.

3. Foreign Subsidiaries

Foreign subsidiaries play an important part in several Belgian industries. Industries in which more than 50% of output is produced by foreign subsidiaries of multinational enterprises from large countries include car manufacturing, agricultural equipment and tractors, oil, telecommunications, and pharmaceuticals. Multinational enterprises from small countries are strong in household appliances, radios and TVs, and light bulbs. In margarine and dairy products the foreign position is considerable but not dominant. The share of the foreigners is smaller than 25% in clothing, textiles, furniture, beer, and ferrous and nonferrous metalmaking. It is clear that foreigners dominate mass-market industries. The position of foreigners from small countries in household appliances and related products comes from the exceptional position of the Dutch company Philips, which has its headquarters within a short distance of the Belgian border. The low share of foreign companies in the beer industry is due to the fact that beer is a matter of Belgian pride which has enabled local companies to maintain a strong position against foreign competitors and to develop international activities of their own.

Foreign subsidiaries belong to managerial hierarchies and thus contribute to the spread of managerial capitalism. Although foreign subsidiaries are usually wholly owned, foreign control is not complete. A study covering the early 1970s shows that of 317 foreign companies only 20% felt that foreign control was strong.

4. Small and Medium-sized Firms

Not much can be said in this paper about small and medium-sized firms. Such companies hold strong positions in traditional industries, such as leather, textiles, clothing, diamonds, printing, and publishing. In these firms the owners supply the risk capital and make decisions. As long as successors can be found within the family, the firm remains within the mold of family capitalism. When no qualified successors can be found, professionals are hired to run the business. The family then restricts itself to risk bearing and decision ratification. In this way family capitalism has moved closer to financial capitalism in recent years.

III. Concluding Comments

This sweeping review of the comparative position and development of large enterprises and managerial capitalism leads me to the following comments. Managerial capitalism is hard to study as a stage in the development of market economies. The Belgian case illustrates that various capitalistic systems can coexist for decades. Managerial capitalism does not emerge as a successor to financial capitalism or family capitalism. Managerialism appears to be a response to the organizational needs of technologies, products, and markets in specific industries. This helps explain why country size is not a decisive factor for determining the comparative position of large hierarchies from small countries in the European economy.

Industrial structure (not industrialization) is likely to be more important.

This paper has drawn attention to the growth strategy of large enterprises in small countries. In these countries enterprises could not base their growth on the domestic market. Therefore they could not compete with the giants from large countries, and this might have reduced the development of managerialism. But cross-national comparison and Belgian history show that an alternative route was possible. Enterprises in the small countries had to use their technological capabilities to produce quality differentiated products for specialized markets. These markets were large, but they were not mass markets. Not all countries were equally successful in following this strategy. In the countries that were more successful, financial capitalism and managerial capitalism hold stronger positions.

Multinational enterprises play a crucial role in the spread of managerial capitalism. For a country like Belgium, which has few large enterprises outside the basic industries, the genesis of managerialism has come with the entry of foreign subsidiaries into the country.

These conclusions are no doubt somewhat tentative. Their confirmation awaits more data about the small countries. The detailed story of the development of managerial capitalism in small countries promises to provide challenging new insights into its driving forces.

NOTES

1. Alfred D. Chandler, Jr., *The Visible Hand: The Managerial Revolution in American Business*, Cambridge, Mass., Harvard University Press, 1977.
2. E. F. Fama and M. C. Jensen, "Separation of Ownership and Control," *Journal of Law and Economics*, Vol. 26, No. 2, 1983, pp. 301–25.
3. Herman Daems, "The Determinants of the Hierarchical Organization of Industry," in A. Francis, J. Turk, and P. Willman, eds., *Power, Efficiency and Institutions*, London, Heinemann, 1983.
4. The data used here are part of a large ongoing data-gathering

project on 313 large European enterprises, made possible by a special grant from the Belgian Ministry of Science. The project is called **PREST** and is carried out by **INCAP** at the Department of Applied Economics of Katholieke Universiteit Leuven.

5. Richard E. Caves, *Multinational Enterprise and Economic Analysis*, Cambridge, Cambridge University Press, 1982.
6. Herman Daems, *Holding Company and Corporate Control*, Leiden and Boston, Martinus Nijhoff, 1978.
7. Leo Sleuwaegen, *Location and Investment Decisions by Multinational Enterprises: Theoretical and Empirical Essays on the Operations of Multinational Enterprises in Belgium and Europe*, Doctoral Dissertation Series, No. 55, Katholieke Universiteit Leuven, 1984. Daniel Van den Bulcke, *De Multinational Onderneming, een Typologische Benadering*, Ghent, Serug, 1975.
8. Fernand Baudhuin, *Histoire économique de la Belgique, 1914–1939*, Brussels, Études Bruylant, 1944.
9. Baudhuin, *Histoire économique*.
10. Daems, *Holding Company*.
11. Philippe De Woot and Xavier Desclee de Maredsous, *Le Management stratégique des groupes industriels*, Louvain-la-Neuve, Cabay, 1984.

Comment

Reiko Okayama
Meiji University

Professor Daems's paper focuses on the development of large hierarchies in small countries in Europe, with particular reference to the case of Belgium. He sees the development of large hierarchies as being closely, but not perfectly, connected with the rise of managerial capitalism. Here managerial capitalism is defined as a "system that separates risk bearing, decision ratification, and decision making." This close connection between the development of large hierarchies and the rise of managerial capitalism is seen to have brought about efficiency gains that can be made in large hierarchies by entrusting these three functions to separate economic agents. What forces would drive large hierarchies in small countries toward managerial capitalism, since they have the disadvantage of small domestic markets?

Professor Daems tries to answer this challenging question. Through his careful examination of the development of firms that employ more than 10,000 individuals in small European countries, particularly Belgium, he presents very interesting conclusions. These conclusions are tentative, as he says in his paper, but extremely stimulating. Let me review them, which hopefully will lead to useful discussion on the nature and characteristics of managerial capitalism.

First of all, Professor Daems concludes that the size of a country or domestic market is not a decisive factor for the development of managerial capitalism. He finds through a cross-national comparison that an alternative route to managerial capitalism in these small countries has been found in the technological capabilities of enterprises, through which firms have been able to produce quality differentiated products for specialized markets. These markets are

large, but not mass markets. When large enterprises from small
countries become successful in mass markets, it is because these
enterprises have positioned themselves with quality differentiated
products in higher-priced segments of mass markets. Sometimes the
companies have entered these markets because an early innovation
has given them a first-mover advantage in the market, making the
company competitive against foreign enterprises from large countries. Thus Professor Daems emphasizes the significant role of
advanced technology in the growth strategy of large firms in small
countries. This explains lucidly how a considerable number of large
hierarchies have achieved success in quality-segmented markets.

In addition, I am particularly interested in Professor Daems's
remark in regard to Belgium that the management of large hierarchies remains largely in the hands of engineers, who have led these
firms through their long history. It would be a great help if he
could comment further on the careers of these engineers, including
their educational, training, or professional background, as well as
the way in which they acquired their position within management,
by promotion up the company ladder or by entry from other
companies.

Second, Professor Daems points out that managerial capitalism
has coexisted with family and financial capitalism in Belgium.
He also maintains that managerial capitalism does not emerge as
a successor to financial capitalism or family capitalism. As long as
we understand managerial capitalism as an economy or sector
that is dominated by managerial enterprises, we see that three types
of capitalism coexist in the larger economy. However, when we
consider the growth of firms with increasingly advanced technology,
it seems plausible that family-dominated and financially dominated
firms are transitional stages toward managerial ones.

Third, Professor Daems identifies four types of companies in
Belgian industry: large Belgian-owned and -operated firms, companies affiliated with Belgian financial or industrial groups, subsidiaries of foreign multinational enterprises, and small and medium-sized Belgian companies. Managerial capitalism in his paper
is seen as being most likely to be associated with the first and third
types of firms. The second type of firm is related to financial capital-

ism, and the fourth type to family capitalism. Financial and family firms as well as foreign multinationals appear to have been of relative importance to the Belgium economy in their own ways.

A further point that Professor Daems makes tells us that three of the six firms that belong to the first category, large hierarchies, and that hence are assumed to represent managerial capitalism, are partially owned by financial groups. Can we conclude from this point that the development of managerial capitalism in Belgium has been retarded by financial groups' control over industry? My knowledge of Belgian history is almost nil. I would like to have further information concerning the relationships between financial groups and their affiliated companies, particularly the effect of decision ratification on the decision-making process and the degree to which this ratification puts practical restraints upon the affiliated firms' policy making.

Before closing my comment, I would like to raise a question: From the picture that Professor Daems has drawn of managerial capitalism in small countries, particularly in Belgium, I cannot help feeling that large-scale domestic markets and also large-scale throughput are still decisive for the development of managerial capitalism, especially if we consider that there are only three large hierarchies that can be put into the category of managerial capitalism and that multinational subsidiaries have played an influential role in the Belgian economy.

Summary of the Concluding Discussion

Hidemasa Morikawa

The concluding discussion began with the presentation of the main issues raised by the participants in the course of the three-day conference. As the project leader, I selected the following outline of topics for discussion.

I. Emergence of managerial capitalism and managerial enterprises
- A. Definitions—managerial capitalism, managerial enterprise
- B. Chandler model—theoretical framework for the process of the emergence of managerial capitalism
- C. The experience of prewar Japan—deviation from the Chandler model

II. Background and speed of development of managerial capitalism
- A. The background—cases from Japan
  - 1. Can we identify the "progressiveness" of owners in the emergence of managerial enterprises in each country?
  - 2. Can we conclude that managerial enterprises are inevitable despite the differences among countries and among industries?
- B. Speed of development of managerial capitalism
  - 1. Measure of speed—the proportion of inside directors to outside directors
  - 2. Differences among countries: comparisons between the United States and Europe, Britain and Germany,

      large industrialized countries and small industrialized countries, and industrialized countries and developing countries

3.   Education and managerial development as important factors affecting the speed of development of managerial capitalism

The concluding discussion however, did not proceed according to this outline, but shifted from topic to topic. Therefore, to present the results of the concluding discussion coherently, I will summarize it in terms of the main issues instead of following the actual sequence of the discussion.

Definitions

Reconfirmation of the definitions of managerial capitalism and managerial enterprises was the first main topic. Managerial capitalism was defined as "a capitalist economy in which managerial enterprises dominate" and managerial enterprises as "firms in which representatives of the founding families or of financial interests no longer make top-level management decisions—where such decisions are made by salaried managers who own little of the company's stock." According to these definitions, formulated by Alfred D. Chandler, Jr., the point is that managerial enterprises are not the same as large enterprises with managerial hierarchies. Hidemasa Morikawa stressed this point in a paper read on the first day of the conference. Although no one opposed this argument, some participants regarded managerial hierarchies as the decisive factor in the emergence of managerial capitalism. Whether we should account for managerial capitalism on the basis of the emergence of managerial hierarchies was the basic definitional issue.

The Chandler Model

A second point concerns the applicability of the Chandler model. Morikawa pointed out that the Chandler model is an ideal type or framework on the basis of which we can collect and analyze historical materials. It is predictable that differences will arise between his model and the historical facts.

Chandler himself conceded that his model is an ideal type and that every country will present its own variations in the development of managerial enterprises. He argued further that managerial enterprises are not necessarily identical with managerial hierarchies. He also noted the early emergence of managerial capitalism in Japan and its distinctiveness. In these respects Chandler and Morikawa seem to be in agreement.

Chandler, however, focused on the development of managerial hierarchies in modern Japan, omitting any explanation of the relationship between this and the development of managerial enterprises. He commented that the characteristic complexity of Japan's business enterprises fostered the development of managerial hierarchies. Furthermore, near the end of the concluding discussion, he pointed out that managerial enterprises become indispensable only when they are required to integrate the technological scale with marketing. Thus, his own arguments indicate that Chandler regards managerial enterprises and managerial hierarchies as virtually the same.

Chandler did insist that in an enlarged managerial hierarchy, outside directors are obliged to lose influence. His argument, however, is not inconsistent with many cases in which salaried managers dominate the top management of a company that lacks a large, complex managerial hierarchy.

Gourvish presented five categories of enterprises to identify the characteristics of managerial enterprises in relation to managerial hierarchies. His categories are (1) salaried-manager dominated, without a managerial hierarchy; (2) salaried-manager dominated, with a managerial hierarchy; (3) owner dominated, without a managerial hierarchy; (4) owner dominated, with a managerial hierarchy; and (5) both owner and salaried-manager dominated, with a managerial hierarchy. Gourvish argued that his categories 1 and 3 are not managerial enterprises and category 2 is, but reserved judgment on 4 and 5.

Chandler's remarks supplemented Gourvish's in some respects. First, Chandler commented on the need to pin down the definition of the term "dominate" and to assess the composition of inside full-time directors and outside part-time directors on the board of

directors. Second, Chandler agreed with Morikawa in categorizing
1 and 2 as managerial enterprises from the point of view of defining
a managerial enterprise as one in which salaried managers make
top decisions. Chandler regarded enterprises in category 5 as not
being managerial enterprises, disagreeing with both Gourvish, who
had reserved judgment on that category, and Morikawa, who
regarded them as managerial enterprises with the reservation that
salaried managers must significantly outnumber owners.

Chandler presented the following four types of enterprises: (1)
Personal enterprise: All directors are owners, and there is no difference between inside and outside directors and no hierarchy.
(2) Family enterprise: Inside directors are full time and are managers; outside directors are part time and represent the family.
(3) Financial enterprise: Inside directors are full time and are
managers; outside directors are part time and primarily represent
large nonfamily investors. (4) Managerial enterprise: Outside directors are selected by salaried managers.

Morikawa's paper argued that managerial enterprises developed early in the Meiji era, and Chandler frequently raised the
question of why in Japan family and financiers remained involved
so long despite the early development of managerial enterprises.
Although Chandler understood from Morikawa's reply that in large
family- or financier-dominated enterprises top authority was often
delegated to salaried managers, he did not accept the classification
of such enterprises as managerial enterprises. As his categorization
shows clearly, Chandler's image of managerial enterprises is so
rigid that he identifies only one type of enterprise as a managerial
enterprise: that in which salaried managers select outside directors.

In response, Morikawa contended that if we adopted Chandler's
rigid criteria for managerial enterprise, it would be almost impossible for any enterprise in any country except the United States to
have attained the managerial-enterprise stage in the prewar period.
At the very least, the enterprises identified as managerial enterprises
in prewar Japan would fail to meet the criteria. But if enterprises in
which salaried managers select outside directors can be called
managerial enterprises, why cannot enterprises in which the authority for top-level decision making is delegated to salaried managers
(inside directors) by "progressive" owners be called managerial

enterprises? T. R. Gourvish also cast doubt on Chandler's views in this respect, suggesting that even when salaried managers select outside directors, managers by no means dominate their enterprises and stand in fear of being fired by the owners. Lazonick also mentioned that salaried managers, paid their salaries by the owners, lack ultimate authority for top-level decision making; their decisions can be rejected by the owners.

Consideration of the progressiveness of owners, a point raised in Morikawa's paper, would have led to effective discussion of these interesting issues. It is to be hoped that this issue, together with William Lazonick's proposal emphasizing the central importance of organizing salaried managers within the organization from the viewpoint of job security, will be addressed in later discussions.

Chandler's four types of enterprises also stimulated other discussion. Hartmut Kaelble asked Chandler if his four categories represent developmental stages in a historical progression. He also raised the question of whether there is a relationship between managerial enterprises and performance. Instead of answering Kaelble's question about historical development directly, Chandler posed another question: Why did financier-dominated enterprises in Germany and family enterprises in Britain survive until recently yet did not survive in the United States? He linked these differences to the historical backgrounds and social values of each country. To Kaelble's other question, concerning the relationship between managerial enterprises and performance, Chandler worked out the following instructive answer: What is important is not whether the enterprise is a managerial enterprise but whether it has a technologically based hierarchy.

Herman Daems emphasized the importance of managerial hierarchies and seemed to define a managerial enterprise as one in which the managerial hierarchy is dominated by salaried managers. In this connection he brought up important issues that should be examined further: variations among countries in the function of the board of directors, and the influence of the capital market as the signal permitting financiers to enter the board of directors. He argued that financiers as outside directors are required for any company to increase its ratification ability.

Financial Capitalism

Gourvish, Lazonick, and Etsuo Abe discussed the financiers' control of British railway and other large companies. The discussion related this issue to the question of whether these companies were type 3 in the Chandler model. Gourvish explained that British railway companies would belong to a position midway between types 3 and 4, with some conflict between major shareholders and salaried managers. Lazonick commented that financiers as outside directors in British railway companies and iron and steel companies could be regarded as specialists in analysis and as part of the managerial hierarchy. Since they could not take the place of salaried managers, their control did not necessarily mean financial capitalism. He added that the aristocrats who took charge as directors of British railway companies to raise the companies' prestige could not have been part of the managerial hierarchy because they had no managerial abilities. Abe pointed out the interlocking of outside directors in the British railway companies and iron and steel companies and categorized them both as a variant of type 3 in the Chandler model.

P. N. Agarwala referred to the backwardness of managerial capitalism in India. He stated that business enterprises in India, including types 1 through 3 in the Chandler model, are headed by families, financiers, and outside directors. The outside directors are not always representatives of the families or financiers but are socially respected, highly talented men. In one case, one man was an outside director of 65 different companies in India. Salaried managers are also hired, but a number of them are not professional managers but people connected with aristocrats and owners.

Measures of Development

Unfortunately, there was insufficient time for discussion of the question of the speed and extent of the development of managerial enterprises. Daems raised the issue of how to measure the speed of development. Morikawa adopted the changing proportion of inside and outside directors as a measure in his paper, but Daems had doubts about its applicability in international comparisons.

Chandler agreed with Daems on the grounds that the proportion of inside and outside directors is of no use in measuring the actual situation when, for example, the proportion is 50:50. No substitute for this measure was suggested, however. Gourvish proposed another measure based on observation of whether inside directors or outside directors play the major role in decisions concerning price, growth, and labor problems. Further light on this problem would require access to company records that show the decision-making process.

Managerial Capitalism in Japan

Since the project leader's paper was based on cases from Japanese business, interest was focused on the Japanese case. Chandler pointed out the significance of managerial intensiveness in modern Japan, brought about by several factors. He referred to such factors as the transfer of technology ("complexity of getting started in terms of technology"); the large number of highly educated employees; the complex, diversified, and hierarchical structure of the zaibatsu; and the zaibatsu's worldwide distribution networks. He also remarked that the lack of vertical integration within Japanese manufacturing companies, including those in the cotton-spinning industry, in the prewar period stemmed from their reliance on the trading companies.

Chandler's remarks revealed a few misunderstandings. For instance, among the zaibatsu only Mitsui had a big trading company with a gigantic worldwide distribution network. In other words, few of the big prewar Japanese trading companies grew from a zaibatsu base. Nonetheless, it was fascinating to hear the non-Japanese scholars' views of Japanese business.

All the non-Japanese participants addressed the question of the development of managerial hierarchies in Japan and its intensiveness. Chandler evaluated this as the cause of Japan's present industrial success. Lazonick commented that management in Japan is more intensive than in Britain and, referring to the Gerschenkron model, explained Japan's success by the fact that Japanese businessmen had made a coordinated effort to build a complex managerial organization to overcome Japan's backwardness. He raised the question of how Japan could develop managerial organizations so successfully. Morikawa replied that Japan's present industrial success was due to the appropriate functioning of managerial hierarchies completed after World War II on foundations laid in the prewar period by salaried managers who contributed to the growth of Japanese industrial power by securing top authority for strategic decision making.

Agarwala commented on the zaibatsu and Japan's educational system. He pointed out that the compulsory educational system is the basis of Japanese managerial capitalism. He also stressed Japan's simple, unified social system, in striking contrast to India's heterogeneous social system deriving from the caste system, the past colonial experience, and the individualistic way of thinking of the people.

Kaelble remarked that a feature Japan and Germany have in common is an unfavorable environment for economic development that made managerial capitalism inevitable. He also compared the two countries in terms of the availability of salaried managers. In Germany, he said, salaried managers were less scarce than in Japan; they were scarce in the 1850s but abundant in the 1890s. He also remarked that salaried managers were less powerful and played a less important role in Germany than in Japan because of the spread and influence of business families.

Referring to the Japanese educational system, Mark Fruin pointed out that one of the main causes of Japanese business development was success in developing a well-structured educational system from elementary school to the university level.

Finally, Keiichirō Nakagawa mentioned the cultural aspects of the development of managerial enterprises in Japan. Citing the Sumitomo and Kikkōman cases, he stressed the importance of the integrating function of familism in Japanese business.

This exchange of information was a valuable part of the concluding discussion. Although many issues remained to be discussed, the time limit forced us to end the discussion at this point.

Overall, at the end of the concluding discussion our impression was that we needed to collect more cases and more data from the various countries for better understanding of the emergence and development of managerial capitalism and managerial enterprises and to promote refinement of our theories. We hope to continue our research and to convene another conference on this theme.

MEMBERS OF THE ORGANIZING COMMITTEE

Chairman: Yonekawa Shin'ichi (Hitotsubashi University)
Fukuo Takeshi (Tokyo Keizai University)
Kobayashi Kesaji (Ryukoku University)
Miyamoto Matao (Osaka University)
Okochi Akio (University of Tokyo)
Yamasaki Hiroaki (University of Tokyo)
Yui Tsunehiko (Meiji University)
Secretariat: Abe Etsuo (Meiji University)
Johnston, William (Harvard University)
Nonaka Izumi (Aoyama Gakuin University)
Ornatowski, Gregory (Harvard University)
Sato Hidetatsu (Konan University)

Participants in the Second Meeting of the International Conference (Third Series) on Business History

Agarwala, P. N.
(Educational Consultants (India) Ltd.)
Amakawa Junjiro
(Kwansei Gakuin University)
Chandler, A. D. Jr.
(Harvard University)
Daems, Herman
(Katholieke Universiteit Leuven)
Daitō Eisuke
(University of Tokyo)
Fruin, Mark
(Osaka University)
Gourvish, Terry
(University of East Anglia)
Hashimoto Jurō
(University of Electro-Communications)
Kaelble, Hartmut
(Freie Universität Berlin)
Kikkawa Takeo
(Aoyama Gakuin University)

Kobayashi Kesaji
(Ryukoku University)
Lazonick, William
(Harvard University)
Miura Takayuki
(Fukuoka University)
Morikawa Hidemasa
(Yokohama National University)
Nakagawa Keiichiro
(Aoyama Gakuin University)
Okayama Reiko
(Meiji University)
Shiba Takao
(Kyoto Sangyo University)
Suzuki Yoshitaka
(Tohoku University)
Yamasaki Hiroaki
(University of Tokyo)
Yonekawa Shin'ichi
(Hitotsubashi University)
Watanabe Kishichi
(Kyoto Sangyo University)

Index